Convicted
in the
Womb

Convicted in the Womb

One Man's Journey
from Prisoner to Peacemaker

Carl Upchurch

BANTAM BOOKS

New York   Toronto   London   Sydney   Auckland

CONVICTED IN THE WOMB
A Bantam Book

PUBLISHING HISTORY
Bantam hardcover edition published September 1996
Bantam trade paperback edition / September 1997

ISBN 0-553-37520-2

Published simultaneously in the United States and Canada

Bantam Books are published by Bantam Books, a division of Random
House, Inc. Its trademark, consisting of the words "Bantam Books"
and the portrayal of a rooster, is Registered in U.S. Patent and Trademark Office and in other countries. Marca Registrada. Bantam Books,
1540 Broadway, New York, New York 10036.

PRINTED IN THE UNITED STATES OF AMERICA

TO MY LOVING WIFE,

Andrea

CONTENTS

Introduction   ix

PART I: NIGGERIZATION

1 South Street   3
2 The Bureau for Colored Children   15
3 YDC and Glen Mills   31
4 Camp Hill   51
5 Fort McClellan   62
6 Milan   74
7 Lewisburg   81

PART II: DENIGGERIZATION

8 Break of Day   99
9 Starting Over   111
10 Progressive Prisoners' Movement   125
11 Back to School   133
12 Maria   145
13 Council for Urban Peace and Justice   154
14 The Summit   165
15 Ripples   186

PART III: ANTINIGGERIZATION

16 Empowerment   197
17 American Apartheid   209
18 Leadership   218
Epilogue   233

INTRODUCTION

I was a nigger in the womb. Not just black. Not just male. A nigger. The contempt for my people—every assumption, insult, and slur—was trimmed and tailored for my infant shoulders before I was even born. A culture of low expectation, violence, disrespect, and degradation which was imposed from the outside began germinating in the earliest moments of my life. An environment saturated with raw immorality enveloped me as soon as I entered the world. It took me more than thirty years to learn that, unlike being male or being black, being a nigger wasn't coded into my DNA.

I was niggerized by my mother. Her tolerance of drug addicts, whores, pimps, dope sellers, hustlers, sexual deviants, and foul-mouthed gangsters impressed on me the hollow value of my existence at an early age. My emotional development was accompanied by insults and put-downs: "You're a dumb cocksucker." "You're a stupid motherfucker who ain't never gonna be shit." "You're just like your lazy-assed father."

The venom that poisoned my mother's tongue did not originate with her. She learned to be a nigger from her own mother, who had learned it from *her* mother, in a destructive cycle that reached all the way back to the first African natives, whose capture and subsequent slavery in this country initiated a legacy of violence and self-loathing that would be bequeathed to generations of African-Americans to come.

I was niggerized by my family. My uncle Haywood was a convicted rapist. My grandmother, who virtually raised me, was a prostitute. My father, whose affection my mother never could secure, spent most of his life in and out of bars and street fights, never taking responsibility for me. And my uncle Joe, the family hero, went to the electric chair on February 25, 1952, for a two-dollar robbery of a South Philadelphia wine joint, during which he and his accomplice had viciously beaten the proprietor to death. My family was proud that Joe went to the electric chair—doubly proud that he had done so without whimpering or pleading for his life. Needless to say, the values I learned as a young-ster are not the ones you'll find in the pages of a William Bennett anthology.

I was niggerized by my environment. In South Philly, violence was so commonplace that I grew up believing it was the solution to every problem. I emulated the people I saw—hoodlums, gangsters, and slick criminals whose chief agenda was to hustle, or "get paid," at any price. My heroes were those who were quick with a fist, a knife, or a gun; those who were best at a deal, a fight, or a con. I would have done anything to get their approval. In 1969, for example, a young woman in our neighborhood stole twenty-five bundles of heroin from one of the guys I looked up to. "Smoke the bitch!" he told me, and he gave me fifteen hundred bucks to do her in. Without a second thought, that night I took my .25 automatic, climbed in through her bedroom win-dow, clamped a pillow over her head, and pumped five shots into the pillow. I found out later that she hadn't died, since only one bullet had hit her in the jaw, but I got to keep the fifteen hundred bucks anyway.

I grew up believing that I deserved society's contempt just because I was black. With each day of violence, destruction, disappointment, and rejection; each stabbing, each shooting, each fight that I witnessed; each bitter word from my mother, each meal that was not provided, each time I had to go to school in dirty clothes, I retreated further inside myself to a place of empty darkness and growing anger. And with each retreat, the armored wall I kept securely around me became less penetrable.

Once a shy, awkward, melancholy youngster, I had to mimic what surrounded me in order to survive. Motivated by anger and a profound sense of worthlessness, my behavior became that of a self-destructive, self-loathing creature living only from moment to moment, impulse to impulse. If I wanted what someone else had, I took it. If someone messed with me, I punched him or kicked him or stabbed him. All that mattered was getting what I wanted, *now,* no matter whom I hurt or how much I jeopardized my own well-being. I had no remorse. I didn't care who or what else existed, or even what happened to me. I was governed by a careless, heartless ruthlessness fostered by a pervasive sense of inferiority.

I was thoroughly niggerized.

———————

The fact that I'm neither dead nor still in prison is due not to any government program or fancy rehabilitation center but to some folks I met in prison—poets and playwrights, activists, theologians, and philosophers. Desperate to pass the time during a stretch of solitary confinement, I opened up a book that happened to be propping up a table in my cell. It was a slim volume of Shakespeare's sonnets, and reading it started me on a journey of self-discovery I never could have foreseen. William Shakespeare somehow reached across the centuries to me and cradled my tortured soul. For the first time in my life, I began to understand that violence wasn't the only lens through which I could look at my life.

Although *nigger* is a volatile, abusive, oftentimes taboo word to most African-Americans, I use it here intentionally, though with no wish to offend. After examining my former behavior, my history, my psyche, the environment that produced me, and all the other forces that reinforced my destructive, hateful existence, I find *nigger* to be the most accurate word to describe who I was then. I couldn't deniggerize myself—stop being a nigger—until I understood how I had come to be one. Niggerization is everything that happens to millions of poor African-Americans who grow up in niggerizing environments, as I did.

Once I had read enough, learned enough to identify that process, I then had to reconstruct myself as a decent and worthy child of God, painfully peeling away the layers of filth that covered me. This deniggerization, this de-savaging of my soul, began with Shakespeare; it continued in my voracious exploration of literature. Authors as disparate as Mark Twain and W.E.B. Du Bois, Carter G. Woodson and Victor Hugo, Malcolm X and Maya Angelou challenged me, inspired me, and taught me endless lessons. Through them I have found the soul I had thought forever lost.

Discovering, through the words of others, that choices were available to me was liberating. I realized that I could choose to wallow in niggerhood—shooting drugs, robbing people, going to jail, disrespecting people—or I could choose to rediscover my humanity and work against being a nigger for the rest of my life. I chose the latter.

———

The culmination of all my struggles has been the gut-deep realization that there is more to this process than niggerization and deniggerization. A third step, mandated by our faith and by our obligation to our African-American brothers and sisters, is *anti*niggerization. It has the potential to be our salvation.

We have a responsibility to work actively against niggerization on behalf of our children. Antiniggerization means taking responsibility, both as individuals and as a group, for our contribution to the niggerization that exists inside each of us, then vigorously challenging that process wherever and whenever we see it. It requires that we understand our history, including both the legacies and the limits of traditional black leadership. It requires us to understand that the power structure of this country, whatever its color, will not respect us unless we demand its respect. It requires that we learn how to deal with one another irrespective of race, class, or creed.

Antiniggerization requires commitment to a truth that transcends traditional icons—black, white, liberal, conservative, the NAACP, the Urban League, the SCLC. The symbols that have heretofore defined our struggles and our liberation must be reevaluated in the context of today's realities, must be held to a higher standard.

One powerful example of antiniggerization is the 1993 gang summit in Kansas City. If there is one lesson to be learned from this event, where a courageous group of young men and women empowered each other to live without violence, it is this: We can love each other, respect each other, care for each other, and yes indeed, embrace each other for the common purpose of saving our children. They too were convicted in the womb—the womb of social injustice, of economic inequity, of hypocritical churches, of death and destruction. The gang leaders who came together in Kansas City planted a seed. Now each of us must continue to work for antiniggerization.

I never had a chance to start out as anything but a nigger. But God kept me in his hand. Some pivotal people, both real and fictitious, have inspired me to persevere through the years of hard work—sometimes painful, sometimes agonizing, sometimes rewarding—that brought me to where I am today.

Patterns of social and economic and political immorality produced the environment that spawned me, I now know, and I'm mad as hell about what was done to that little boy and to millions of kids like him before and since. Instead of reacting with violence, though, I have started to use my anger to challenge the evil process of niggerization, both in ourselves and in our country—creating the Council for Urban Peace and Justice, helping teenagers understand the consequences of the choices they make every day, bringing together gang leaders from all over the country to talk to each other about ways to live, not kill.

We must take control of our own destiny. It's time we stood up to the forces that have *niggerized* generation after generation of our children, and said, "Enough!"

On a brisk but sunny day in 1963, I stood on the corner of 13th and South streets in South Philadelphia with Butch, the leader of our gang. A few days earlier, one of our cornerboys, Paul, had been beaten up. They had smashed him up real good, kicked his face on the curb, kicked him while he was down. Butch and I were talking about how we were going to get somebody. We knew who was responsible, and we knew we had to get them now.

We walked about twenty blocks up to 17th and Wharton and found what we were looking for—eleven or twelve guys from 15th and Clymer, one of the three gangs we ran up against. They were there playing basketball, but when they saw Butch and me, they broke and ran. We managed to catch one guy and throw him over the hood of a car. I held him down by his neck while Butch unfolded his knife and started stabbing the guy in the back. The kid was wearing this bulky insulated jacket, so at first I didn't see any blood. I yelled at Butch, "Kill this motherfucker! Stab this motherfucker, Butch!" I could see one of the other guys trying to get up enough courage to come back and help his friend, so I hollered at him to stay away.

Butch kept pumping the knife into the guy's back, but I still didn't see any blood. It made me mad; I wanted to fuck this guy up bad. I yelled at Butch again. "Butch, you ain't stabbing this motherfucker. Stab this motherfucker, man! Kill this motherfucker!"

Then all of a sudden the guy's coat, which was shredded by now, fell to pieces, and I saw his back. It was sliced up bad; the blood I hadn't seen till then had soaked his clothes all the way to the ground. Butch didn't stop; he just kept pumping the knife in over and over again. One time the knife hit the guy's spine and folded up on impact, cutting Butch's hand. Butch opened it back up and stabbed the guy one more time, then he threw the knife down and we ran.

Back on our corner, where the rest of the guys from 13th and South were hanging around, they looked at our blood-soaked pants and knew something was up even before Butch said, "We got somebody." Everybody started asking questions, wanting the story: "Butch, what'd you all do?" "Hey Spoon, you all fuck that nigger up?" "Yeah," I said, "we fucked that nigger up."

We hung out on the corner and talked about it for a while. I was thirteen.

April 1993. The church was overflowing that Sunday in Kansas City, though the "congregation" was unlike any I had ever seen. They wore ball caps cocked back on their heads or knit stocking caps pulled down over their ears. Most wore Starter jackets long enough to hide a considerable arsenal. They stood rigid, looking tough and impenetrable. Hanging prominently around virtually every neck were loosely tied bandannas in many different colors, markers of gang allegiance that signify both identity and status. The colors were the clearest indication of the divisions among these seemingly identical youths.

On Thursday, the first day of this national gang summit, they would have killed each other for any number of reasons—retribution, honor, spite—maybe even on sight. During the eight months I had worked to make the dream of a national gang summit a reality, my worst nightmare was that it would explode into violence. But after three days of continuous talks at this gathering of gangbangers, things changed.

One Blood and one Crip, both tough, each sworn to lifelong enmity of the other, stood facing each other at the pulpit of St. Stephen's church that Sunday morning. As I watched from the back of the church, they did something unimaginable: together, they removed their colors from around their necks and threw them to the floor. This was an act at once of deadly betrayal and of unprecedented peace. The church broke into thunderous applause as nearly 250 gang members and community leaders rose to support the courageous gesture.

The two hardened gangbangers, who had previously reacted to everything in their lives with violence, stood side by side, fighting for composure. After embracing his former adversary, the young Crip spoke with some difficulty:

> *I have something to say that is really moving me to tears. I've been gangbanging for twenty-two years. I come out of Compton, California. I moved to Portland, Oregon, selling drugs, banging, and putting the destruction into their community.*
>
> *I ran into a brother—that's right: Akili. The brother is standing here today. The brother is a Blood. Today, I take my rag and I say, from now on there's a counterrevolution in progress. When you hear "Crips and Bloods," don't let it scare you, because we have a counterrevolution. This is the brother I tried to kill. This day I love him.*

Jim Wallis of Sojourner *magazine believed that this single act—throwing down their colors and proclaiming they would work for peace—could be a historical turning point for America's cities.*

For me, it was the highlight of the summit, and it remains my hope for the future.

PART ONE

Niggerization

One

I am three years old, sitting in my high chair with my back to the kitchen window. The sun shining down on the back of my head is blistering, and the apartment is stifling hot. Gomere, my grandmother, is feeding me lunch while she and Luke, my grandfather, spar back and forth. The heat is making me cranky and irritable as their argument escalates.

Neither the heat nor the shouting are new to me, even at three. Still, I feel tense, an anxiety that comes from not knowing what will happen next.

Gomere finally reaches her limit. She puts down the food and goes out the kitchen door toward the bathroom. Her behavior scares me, and I begin to cry. Luke sees where she is headed, and he knows why. He takes off running, past my high chair and down the steep flight of stairs descending to the street. For a brief moment, I am left alone in the kitchen, not knowing what their disappearance might mean for me.

Luke is halfway to the front door when Gomere comes out of the bathroom with a gun. She aims down the stairs, screaming, "You cocksucker! You know not to mess with me!" She fires then—four, maybe five shots—each one a deafening explosion. Then she comes back to where I am sitting, swearing at Luke under her breath. "Gomere," I say, "you shot Luke." She puts her arms around me. "You shot Luke," I repeat. "Yeah," she says, and then, "That cocksucker. Who does he think he is?"

I'm not sure I ever did finish my lunch.

I found out later that only one bullet had hit him. It took a piece out of the right side of his skull, but somehow he made it to a hospital, where they stitched him up.

———

This is my earliest childhood memory. Clearly, niggerization already had me in its grip. My world had already condemned me to a life of crime—I just didn't know it yet.

The apartment we were living in that hot afternoon in 1953 was on South Street in South Philadelphia. It was located above Ben's Shoes, in a dull gray building owned by Ben. A narrow, steep flight of stairs led from the street up to a hallway where the communal bathroom was located. The door next to the bathroom led into our apartment. Inside the apartment a flat, moldy smell hung over everything.

That apartment was always hot and muggy, even in the winter. A large brown table stood in the middle of the room, and the chairs around it always smelled like wet clothes. To the left of the door was my high chair, with the single kitchen window right behind it. Next to the high chair, a stand held a television that blared soap operas all day long. In fact, many of my childhood memories are revived if I hear the theme music to *Guiding Light*. And I always knew it was lunchtime when I heard the *Search for Tomorrow* theme. We couldn't afford a television, so we got one that you had to put a quarter in every half-hour. At the end of the month a man would come and collect the money, and at some point, I guess, we would finally own it. Somebody figured out a way to rig it, though, so it was always on.

On the other side of the door, the old icebox had rust stains trickling down the sides. When I was a few years older, Gomere would give me a quarter to get a block of ice when the ice truck swung through the neighborhood. The fresh ice offered temporary relief from the dirty, rusty smell that spewed forth whenever the icebox was opened. We kept a rat trap beside the stove, and it was Gomere's job to empty it every morning. Although I never heard it snap during the night, it needed emptying almost every morning. Dirty window ledges, grimy linoleum, and piles of garbage were standard, even though sometimes it seemed as if someone had made an effort to clean up from the Friday or Saturday night before.

An old pee-stained mattress lay on the floor in the left corner against the wall across from the door. Inches above it was a sink with mold and rust covering the bottom. The brown rusty water had to run for a while before it ran clear. Colonies of cockroaches scurried across the gray-and-white linoleum and up behind the wallpaper. I used to lie on that mattress at night and pull the blanket up over my head, afraid that they would crawl across my face as I slept.

To the right of the mattress was the doorway to the bedroom. It had no door—all that separated the bedroom from the kitchen was someone's dress, or maybe a bedsheet, tacked up on the ceiling. The communal bathroom had a splintering, cracked wooden floor. The plaster on the walls was chipped in places and turning moldy in others. The white porcelain of the sink, toilet, and tub was stained, but at least they usually worked.

When we were on welfare, the welfare lady would come once in a while to take inventory to make sure we didn't have more stuff than the welfare check allowed. Fooling her became almost a game for us. When my uncle John went into the air force, he gave us his new television. Whenever the welfare people came, I had to hide it under the bed so they wouldn't cut us off. We drilled a hole in the door so that when somebody knocked, we could see if it was the welfare lady. Then I'd run around hiding the stuff we weren't supposed to have.

We shared the bathroom with Miss Kate, who lived in the front apartment. She was the only white person in the neighborhood. I think she lived there because her boyfriend, Ike, was black. She never seemed out of place, and nobody ever treated her differently because she was white. I remember most how kind she was. Ironically, though, some of my earliest memories of violence are connected to Miss Kate. Ike used to beat her up every night. I'd lie on my mattress, listening to the noise coming through the wall, thinking, "Ike beating up Katie again," and wishing I was big enough to hurt him the way he was hurting her.

Miss Kate and I loved each other. Every afternoon she would send me to get a half-pint of butter pecan ice cream. Before I gave it to her, I would always steal a little taste, dragging one finger around the mound of ice cream, then smoothing it out and putting the wax paper back in place. When I finally confessed, I discovered that she'd known it all along. When I asked her why she'd never said anything about it, her answer cemented my love for her: "Because God gave you to me." Miss Kate and my mother had been pregnant at the same time and had even gone into labor on the same day at Jefferson Hospital. Miss Kate's son died at birth, and she never had any other children. She loved me like the son she never had, and I had an emotional bond with her that I never had with my own mother.

My mother was a beautiful woman, like all the Upchurch women— tall and shapely, with a rich, dark complexion. She was only twenty years old when she had me, and eighteen when she had my sister. My mother and my father, Martin McGill, never got married. Although he didn't live with us, my father would come around once in a while. I got the feeling that my mother truly loved him, even though he never showed much interest in her. I don't think she ever got over the pain he caused her.

My mother would turn men's heads as we walked down the street together. During my early years, she was in her twenties and very lively, not much more than a child herself. She was susceptible to sweet talk, and various men were in and out of the apartment, but she was no prostitute. She loved to go out and have a good time, but she spent most of her time hanging around the apartment talking with whoever was around. Her occupation, at least until I was six, was collecting welfare checks. I don't remember her ever being happy.

My relationship with my mother was always very distant and very tense. I never called her Mother; I called her Teeny, like everyone else. In her eyes I was no good, dumb, lazy, and conniving. Our relationship was overshadowed by her criticisms of me, and there was never a time when I felt she approved of me. I don't remember ever receiving affection from her, ever hugging her or being hugged by her. As a person, she was strong, direct, and no-nonsense. As a mother, she was stern, authoritarian, cold, and insensitive. Her favorite line was "I can't accept no weak motherfucker." I spent all of my childhood, and way too much of my adulthood, trying to stimulate a caring response from her.

Luckily for me, my mother's mother, whom I always called Gomere, was quite the opposite of my mother. She always had time for me; she loved me, kissed me, embraced me, and talked with me. I was her favorite grandchild, and she was very protective of me. Gomere was in her forties then, and I thought all grandmothers must look like she did. Her big black bare feet had corns on them. Her hands were soft but looked as if they spent a good deal of time in dishwater. I remember her soft, bosomy hug when she squeezed me to her. I'd sometimes lie down on her while she took her afternoon naps. It was a warm, comfortable feeling.

Gomere was tall, shapely woman and clearly had been very attractive in her youth. Around the apartment she always wore a housecoat and no shoes, but I distinctly remember her "other" look, when she was getting ready to go out on the town. She had a patent-leather belt with a big buckle that she strapped real tight around her waist. Gomere loved flowers and bright colors, and she'd wear very tight skirts and full, ruffled blouses. And she'd cram those feet into high-heeled shoes.

Gomere was the only one in the house working when I was very young. She cleaned for white people, and some guy named Jimmy was her pimp. Because she was discreet about the activities she performed as one of Jimmy's girls, it was not until years later that I realized what it meant for her to be "working" for Jimmy. To us kids, Jimmy was just a friend with a wonderful personality. His movements were smooth, calculated, always in slow motion—what I now call "ghetto suave." When he saw us on the street, he'd always slip some change into our pockets.

From my point of view, Gomere was a true matriarch, holding up all the responsibilities her role entailed—leader of the family, disciplinarian, and breadwinner. Even though there was never enough money to feed the whole family, we always knew that she would bring something for dinner. I was long gone from South Street before I found out that she had stolen meat and eggs from local stores so that we could eat.

Gomere had six kids, and they were always in and out of the apartment. We were family. No one had much money, but we all stuck together, with Gomere staunchly at the head of our household. Anyone who could put in two dollars for rent was welcome to stay with us. At the time of the shooting, my mother and I, Gomere, Luke, my mother's sister Nita, and Nita's two children, Frankie and Toby, were all living together.

My mother and Nita were very close. Nita was about five feet four, not as pretty as my mother, but not unattractive either. Like my mother, she hung out and collected welfare. Nita was warm and always kind to me. She liked to tell jokes, and she had a gold tooth that showed when she laughed, which was a lot. Nita was the kind of person who spoke her mind. She didn't take any nonsense from anybody, and it wasn't uncommon for her to punch some guy in the stomach. She also liked to play with words. One of her favorite expressions was "Suck my puss-simmons," and every time she said it, she'd follow it with a sheepish "Oh, I'm sorry," as if it had just slipped out. One of her other favorite lines was "Is this motherfucker crazy, or was he just in the service?" Her spirit and her sense of humor may have appeared vulgar to others, but they were part of what endeared her to me. She kept me laughing throughout my childhood.

My mother's sister Lil lived with us sometimes too, but she and my mother weren't really close. Lil was the youngest of my mother's sisters, the most sensitive and the most intellectual. She was bright and beautiful, the only one to graduate from high school and probably the most "normal" of all my mother's sisters. She often stayed with her boyfriend rather than with us. She was the kind of woman who never had sex with a man until she really liked him, which was not the general rule in our house.

Uncle Haywood, the eldest of Gomere's children, came to stay with us now and then too. He was a conservative-looking man with a short, stocky build and a wonderful smile. He was very athletic—he probably could have been a professional baseball player. Tough and quick to defend his family, we all liked and respected him for his strength. He couldn't read his name unless you spotted him most of the letters, but he could do just about anything with clocks or cars or construction. He had an annoying habit of flicking at my head with his thumb and middle finger, or throwing punches at me to see how tough I was. Unfortunately, I was more sensitive than tough during those early years, and although I liked him a lot, most of the time when he came over, I moved across the room and sat near somebody else. At some point during my early childhood, Uncle Hay was incarcerated for rape at the State Correctional Institution at Camp Hill—a place I would one day come to know myself.

Uncle John, my mother's other brother, was very different from Haywood—taller, for one thing, and a little rounder because of his weakness for fried foods. He couldn't do anything with his hands and wouldn't have known a battery from an accelerator. Mostly self-taught, he had an avid interest in art, theater, literature, and music. He loved language and quoted Shakespeare as easily as if it were street talk. Some people called him Professor, and he was often teased about his intellect, but John was also street-wise and keenly understood his environment.

Of all the people who lived with us then, my memories of Luke, my grandfather, are the most vague. He was dark skinned, somewhat husky, but well built. I don't remember his face or what he did for work. But then he and I weren't very close, and he wasn't always around. Oftentimes, after he and Gomere had been fighting, he'd stay away for days at a time. How long usually depended on the severity of the fight. His absences seemed to be based on some sliding scale of banishment that only he and Gomere understood.

When I was about ten or eleven, Gomere had another baby, a girl named Tonie. Since she looked completely different from my mother and her sisters, we all figured she wasn't Luke's baby, but nobody remembers Tonie's father. She looked more like me than my real sisters, so I always thought of her as my little sister. My mother and my aunts were all jealous because it was obvious that Tonie was Gomere's favorite of all her children. Tonie could do no wrong. When she got a little older, they would tell Gomere that she was running around or doing things with boys, but Gomere wouldn't listen. She always defended Tonie by saying, "Now, just because she's with some boys, you go and think the worst of her."

I didn't see much of my older sister, Stoney, because she lived with my father's mother almost the whole time we were growing up. We became very close after my father died, when she came to live with us because our grandmother was too old to take care of her. Stoney's complexion was lighter than mine, but we had very similar features, much like our father's. Her looks were so striking that once *Jet* magazine wanted to do a centerfold of her, but she turned them down. Her childhood was very different from mine because she wasn't surrounded by the violence of South Street. Moving into our neighborhood was a big adjustment for her.

My brother, Seppie, is four years younger than I, and my sister Deenie is six years younger. They looked different from Stoney and me and were both much quicker to anger. Their father, John Pearson, was a quiet, authoritative, serious man. He owned a candy store across the street, but it didn't make much money because his real occupation was wino. He filled a fatherly role for me for a while because he was the first young man who stayed in our house, but he died before Seppie and Deenie were old enough to know him very well.

Actually, our apartment was the hip place in the neighborhood. People came from everywhere to get high, sell booze, and play cards.

Parties were regular events, not just on the weekends. The two-room apartment would fill up with dope dealers, pimps, prostitutes, and other characters. People would get drunk, smoke pot, or even have sex right in front of everybody else. Mostly it was men and women, but one night, after my cousin and I played guns on the bed in the kitchen until we fell asleep, I woke up in the middle of the night and saw two women on the floor having sex. I wasn't shocked, but I remember being scared by the look on the one woman's face. Her eyes were rolling back in her head. I'm sure the adults all thought, as adults tend to do, that we children were asleep or too young to understand. I never thought there was anything odd about all the stuff that happened there, and I always had a good time when people came over because they would be smiling and horsing around.

Almost every party, though, would end in some sort of violence. Once Haywood slashed John across the back with a straight razor, as I was watching; I watched my father, a devastating boxer, knock a guy over a car; I watched some man punch Aunt Nita in the stomach when she was pregnant. My feelings toward these people didn't change, though, because such behavior was standard, even expected, at these gatherings.

The people who came to party played with me and patted me on the head as I ran around the apartment. I liked Puny, a skinny guy who was always telling jokes and getting beat up; I liked Ralph, who was always laughing and trying to screw every woman there; I liked Roosevelt, a big, jovial man who taught me how to play chess. And my family was my family. Like any other kid, I cared about them and what happened to them.

The parties were fun, with everyone laughing. And despite all the violence, I never felt that any of them were bad people. I never felt afraid of them. What I did feel, though, even at the age of three, four, or five, was a kind of emptiness that shadowed the stretches between the parties. Later I figured out that they felt it too and partied so hard to avoid its stark reality.

———

Until I was five years old, I observed everything on South Street from my perch on the front steps of our building. I was never interested in playing sports with all the other kids in the neighborhood. I was a curious child who enjoyed watching things, and I was most content to be left alone. Even after I started school, I still sat there when I could, absorbing the sights, smells, and characters of the neighborhood. Everyone knew me, and I knew everyone. At the time, South Street was a neighborhood in transition, a bit run-down but on the cutting edge of what a good black neighborhood could be. It was somewhat avant-garde, with a diversity of ethnic flavors—Italians and Jews owned most of the stores, and blacks lived in most of the second- and third-floor apartments.

Each morning the shops opened, unfurling their colorful canopies to reveal fruits, meats, and other wares, and life cranked up to a vibrant pitch. Fresh fish was sold on the sidewalk, and the smell of newly baked pastries hung in the air. There were music and art galleries on the nearby streets—South, Pine, Spruce, Lombard—alongside clothing outlets. It was a wonderful mixture of shops. A person could eat ham hocks and black-eyed peas on South Street, then go to a highfalutin poetry reading on Lombard.

Miss Marie, who was Italian, worked at a Jewish-owned store down the street where my mother would often send me to buy Pall Malls, Carnation milk, and orange juice. Miss Marie would write down how much we owed, and at the end of the month when we got our welfare check, I would take her some money to pay it off. One time as I was bouncing home, the bottom of the paper bag broke and a bottle of orange juice crashed to the pavement, shattering at my feet. I was too scared to go home to my mother without it, so I ran straight back to Miss Marie, who gave me another bottle without even writing it down.

I knew all the people in the stores, and most of them were good to me. We bought everything on credit, even the new shoes we got every Easter from Ben's. Sometimes late at night, when I was a little bit older, I would sneak up to the canopy-covered fruit stands and take some oranges, or I'd steal ice cream and potato chips from a store. I never got caught, and I've always felt they must have just looked the other way.

There was a restaurant called Dave's that sold soul food long before it became popular. Fifty cents bought a huge meal of black-eyed peas, corn bread, navy beans, collard greens, ham hocks, chitlins, rice, gravy, and plenty of hot sauce for seasoning. Dave also provided a big vat of orange juice with a dipper so his customers could squelch the fire from the hot sauce.

The music store across from our apartment had speakers aimed out at the street. As I sat people-watching, the South Street goings-on were set to the sound of Fats Domino singing about Blueberry Hill. When the music was playing, the atmosphere on South Street was fantastical. I'd spend hours daydreaming about the people I watched, about their lives, which all seemed so different from mine.

I remember a woman walking down the sidewalk with one child in a stroller and another trailing behind. She kept turning to the one behind her to make sure the little girl could catch up. I dreamed that I was her child, that it was me she was checking on. I desperately wanted someone to look at me the way that woman looked at her daughter, to have someone care about me the way she so obviously cared.

At five-thirty every afternoon, when the stores closed and the music stopped, stark reality would close in, pulling me roughly from my daydreams. In the next few hours, South Street would be transformed from a hustling, bustling business district to a strip with a pulsating night life. All the best black entertainers performed on South Street, and it became internationally known, drawing performers from all over the country, just like Harlem in the 1920s. Hip white people flocked in from the suburbs to Pep's Musical Bar to party and hear Dinah Washington, Sam Cooke, and Max Roach—all giants. I loved to watch whites and blacks, pimps, prostitutes, and performers, all dressed up for the evening, coming and going, laughing and smoking. I stood in the back of the Royal and the Standard theaters and listened to Miles Davis, unconscious that I was in the presence of genius.

When I was older, maybe eight or nine, I would walk over to a club on Lombard Street, watch through the window, then sneak in and listen to the poetry through the foggy cigarette smoke. Of course, I didn't know that what I was hearing was called poetry; I just knew it had a different rhythm. And even though I didn't understand much of what the poets were saying, I was fascinated by how they said it. Everybody else seemed fascinated too, so I figured that the people onstage must be saying something significant. The stark images during those poetry recitations stayed with me long after I walked home.

I was particularly absorbed by how whites did their business and socialized, and by how differently they dressed compared with people I knew. The white guy in khaki pants and cloth shoes, a beret on his head and a cigarette in his mouth, was so unlike the black guys who hung out on the street corner, with razor-sharp creases down the center of their pant legs. Those cultural differences fascinated me.

Day and night, a lot of illicit business was carried out right alongside the legitimate transactions. The pimps and prostitutes were out all the time, and so were the players, the macks, and the dope dealers. They were everywhere—on the corners, in front of our building, in the bars—as much a part of the daily routine on South Street as anyone else. I watched dealers sell marijuana and heroin, pimps grab their whores by the hair and drag them down the street. I watched people get stabbed or get slashed across the face with a straight razor.

By the time I was five, I knew more about the streets than most kids ever do. Violence was part of life on South Street. Everyone just took it for granted. I certainly never thought of it as shocking or even out of place. But it twisted me as surely as it twisted everything on South Street.

Two

THE BUREAU FOR COLORED CHILDREN

When I was in the fourth grade, my class made American flags for May Day. Before my flag was finished, the white crayons were all used up. The closest color to white was yellow, so I used it, thinking how smart I was to have done that.

The teacher walked up and down the rows, looking at each flag. When she got to mine, she grew very angry. She shoved me and yelled about how dumb I was to put yellow on the American flag. Putting a big yellow streak down the middle would make people think our country was cowardly, she said.

I began to cry. I had no idea what had made her react that way. Then she said something like, "People like you may not understand how important it is to put white on the flag, but we Americans do." She didn't call me a nigger or even an African-American, but she didn't need to. I knew what she meant. That woman, who should have been nurturing my development, made me feel like a criminal. She made me feel stupid. She made me feel worthless.

I reacted in my accustomed way: My outside shell got a little tougher, and my inside self retreated a little deeper. And I decided that I had had enough of school.

———

I pretty much ran my own life from the time I was four years old. Before I started school, I stayed out on South Street all day long, dreaming and watching people on the steps or wandering around. I had a good reason to stay away from the apartment—my mother. She was one of too many young black girls having babies out of wedlock and had come to motherhood a child herself, unwilling and unprepared. She had inherited my grandmother's niggerized outlook on life and herself, and passed it on to me without a second thought.

She mostly left it up to her mother to raise me, but when she couldn't avoid it, she parented me using the only skill she had—insults: "You'll never amount to nothing in your life." "You'll be a thief or a bum or a dope seller." "You're just like your father." "You ain't worth shit!" As a child, I believed every word she said.

Out on the streets I got a sense of power that I didn't have at home. I went where I wanted, did what I wanted, and took what I wanted. South Street and its surroundings were colorful and lively, and I couldn't get enough of the sights and sounds. From the time I could get down the stairs alone, I roamed—first with my eyes, later with my feet, watching adult interactions and acquiring wisdom far beyond my years, despite the absence of the love and nurturing that all young children need. By the time I was old enough to go to school, I had life as I knew it all figured out.

Now suddenly I was expected to sit in a room and communicate with a bunch of strangers in an entirely new way. Compared with South Street, school was artificial and pointless. I had received no preparation to help me adjust to it or do what was expected of me. At home no one had ever asked me to sit and listen attentively, or cooperate, or share, or learn, or read, or be considerate. Today, as a father, I realize that parents have the power to inspire children or beat them down, to encourage them to dream or to break their spirits. No child can suddenly become responsible, clean, courteous, respectful, attentive, caring, considerate, and cooperative without being exposed to these type of behaviors during the first five years of his or her life. Without models, without instruction, without emotional nourishment or intellectual preparation, a child cannot possibly perform to the standards set by society.

Everything I had experienced in my childhood was the opposite of what I needed to survive socially, intellectually, and psychologically at school. I had gone to no preschool; I had not had to struggle to learn how to share. In my childhood world of drugs and pimps and lies and fights, no one had checked my spelling, read me stories, helped me add, or asked me what I was learning. I had been socialized at home under the most negative emotional conditions; as a result, my socialization in school felt like an assault to my culture and values. My teachers brutally berated me for not being what I had never been taught to be.

Getting me to school each morning wasn't a priority for my mother, since she had never considered it a priority for herself. She never got up early enough to help me get ready. She showed up just in time to rush me out of the house. "Get outta here!" she'd shout. "You're gonna be late!" And I was late—nearly every day. I went to school without breakfast, without a bath, without clean clothes, and without my hair combed. Just getting out the door was humiliating, and it didn't get any better once I got to school. As I ran up to the classroom door each morning, I saw scorn on the other children's faces. No one ever said "Good morning, Carl"—not even the teacher. I walked quietly to my seat, and spent the day being either as disruptive as possible or as withdrawn as possible, depending on my mood.

Having had no breakfast, I was hungry all day long. Each Friday we had to bring twenty-five cents to pay for our graham crackers and milk. All too often I didn't have the quarter, so I would sit and watch while the other children ate their snacks, never daring to ask if someone would share with me. Even though the teacher knew I couldn't afford the snack, she never took it upon herself to spare me the embarrassment of being poor. Eventually, I began to steal graham crackers out of the cabinet in the classroom.

Each day at recess, the other kids took off their school shoes and put on sneakers. Of course, I had no sneakers, and the other children wouldn't play with me anyway, so I just stayed inside most days.

In class, the other students told the teacher they didn't want to sit next to me. I must have smelled—my body and my clothes were always dirty. The other children, especially the white kids, wore new clothes and had nice things. They were all clean, and their hair was always combed. I decided, at some point, that if a girl had clean white socks, rolled over at the ankle, she was really something. I hated looking and feeling dirty, but since I had never been taught basic grooming, I didn't even know how to fix what was wrong. I wasn't dumb—I knew the other kids had something I didn't. I was just too young to know what, or why.

My kindergarten teacher was named Miss Burton. I thought she was God and that all teachers in the world were like her. They weren't. From first grade on, all of my teachers were white—Miss Burton was the only black teacher in the school. Up to this point I had learned a lot about white people from South Street: Most all the shop owners were white, and all the people who had money and nice clothes were white. School verified my impressions. Everyone who was in a position of power was white. Everything they taught us felt white. The white students were cleaner, and they were treated better—the teachers paid more attention to them.

My teachers had racist tendencies. I did not understand it as racism yet, but I understood very well what it felt like. The white teachers brought their white values into the school—values that negated my world entirely. The message was subtle, but it was clear to me: everyone I respected and loved was considered ignorant, irresponsible, and good-for-nothing. They weren't even represented in our schoolbooks.

Our first-grade reading books, for example, were the *Fun With Dick and Jane* series. We read about perfect white Jane and perfect white Dick who played with their perfect dog, Spot, while their perfect white parents looked on. Only a teacher who was utterly insensitive to who we were could have chosen such books. I couldn't have articulated it at the time, but felt that they were making fun of me.

Even though I hated the books they made me read, I was a good reader. Reading was the only part of school that was bearable. We were seated in rows, boy-girl-boy-girl. I was the anchor in my row, meaning I sat in the last seat. Every day each person had to read an assigned passage out loud. As the anchor, my performance would determine whether my row got a gold star or graham crackers and milk at the end of the week. A girl named Gloria sat in front of me. I would get so wrapped up in winning the gold star, I would try to help her when she got stuck, momentarily forgetting what the other kids thought of me. But she never accepted my help, even though she couldn't read very well and even though it might mean losing out on the treat or the star. She just turned around and hissed, "Don't help me, Carl," slapping the air with her hand.

Over and over again, the humiliation, embarrassment, and alienation that I felt at home was duplicated at Nathaniel Hawthorne Elementary School. I decided I must not be good enough to be there. I didn't look like I belonged there, I didn't feel like I belonged there, and I was made to believe I wasn't smart enough to belong there. I never had a group of friends, black or white. I had one friend, Stanley Grogin. He came from the same kind of environment I did, and we clicked on almost every level. One of the reasons I went to school for as long as I did was that I saw Stanley every day there.

A child who is shunned for being smelly, poor, and dirty knows it. But that child has the same desire to be liked and accepted as any other child. When a child learns that showing off is the only way to get attention, he will assume that this is the way to get people to like him. If the only way he can show off is by being negative, nasty, and obnoxious, he will do that, but in doing so, he will push the other children away without ever knowing why.

I knew the other kids didn't like me, but I didn't know how to change myself so they would. I had never been taught how to have healthy interactions with people. In my experience people were classified as cocksuckers and motherfuckers, bitches and whores. My body odor and my lack of sneakers were just a small part of what I was up against.

Each year at school was worse than the last. When I turned nine, three-quarters of the way through fourth grade, I just stopped going. My mother didn't know it for a while because she still saw me leave for school every morning; I just stayed out of her sight and hung out on the street. But the school authorities caught on pretty fast and dragged my mother into the counselor's office nearly every day. My mother did everything she could think of to force me to go back so the school would leave her alone. She screamed at me, she beat me, she withheld things, she made me stay in the house, she cursed me. I had made up my mind, though. I wasn't going back, no matter what. And once the school finally stopped bothering her about it, my mother lost interest.

———

At that point, I began wandering farther away from home, all over Philadelphia. The city was full of fascinating places, and every day I saw something new and interesting. If I got curious about what was inside the big, clean, impressive buildings downtown, I went up and tried the door. They were hardly ever locked, so I just went on in. I wandered into old museums and private clubs and noticed that they all had pictures of important-looking white men hanging on the walls. The clubs had huge leather armchairs, and I liked to sink into them and rest. We never had chairs like that back on South Street. Sooner or later someone would come along and see me. "Son," they would ask politely, "are you waiting for someone?"

"No, I'm just sitting here resting," I'd say carefully.

"You know no one is permitted in here," they would say, meaning that I wasn't allowed in there.

"Oh, okay," I'd say, trying my best to sound very tired or disappointed.

Usually they would soften up and tell me I could stay awhile longer. I'd sit there until I got bored or thought of something else to do.

Some days I would walk until I came to cobblestone streets lined with huge three-story brick houses. Through the tall windows I would see lots of fancy furniture. Giant steps led up to massive double wooden doors. I would go up to a house and try the door. Hardly anyone locked their doors in those days, and sometimes I just walked in. I liked to poke around and sit in the big comfortable chairs. If I found something to eat, I grabbed it. And if I saw anything else that interested me, I'd take that too.

I saw the rich Philadelphia bigwigs—the Wanamakers, the Snellenbergs, the Kelleys. But then, all white people looked rich to me. They interacted in ways so different from anything I'd known. They were polite. They smiled and made small talk. They greeted each other with "Good morning," helped each other in and out of cars, and shared lunch in fancy restaurants. I watched what they wore, how they walked, and what stores they went into. And yet as much as they fascinated me, they were a constant reminder of what I didn't and couldn't have. In their presence I felt appreciative, curious, envious, offended, and angry all at the same time.

It didn't add up. On one level, I believed all the insults my mother hurled at me, and all the disdain I had felt at school, and I felt worthless and bad. But on another level, in my heart of hearts, I didn't believe that I was a nasty, horrible little boy. White people clearly lived in a separate world, but I didn't understand why they shunned me or why little white kids in clean uniforms skipped to school as if they didn't have a care in the world. I didn't understand why they had things and I didn't. Somewhere deep down I felt that something was terribly wrong. I could see clearly the difference in how whites and blacks lived, but I didn't yet fully understand it. All I knew was that white people were clean, happy, wealthy, considerate, and well fed, while black people weren't any of those things. My nine-year-old mind could do the equations: White meant good, and black meant bad.

At this point I discovered I was invisible. My presence in the white world of downtown Philadelphia went totally unacknowledged. Back on South Street, everybody knew me, I was part of the action. Here I was an observer, even an intruder, and as my actions became bolder, my real self retreated further inward. No one spoke to me, no one looked me in the eye. White people noticed me only when I was obnoxious enough to draw their attention.

I learned quickly to survive on my wits. Everything I needed in the way of food or clothing was there for the taking. This was important because it freed me from dependency on home or school. When I got hungry, I stole a hot dog or a bag of chips or an apple. If I saw a shirt or a pair of shoes that I liked, I took them too. Taking money out of a cash register was simple: I sent the clerk around an aisle or outside to get produce, then grabbed a few bills out of the drawer. They didn't let kids into the movie theaters until after three-thirty, so I would sneak in the side door and watch until I got caught and thrown out. Sometimes I went into a restaurant and ate as much as I could. When the check came, I ran. I learned to lift women's wallets out of their purses. I never thought of myself as bad or as breaking any laws. I was just taking what I needed to live.

One time when I was exploring in Snellenberg's department store, I saw a package of nice white T-shirts. It didn't matter what size they were, I just had to have them. I went right outside with them and put on a clean shirt. It wasn't a question of right or wrong; it was a question of getting a clean shirt in order to be accepted and acceptable. It makes no sense to tell a nine-year-old child in a dirty, stinking shirt not to steal; somebody should just give him a clean shirt. We are forever asking our children to justify the decisions they make. Shouldn't we also ask ourselves to justify a culture that forces them to make such decisions?

Anytime I was caught stealing, the worst punishment I ever got was a slap on the wrist. "Don't do that no more," the shopkeeper or cop would say. But the next day I would do the very same thing. Even when I got taken to the police station, which happened fairly often, nothing ever came of it. They talked to me and wrote stuff down, but they always let me go. I was very small for my age and pretty cute, and I learned real fast that being cute could get me out of trouble most of the time. When a store owner asked, "Why are you stealing? Don't they feed you at home?" I'd give him a good sob story, and he'd let me go, usually with a piece of fruit for good measure.

But one day the rules changed. I was wandering around downtown, and a boy rode past me on his bike. He got off and went into a store, leaving the bike out front. I wanted that bike the minute I looked at it. It wasn't that I wanted it to ride around Philadelphia—nothing beat walking. I wanted that bike as a status symbol, to ride around the neighborhood where other kids would see me. So I climbed on and rode away.

The boy saw me take off and yelled. A policeman nearby came after me and knocked me off the bike. He dragged me back to the store and called a paddy wagon, which took me to the police station. When they looked at my record with its long history of petty thievery, they decided to send me to the Youth Study Center (YSC) on a charge of "malicious mischief." I lived there off and on from the time I was nine until I was fourteen.

YSC was a holding tank where kids stayed until the courts could figure out what to do with them. It looked and felt like a hospital: cold, sterile, and impersonal. Each floor had a wing for boys and another one for girls, and each floor housed a different age group. The third floor was for the younger children, the fourth floor held ages eleven through thirteen, and the fifth floor was for the big tough guys, regardless of age. (They were usually fourteen or fifteen.)

When I got to YSC that first time, they put me in a room and locked the door—from the outside. I was more confused than scared. My police record dated only back a year or so, to when I was eight, so why were they locking me in a room? I was sorry I had taken the bike, not because I felt it was wrong but because I didn't want to get in trouble. During future stays at YSC, I'd meet a guy who was there for stealing and I'd think, "This guy is a thief," never realizing that what I had been doing was also stealing. I always saw my actions as somehow different. Even later, in the penitentiary, I still thought I was different. Now I know we were all part of the same vicious cycle.

The day of the bike incident, my mother came and got me out of YSC before I had to spend the night there. But after that first real arrest, things happened fast. For one, I no longer got away with petty theft. I'd get caught, go to court, go to YSC, be back on the streets for a while, get caught, go to court, and go back to YSC. I got to know all the counselors, and each time they'd say, "You back again, Carl?" After a series of arrests for shoplifting, receiving stolen goods, conspiracy, assault and battery, trespassing, and larceny, the judge decided to keep me at YSC until the juvenile system could decide what to do with me.

In some ways YSC was better than home. We all received clean shirts, pants, and socks, but we kept our own shoes. Everyone got blue pants and a pullover V-neck cotton shirt like the ones hospitals used. The third floor had green shirts, the fourth floor wore white, and the fifth floor wore navy.

I even got my own room. It was small, with nowhere to sit except the bed, but I had it all to myself. It had a ceiling light but no switch; it was turned on in the morning and off at night. The room had a small sink with a button you had to push to get hot water. They gave me tooth powder, a toothbrush, Pencor soap (made by the guys in the penitentiary), and toilet paper. Eventually I learned that on every floor, in the last room of the boys' section, there was a hole in the wall. Usually you could look through and see a girl's eye staring back at you, and if you were careful, you could sit and talk to her. It was considered a great stroke of luck to get the room at the end of the hall.

Everything we did at YSC was regimented. The twenty-one boys in each unit ate together three times a day. We marched everywhere we went, and we had to be silent at all times. We even had a special way of getting into the elevator: we marched in facing the back, then all at the same time, when the signal was given, we turned around and faced front. I couldn't walk where I wanted or say what I wanted; I just watched the clock, waiting for the next meal.

I loved breakfast. We were given milk and hot cereal, and we could take as much toast and apple butter as we could eat. Lunch and dinner were hot but bland. Usually we had carrots or peas, some kind of meat, and potatoes. It was served on trays that were sectioned off to keep the food from running together. There never really seemed to be enough, and I was always looking forward to the next meal.

Every day, after each meal, came recreation time in the day room. We played cards, checkers, and chess and were allowed to watch TV for two hours each evening. The day room had big windows overlooking a huge park. Fist fights broke out in the day room all the time, sometimes over a game or something else minor, but usually as a result of frustration at being caged in. Every new kid, it seemed, tried to throw a chair through those windows, but the chair just bounced off. The people at YSC weren't dumb enough to make the windows out of real glass.

The window in my room looked out over the same park as the day room. I spent a lot of time standing there with my face pressed against the glass, watching the children play outside. They would stop on their way home from the private school nearby. They put down their books and climbed around the statue in the middle of the park. They laughed and ran. They were free. They were white. And I was not one of them.

All of the subtle yet disconnected messages of my childhood coalesced as I stood watching those children. That window came to symbolize the distance between me and them, between me and white people in general. They weren't locked up as I was—they were free to run and laugh and play. But more than that, those kids had something I would never have: a childhood. They were free to be children. Nothing inside me felt childlike.

From then on, it became increasingly clear to me that my life was controlled and dominated by white people. Everyone I encountered who was happy and wealthy and good was white. Not only were they all white, but they all responded to me with a strange combination of suspicion and indifference. The human spirit cannot take such denigration for very long without building a defense against it. And that's exactly what I did.

Luckily, there was one counselor at YSC who made an impression on me. He was very supportive, even though he saw me come back time and time again. He would say, "Carl, you've got a lot more than you realize. You can do anything you want to do." I couldn't find any reason to believe it—I was already too beaten down to believe anything positive about myself. But still I liked hearing him say it, and it meant something to me. He was the first person who had ever offered me encouragement.

Another counselor, Mr. Threadgill, who was also black, was hated and feared by all the kids. He was more patient with the little kids than with the bigger ones, but he didn't take nonsense from anyone. He was fair, but he didn't tolerate any foolishness. He didn't play with us, and he didn't consider our being at YSC a joke. If someone crossed him, he would slap them halfway across the room. He was tough, which impressed me. I never got close to him, because I was afraid of his toughness, but I watched his every move and respected him from a distance. He was killed in a car accident during one of my stays at YSC. When they told us he was dead, no one cried. But then again, no one cheered either.

At the end of a four-month stay at YSC, when I was still just nine years old, I went to court—at 1801 Vine Street—where I was sentenced to the Bureau for Colored Children (BCC). Back at YSC, they called my name over the speaker: "Carl Upchurch, you'll be leaving today." I thought I was going home. A black social worker picked me up. In the car, when I asked him where I was going, he said, "You're going to the farm." I had no idea what he was talking about.

We drove out to Pomeroy, Pennsylvania. The YSC social worker dropped me off at the bottom of a hill, where another social worker was waiting for me. I had gotten out of the car and closed the door, when it suddenly occurred to me that I didn't know how long I had to stay at "the farm." By the time I turned back to ask the YSC man, he was already driving off. I ran after it until I knew I wouldn't catch him. I asked the new social worker about it as we walked up the hill, and again when we got to the cottage, but I got no answer. The truth was, I was supposed to stay at BCC until Social Services deemed it appropriate for me to leave, however long that took.

We went up a long driveway that led to several cottages. To my amazement, the place really did look like the farms I had seen in pictures. We slept in a cottage, older kids downstairs, and younger kids like me upstairs and across a creek was a two-room schoolhouse.

They gave me new clothes, stamped *1*, which was my number. They gave me a suit for Sundays and dress shoes. We always had clean clothes and clean sheets. And I finally learned how to wash and groom myself.

There was plenty of good food and fresh fruit at BCC. Miss Frey was our cook. She was a wonderful cook but grouchy. Most of the kids thought she was mean and were scared of her bad temper. All I knew was she made the best food I had ever eaten. One night a deer was killed in the road, and she made venison steaks with tons of gravy. It was delicious. Sometimes I'd go to the back door of the kitchen and ask her for a piece of pie. "You always come in here wanting something to eat," she'd bark. "You ever gonna stop growing? Here, take this pie and get outta here." When one of our teams won a big game against another institution, she told us, "Y'all come in here. I made this cake for y'all. Now eat it and get outta here."

In the winter we sledded on the hill; in the summer we played baseball and football in the fields. We were allowed to fish in the lake, and sometimes when we caught trout, Miss Frey would cook them for dinner. There were no fences to keep us in. It was more like a boarding school than a prison. I think part of the concept was that if isolated boarding schools could produce good kids, isolated boarding farms might turn around troubled city kids. In some ways it worked for me. All I was asked to do was get up on time each morning, care for myself, and get my assigned work done. I was given clean clothes, good food, and the freedom to play all day long. I blossomed intellectually, athletically, and socially.

School was required at BCC, but nothing ever happened to you if you didn't go. A nice woman named Miss Jones taught all the grade levels. For the most part I liked school there, even though I sometimes cut class to go fishing with a guy named Cade. Unlike my awful experiences back at Nathaniel Hawthorne Elementary, nobody at BCC was mean to me. I was always clean, and I didn't feel stupid. I did well and still really enjoyed reading. I made friends, even learned how to play the trumpet, and gained confidence as I discovered that, given the right environment, I could excel.

I even learned to make choices about good and bad behavior. For example, each of us got twenty-one cents a week to buy candy. Every time we did something wrong, we'd lose a few pennies. Since I liked having the whole twenty-one cents at the end of the week, I was careful to do as I was told. Unlike YSC, there was no solitary confinement at the farm for missing dinner. It was a much simpler cause-and-effect system: If we missed dinner, we didn't eat. We had to be in the cottage by nine o'clock at night, but they didn't lock the doors to keep us in.

Sometimes, on weekends, they'd take us to a nearby town. We'd go to the movies, which I liked a lot, or to dinner at the home of some "stable" local black family. Those occasions were pretty uncomfortable. The families were always hospitable and tried to make polite conversation with us, but mostly we just huddled together on the couch, all dressed up in our Sunday best and feeling out of place. Social Services had decided that these visits would show us how our lives could be if we got our acts together. But for me they accomplished the exact opposite. They taught me that despite all the good things at

BCC, out in the community, where people saw us only as "the boys from BCC," I was the same lowly person I'd always been.

I learned to play sports at BCC. At nine years old I had never been interested in sports, so I was pretty clumsy at first. When I started playing baseball, I couldn't even catch the ball. But I practiced and practiced with a guy named Jerome Bussey—throwing, catching, batting, and pitching—and got good enough to make the BCC team by the time I was ten. That was the first time I had ever set a goal for myself and worked to reach it. It boosted my confidence to be good at something, and once I got started in sports, I was hooked. I learned how to play football and even did a little boxing.

BCC was the first warm, positive environment I had ever experienced, and the two years I spent there were probably the healthiest of my childhood. I got interested in learning, my athletic ability flourished, my health was restored, and I took pride in myself. By the time my two-year stay was finished, I was feeling good.

Two years. It's a long time for a little kid. A lot of the other kids got out before I did, not because I caused more trouble than they did but because their parents wrote letters or petitioned the judge to release them. When the court sent social workers to my family to see if they were prepared to take me back, my mother must have told them repeatedly that she wasn't. Two years without me around gave her a real break from having to take days off work to find me or pick me up at the police station. She was able to focus on her own life. When I finally came home, she looked healthier. She had moved to a new apartment and was trying really hard to get her life together.

I've often heard that it is common for men to idolize their mothers. I never felt that way about mine. Though I've been tempted to condemn her for her faults as a mother, I've more often tried to understand her. She was young and poor when I was born, undereducated, and living on welfare in a hostile environment. Maybe if she had lived in a different time and place, she might have raised a more loving and cooperative son. But it didn't happen that way for her. Like me, she had been convicted in the womb. Even though she never did any jail time, I'm luckier than she was. She never had a single person in her life who believed in her. I did—at almost every correctional facility I was in—and their cumulative caring is one of the major reasons I'm where I am today.

When I was released from BCC, everything I went back to was negative, dirty, racist, and violent. Instinctively, I reverted to my old feelings and actions. You cannot corrupt a child's spirit, give him a respite from that corruption, then return him to the original environment and expect him to be more moral than others in those circumstances. The respite was better than anything I'd experienced before, but it was only a matter of time before that old stark reality kicked in.

Three

YDC AND GLEN MILLS

One afternoon, Peanut chased Pretty Boy home from school with a knife. Pretty Boy was from the 15th and Clymer gang. Peanut was fast, and each time he got close to Pretty Boy, he stabbed him in the back.

The next week, me and my cornerboys were hanging out on the steps on the 13th Street side of the school, when some guys from 15th and Clymer drove by. One of them pulled out a .22 and fired at us from the moving car. I jumped off the steps and ran after the car, grabbing some empty wine bottles out of a trash can as I went by. I chased the car down the street, throwing bottles at it and yelling, "You punks, you faggots, come on back here and rumble!"

My cornerboys were impressed. I went back, and we sat around talking about how crazy I was. It was then that I noticed my ankle. I said, "Man, something's wrong with my ankle." A couple of my cornerboys took a look at it. "Damn, Spoon, you been shot," one of them said. A .22 bullet had gone through my ankle and come out the other side. We couldn't believe it. The guys took me down to the hospital, where the doctor cleaned off the wound and bandaged it up. I never told my mother.

———

I was eleven years old when I came back from BCC late in the summer of 1961. It was exciting to be back on the streets, where I could do what I wanted. School was about to start, and I was sent to Bartlett Junior High and put in the seventh grade. I lasted there until the following February.

Since I had wandered around on my own so much when I was younger and had been away at BCC for two years, I didn't know any of my classmates very well. But Stanley Grogin, now known as Fish, was still there, and he knew most of the other guys. Fish and I picked up right where we had left off. We quickly got even closer than we'd been in early grade school, when he'd been my only friend. We hung out together, visited each other's homes, stayed out late, played ball, chased girls, went to movies, and played pinball at the corner store. Fish was my "walkie," my best friend. We stood up for each other and shared everything. If I had money and he didn't, he knew I'd give him what I had; if I needed food or anything else, I always knew I could go to Fish. We were inseparable, and I came to love him like a brother.

Fish introduced me to everyone from 13th and South, telling them, "He's cool, man, he's with me." I wouldn't have been accepted if I'd just walked up to these guys. It was because I was with Fish that I was cool—and because we were all from the same neighborhood.

Right away I noticed that everything had geographic boundaries. I was from 13th and South, and so were a lot of the guys at Bartlett. A kid was either from somewhere, like 13th Street or 15th Street, or else he was from "nowhere." If you weren't aligned with anyone, you were free game, so being from "nowhere" meant you'd end up smashed, beat up, or taken advantage of.

I didn't have to go through a rite of passage to get into the gang; the fact that I had grown up in the neighborhood was enough. One of the central tenets of gangs is that you stick with the people you grew up with. It didn't matter whether or not I had been close to these kids or that I'd been away for two years. Most of them had been in and out of detention centers too. It was our responsibility to protect the integrity of our neighborhood, an entity whose importance dwarfed our particular lives. We were from 13th and South. Period.

There is a historical pattern to gang involvement. Young men who grow up in poor urban areas with families who are often unstable or broken by abandonment or death—with family members who unexpectedly appear and disappear—look for alternative sources of identity, nourishment, and security. I was no different. I needed a group to rely on, fight with, steal with, and party with, a group that would function as my extended family. Part of gang culture is the feeling of unity, family, and brotherhood that it brings to young men. Without a gang, you're alone out there, prey for anyone and everyone. With a gang, you're part of a tight-knit group whose loyalty almost always exceeds anything you get from home. I had found my family.

I started hanging around with my cornerboys: Skeeterboo, who lived down the block; Butch, who lived over on Kater Street; Lynn and Booboo McHarris, Harry Bradley, Bubby, Peanut, Fish, Cabbage, and David Felton. Butch was our runner, which meant that he led the gang.

Around this time people started calling me Spoon. A guy named Nelson started it, because he said my head was shaped like a spoon. It wasn't exactly a compliment, but it stuck, and it made me feel even more a part of the gang, which I liked. They'd say, "Spoon, we're goin' gang warrin' tonight, you comin'?" So I'd go, and we'd hang out, fuck somebody up, or sit around smoking. I had started smoking when I was nine, so by now it was no big deal. I started drinking with my cornerboys when I was eleven or twelve, and we'd get a bottle of wine and share it while we hung out.

We were the 13th and South gang. There were other 13th Street gangs: juniors, who were a little older than us, and old-heads, who were seventeen or eighteen. Butch was always the toughest. He was our runner from the beginning, when we were young boys and he could beat up everybody else, and he stayed our runner when we were juniors and even old-heads.

When you're a gang member, you're a member for life, even if you're incarcerated or not really fighting anymore. Every time I was incarcerated, people would ask me where I was from, just as they had when I entered Bartlett Junior High. What they meant was, "What's your gang?" When I said 13th and South, it made me important. It's pretty rare to get kicked out of a gang. One sure way to do it is by ratting on somebody, by being a snitch. If you do that, you put your gang association, your reputation, and your life in jeopardy.

As cornerboys, we got "props" when we did things we thought were cool. "Props" were due, or proper, respect earned from other gang members. They helped build your reputation. We didn't keep track of props the way you do a basketball score, but you always knew who had a lot of them.

I got into 13th and South because of Fish, and I got props for having been away at BCC, but I still had to prove my strength and endurance as a gang member. Some guys went to extremes, like Peanut—he'd run off and stab somebody just for the hell of it. I wasn't that crazy, but if there was something that needed to be taken care of, I was always there.

When we were gang warring, we'd either beat people up or stab them, or else we'd plan a fair-one. A fair-one was when another gang would meet us to fight, one on one. The runners generally fought first, so Butch would take on the runner from the other gang. The warlords, the guys in charge of gang warring, went next. They were usually totally nuts, because they led us into battle. Unsurprisingly, Peanut was our warlord. Finally, we'd each fight one guy for five or ten minutes of all-out, cold-blooded fighting.

The first fair-one I was in, Butch fought Turk from 5th Street, Peanut fought Jocko Jackson, and I fought a guy named Shotgun Gibbs. It was my first chance to show 13th and South that I could take as much as I could give. Shotgun and I were each other's equal, and we fought for about fifteen minutes before I landed one on his jaw that made him bite his tongue. Blood spattered everywhere, and Shotgun hit the pavement, holding his face. When he didn't get back up, I started kicking him. My cornerboys jumped in, saying, "You got him, man. This is fair-ones, you got him." In fair-ones, once you beat a guy, the fight is over. I was now a full-fledged cornerboy.

I liked my new identity as a member of 13th and South. It was good to finally belong somewhere and have a group of friends to hang out with. When other guys reminisced about things I did, it showed me how important it was to have a good reputation. People gave me props for how well I'd fought Shotgun Gibbs and for the day I chased the car down 15th Street, throwing bottles and getting shot in the ankle. I became a sort of legend, which made me even prouder. Nobody did things consciously to enhance their reputation, though, because protecting the honor of the neighborhood and the gang always came before personal aggrandizement.

The teachers at Bartlett spent most of their time trying to manage our behavior; they weren't very successful. I was totally unmotivated to get an education. School still felt confining and uncomfortable, and I still hated it. The only thing that made school worth bothering with was that I now had friends. We spent most of our time protecting ourselves from the other gangs and defending the honor of our neighborhood. Kids from 5th and South, 15th and Clymer, and 13th and South all went to Bartlett, and the gangs had long histories of rivalry. Standing up for myself and the other guys from 13th and South was not a choice but a matter of survival. After school we always grouped together before we left the building, so no one would get fucked up.

As I said, I lasted at Bartlett till February, when I beat up Tommy Jenkins, who hung out with guys from 5th Street. I went into the bathroom one afternoon, and Tommy was there talking shit about one of my cornerboys, Lynn McHarris, saying that somebody had fucked up Lynn during a fair-one.

"I was there, and you ain't got no right talking," I told him. "You're a pussy."

"You ain't calling me a pussy. Who are you?" he asked.

"My name's Spoon and I'm from 13th Street, nigger, and you ain't got no right talking about Lynn 'cause I was there," I said. "How about me and you get a fair-one?"

We told some guy to stand watch outside the bathroom door, and we went at it. I beat him real bad and pushed his head into the sink, then went back to class. Later, the principal came and got me. Little Tommy had ratted. When the principal asked me if I did it, I said, "Man, I don't even know what that fuckin' guy's talking about." I felt no remorse—this had been a fair-one, and as far as I was concerned, we had played by the rules. Being hassled about something so minor was the last straw, and not long afterward I was back on the streets.

The first time I got picked up after that, the juvenile authorities decided to try a new approach and sent me to a special disciplinary school called Daniel Boone. I went there maybe two days a week and stayed out on the streets the rest of the time.

When I got to Daniel Boone the first time, my cornerboy Bubby was already there. He told everybody, "This here's my cornerboy, he's cool." But just like everywhere else, I still had to prove that I could hold check here—that I could control things and stand up for my cornerboys. I did it by boxing. In the coatroom one day, I boxed a guy named Lloyd Nelson, the runner of the Valley gang in North Philly. Lloyd was a good boxer—ultimately he became one of the top middleweight boxers in Philadelphia and won a gold medal at the Pan-Am games. I didn't beat him, but I held my own. He was a hard puncher and fast on his feet, but I hit harder, so we balanced each other out. After my fight with Lloyd, I was a "shot"—a big shot—at Daniel Boone.

The days I wasn't at Daniel Boone, I went back to my usual pattern—wandering around Philadelphia, stealing money or the right kind of clothes and shoes for a cornerboy. We all wore starched khaki gabardine pants, high-top Comforts like old men wear today, rust-colored jeff hats, and long-sleeved, button-front Ban-Lon shirts with starched Highboy collars. I'd started out wearing clothes my mother got at the Salvation Army, but after one of my cornerboys made fun of my "turnover" creases, I quit wearing what she bought and stole my own. Everything, from head to toe, had to be pressed with as much starch as you could use. Gomere ironed my things for me so I looked just as starched as everyone else; we all must have looked like we had lain down on an ironing board. Hair styles were important to us too. Most of us conked our hair, or conked each other's. Mine was conked and combed straight back. I thought I looked like Nat King Cole.

The summer of 1962, when I was twelve, was one of the most memorable ones of my life. I had my cornerboys and a feeling of security. I'd sit on the steps of our building and watch the neighborhood pulsate to Martha and the Vandellas, Marvin Gaye, and the Temptations. I was feeling so good about myself that one morning, when my mother came down the steps and told me to move out of her way, I stood up, made a path for her, and took a bow. All she said was, "What the fuck does that mean?" But I didn't even care what she thought about me. I had my cornerboys, and we were having fun. That's all I needed.

Most of my family was still on welfare, but some were working makeshift jobs. My mother took a job at a place called Metal Masters, a toy factory that paid by the piece. She'd always hated being on welfare, so she was relieved when she finally got the job, and she committed herself to it. She'd get up at four o'clock each morning to prepare for work, and from then until she walked out the door, she always had a lit cigarette and a cup of coffee with Carnation milk within arm's reach. She counted out in advance the twenty-three cents for the bus. It took her a long time to get to the plant, since she had to transfer several times, but she never complained. In retrospect, I think that's when I first saw that discipline in her, though I didn't recognize it then. Her commitment to her work and her determination to improve her life probably affected me more than I understood at the time.

When she started working at Metal Masters, her life got a little better—she could pay her own rent and no longer depended on other people for money. Of course, her working also meant that she continued to have no idea what was going on in my life. In fact, except for

Stoney, my family never even acknowledged that I was in a gang. They probably wondered where I got all the nice clothes, but they never asked. My mother clearly thought she had already spent far too much time trying to keep me in school and retrieving me from the police station. She didn't *want* to know what I was doing.

Being a good athlete was another way of racking up props. My cornerboys and I played sports all the time, and we approached them as vigorously as we did stealing and gang warring. Local counselors and representatives of youth activity groups would come around, form teams, and provide us with equipment so we could play basketball and baseball against some white boys from other neighborhoods. We had some really good athletes: Lynn McHarris could knock a ball for what seemed like a million miles; David Felton could play every sport better than anyone I'd ever seen; and Harry Bradley could pitch a curve ball that looked like it dropped off the edge of a table when it came over the plate.

The holidays were a big time for gang wars. Every New Year's Day, during the Mummers parade in Philadelphia, we went downtown looking for guys to fuck up. All the local gangs were there. The 15th and Clymer, 16th and South, and 20th and Wilder gangs came from one side of Broad Street; Fifth and South, 7th and Kater, and 13th and South came from the other side. We all knew each other. For example, the main guys from 15th and Clymer were Boney Bill, Pretty Boy, Charlie, and Black Bart. And those guys knew that the top props in 13th and South were Butch, Peanut, Fish, and Spoon. Everybody targeted the other runners and warlords; to get them was to get the core of a gang.

This kind of gang warring wasn't like fair-ones, when things were organized and we knew who we were going to fight. This was full-scale war, involving multiple gangs. Anything could happen. One time we caught Shotgun Gibbs and beat him up. I took a starter's pistol, the kind used to start races, and put it in his mouth. When I pulled the trigger, it burned up his mouth and most of his face. Violence had never bothered me; I never thought twice about fucking somebody up like that. In fact, I laughed when Shotgun grabbed his face and went down squealing like a pig. I laughed. I didn't know whether I'd really hurt him, but so what if I had?

One day, Skeeterboo and I went to Gimbels department store. We stole some pants and athletic equipment and stuffed them in a bag. A security guard spotted us and chased us. Skeeterboo made off with the bag, but I got caught and my mother got a call to come down to the police station. When the cops asked her what she thought they should do with me, she said, "Fuck him, leave him in there."

So I took another turn at YSC while I awaited a trial. Eventually I was sentenced to the Youth Development Center (YDC). It had been just over a year since I was released from BCC. I was twelve years old.

———

I arrived at YDC in November 1962. I felt no shame about being there. After all, most of the men in my neighborhood, young and old, had spent time in a succession of prisons. I figured it was a normal pattern of life—YDC was where I was supposed to be.

But things had changed a lot for me during the year between BCC and YDC. I arrived at YDC as a certified member of 13th Street and South, with a reputation. Still, I had to prove that I was tough—that I was no snitch, that I could kick ass, and that I wouldn't let anybody down. I no longer longed for the comfort and security of BCC. The sensitive side of me that had flourished there was deeply buried. Now I focused on surviving on C Unit and being a tough representative for my cornerboys. It was up to me to show people that guys from 13th and South could hold some check.

My cornerboys who passed through YDC while I was there knew they could count on me. There were guys there from other gangs too who knew of me and my reputation. I wasn't known as a monster kick-ass but as someone who would fuck somebody up at the drop of a hat for my cornerboys.

YDC was no pleasant farm sprawled on hills. It occupied an old hospital building deep in the heart of North Philadelphia. We slept locked up in long wards with dormitory-style cots, two or three of us to a cubicle, thirty in each ward. There was one relatively clean bathroom for each ward. When we did something wrong, we were moved to a separate detention unit.

YDC was a much more physical place than either YSC or BCC. We boxed and fought all the time and fielded good baseball and track teams. At twelve, I was too young to play on the institutional team, but I represented my unit in intramurals and played pretty well. Sports became an outlet for some of my anger and frustration, but I also loved the competition and physical play, and the way it felt to be good at something.

Most of my time at YDC I spent either working in the wood shop, fighting, or playing sports. They expected me to attend classes, but I refused to go a lot of times. Sometimes, though, I doodled poetry in the ward, writing what I called gangster poems, about killings and other gruesome things.

There was one teacher, Miss Mines, whom I decided I'd like to impress. A tall, thin woman with light brown skin, she always wore her hair pulled back off her face. She had drowsy-looking eyes, with lids that blinked slowly, and a mole over one side of her lip. I took my poetry to her class and stayed afterward to show her—and to look at her a little longer.

She kept trying to steer me away from my gory verses, encouraging me to write about other things. In December of my second year there, she asked me to write a poem about the new year. I can remember only one line of what I wrote for her: "At your front door, 1964." She suggested I change it to "Loudly proclaiming, welcome 1964." I liked the change and was impressed by how much difference the word *proclaiming* made. Everyone said they loved the poem, and I believed them, even though they weren't all that appreciative of poetry, because YDC was not the kind of place where people lied to try to make you like them. I wrote another poem about the death of John F. Kennedy. The counselors and even my sister Stoney seemed astonished that *I* had written it.

My poem about Kennedy prompted the YDC superintendent, Mrs. Epps, to call me into her office one day. Mrs. Epps was a young professional African-American woman who dealt gently but firmly with everyone. She even took the counselors to task when they didn't treat us sensitively, so we knew she cared about us. I had a lot of respect for Mrs. Epps.

"We want you to go to school here," she told me.

"I don't want to do that, Mrs. Epps," I told her. I still hated school, even though I was at least attending classes pretty regularly.

"You make me mad as hell," she told me. Then she launched into a fifteen-minute tirade about the gifts I had that I didn't use and about how special I was. When she was finished, I started crying. I hadn't cried in a long time.

As Mrs. Epps handed me some tissues, she said, "I wish you were my son." I wished it too.

———

Stoney and I began bonding while I was at YDC. Because she had lived with our father's mother for most of our childhood, we hadn't grown up together, but now she wrote me all the time, and I wrote back every chance I got. Stoney wasn't as close to Seppie or Deenie as she was to me, and she thought it was important that I was her only brother. It didn't seem to matter to her that I was a gang member and always getting into trouble. She loved me unconditionally, and I valued my relationship with her. It felt good to have someone in my family that I felt truly close to.

Two important events in my family happened while I was at YDC. The first I found out about by way of one of Stoney's letters. As always, I eagerly tore open the envelope, only to read that Uncle Haywood had raped her. I was twelve at the time, so Stoney was fourteen. For the first time the violence in our lives struck me in the gut. I had always been able to stow brutality away, without letting myself feel it or analyze it, so that I could continue to function in the world; I had been conditioned to ignore much of it. But I could not and still cannot accept Stoney's rape. I had admired Haywood as a child; now I wanted to kill him.

Stoney had always been the most open and kind person in my life. In her letter she said she had told my mother and grandmother, but they blamed her for it. No one in the family—not Nita, not my mother, not my grandmother—had any sympathy for her. I was the only one she could turn to.

I wrote back asking her to come visit me. When she arrived, I didn't know what to do, so I just held her hand as she told me what had happened. She had come home from school and Uncle Haywood, who was visiting, called her into his bedroom. He asked her to take off her panties. When she refused, he threw her down on the bed and forced himself on her. I didn't know what to say. We just sat there and cried, holding hands. I had never felt so angry, disgusted, and brutalized. In the street, when we were going to finally do somebody, we'd say, "He'll be all right." Before Stoney left that day, I told her, "He'll be all right." I don't know if she knew what I meant by it, but Haywood was on my list.

The second thing happened in March 1964. Mrs. Epps called me into her office. I thought she was going to give me another biweekly pass, which I had been frequently earning. Instead, she said, "Carl, your father has been killed. Your mother is coming on Friday to pick you up, and we're going to sign your release."

I was absolutely stunned. She searched my face for a reaction, but I showed none. I calmly said, "Thank you, Mrs. Epps," and left to pack my things. When my mother picked me up, I was still numb. She took me to the store to get clothes for the funeral. I wore a herringbone blazer, black pants, a black tie, and a black armband.

My father had been a veteran of the Korean War, so three soldiers outside Chew's Funeral Home gave him a twenty-one-gun salute. Each one shot seven times. I didn't know till years later that twenty-one-gun salutes are usually done that way; I just figured they thought he wasn't worth a real one.

It wasn't until I looked in the casket that it hit me that he was really gone. I began to cry uncontrollably. Aunt Lil put her arms around me and held me in what seemed like the warmest and most comforting embrace I had ever felt. I was devastated by the sight of my father lying there. It was the first time I had ever seen anyone in a casket, and I vowed never to do it again.

After the tears came the anger. I wanted to kill Big Nate Williams, the man who had murdered my father. Nate thought my father had been with his girlfriend, who was Aunt Nita. He and my father got drunk and went at each other in a street fight. Nate knocked my father down and kicked his head into the cement, killing him instantly.

I'd never seen much of my father when he was alive. But as a child with no material resources, no emotional support, and no nourishing family structure, the little of him I had seen gave me a lot of comfort. He wasn't around enough to be a "dad" to me, but that also meant that I wasn't exposed to his many negative attributes. When I'd go down to the bar where he'd be sitting with his wino buddies, he'd tell everybody, "Hey, this is my boy here! Hey, boy, what you need? Fifty cents? A dollar? This is my boy, everybody." He loved to brag that I was his only son. "I got a lot of daughters all over the city," he'd say, "but you're my only boy."

It didn't matter to me that he was bragging to a bunch of drunks and druggies, or that maybe it was the alcohol talking. I liked the fact that he took pride in me. After he died I forgot about all the things he hadn't done for me and all the times he hadn't been there. I just knew I'd liked him, enough to be shaken by his death and to miss him afterward. I felt as if something had been taken from me.

Five years later some gangster shot Nate. I was glad.

My father died thirty-two years ago, but in some ways it seems like last week. I still feel the raw emotions of it: I can still close my eyes and see him lying there. I still have questions about the role Aunt Nita played, not only in causing the fight but in refusing to testify, thereby keeping Nate from getting a longer sentence. I've always harbored some ill will toward her for that.

My mother sat on the front steps and cried her eyes out, although

Stoney and I felt that her tears represented no affection for my father. Stoney was every bit as shocked and as hurt as I was, especially because she had known our father much better than I had, having lived with his mother for most of her childhood.

Stoney's rape and my father's murder effectively sealed off the last tiny openings through which anyone, even Mrs. Epps, could have reached the little boy that Carl Upchurch might have been. I returned to the streets tougher, sharper, and meaner.

———

I had been out of YDC only two months when I went into a jewelry store at 12th and Chestnut to rob the cash register. The woman who was working there tried to grab my arm, so I knocked her out. I jumped over the counter and yanked out the money. The cops busted in before I could get away, and once again I was back in court. This time the charge was larceny, but the sentence had a lot to do with my history in the courts and my truancy.

If my record had been shorter, I might have been sent to St. Gabriel's Hall. But as it was, I was headed straight for Glen Mills, where all the other hard-core youths with long records of theft and violence were sent. Word around the neighborhood was that Glen Mills was a brutal place. But I wasn't intimidated. I looked at Glen Mills as just another system to learn, another place I had to prove myself.

My first job was to scope out who was there, connect quickly with my cornerboys, and find out who my enemies were. I connected with guys from Bartlett Junior High, Daniel Boone, YDC, and 13th and South, so I had built-in protection against the guys from 5th and South and 15th and Clymer, who would otherwise have beaten me on sight. I also arrived with a certain amount of authority, based on my reputation.

Glen Mills is in Delaware County, Pennsylvania, twenty miles southwest of Philadelphia. It looked like a rural college campus, with rolling hills, nice houses (which we called cottages), and a large red-brick administration building. Another building had classrooms, a hospital, a gym, a butcher shop, and a bakery. Like BCC, there were no fences or gates to keep us in. I was impressed with the grounds: It was late June, and there were flowers everywhere. I felt comfortable and thought, "I belong here. I can go with this." It seemed like a sweet deal.

The physical beauty of the outside, however, belied the viciousness within. Each cottage was ruled by a group of about five shots. Anyone who wanted to become a shot had to fight all of the current shots, one after the other. If he held up, then he was a shot. If he didn't, he was knocked out and had no say in what went on in the cottage.

New guys would line up for gym, and while we waited, we'd box. As in every other place I'd ever been, boxing or fighting was how you proved yourself. I did pretty well boxing four or five guys, and because I had a reputation of being tough and holding my own, I soon became a shot.

There were eleven cottages—some all black, some all white, some mixed. I was placed in cottage five, along with forty-seven other black kids. The ratio of blacks to whites was about three to one, and the black cottages were always overcrowded. On the first floor of each cottage were showers, lockers, and the kitchen. The dining hall was on the second floor, and our bunks were on the third. The beds were set up ward-style. We had cottage "parents," generally a couple who held college degrees in child development or troubled youth. The "father" counseled us and served as a warden; the "mother" cooked.

Even though no fences or gates or iron bars surrounded the campus, guys rarely tried to skip out. It was a long walk back to Philly, and nobody knew of anyone or anything closer. The Glen Mills authorities could easily find a runaway on the tracks or on the Baltimore Pike. And no black urban gangster could easily make himself inconspicuous in a farmyard. Those who went a month without trying to skip out got to see a special movie as a reward; anyone who had tried to skip had to stay in the cottage. At night we were always locked up.

Usually I spent half of each day in class trying to earn my GED, as I had been advised to do; the other half, I worked in the bakery. I still hated school, but I looked forward to going to work. I enjoyed learning skills that produced a tangible outcome—how to knead bread, grease pans, and make buns and cakes. I seldom made errors and easily worked my way up to first baker. After nine months I was put in charge of pizza-making.

Besides my long record, another reason I ended up at Glen Mills was that the Pennsylvania authorities always sent the better athletes there. I had distinguished myself in sports at YDC, playing baseball, basketball, and football, and it must have showed up in my file. When I arrived, it was the beginning of baseball season, which was my best sport, since I could play four different positions. One day our team played a local high school. I had been hit with the ball three times while up at bat. The next time I went up, I was a little hesitant, afraid that I was going to be hit again, and my first swing was pretty weak. The coach called me aside. "If you strike out, you'll never play for me again," he warned me. I dug in and tried my best on the next two pitches, but I still struck out. Coach Vaughters never put me off the team. I think he knew I had tried my hardest, and that was good enough for him.

Coach Vaughters was in his thirties, a tall, lean African-American man. He had sharp features, sort of like Abraham Lincoln, and didn't smile easily. I think he pretended to be tough because he knew that's what we respected, but he was a decent guy, and I really looked up to him. I worked hard and produced more for him athletically than I had for anyone else.

He kept trying to get me interested in schoolwork, and at one point he even asked me to enter a biology contest. "I know you could win it," he said. "You'll win if you want to, but knowing you, you won't want to."

I did enter, and my entry was a poster about avoiding poison ivy, poison oak, and poison sumac. It said "Stop!" in giant letters across the top of the poster, and something like "If contacted, immobilize . . . and seek medical attention" at the bottom. My poster won first prize. Coach Vaughters was right—I could achieve if I wanted to.

Being at Glen Mills made me even tougher than I'd been. Most people there tried either to break my spirit or to coddle me. I didn't respond to either approach, except maybe to say "Fuck you." Coach Vaughters, though, had found a way to reach me. He knew my indifference was a protective veneer, but he never let it deter him. For my part, I would have died rather than tell him how important his interest in me was. But we both knew he had a lot of influence over me.

When I first started playing for him, I'd pull pranks, run lazily, and not work up to my potential. But as the season wore on, my attitude improved every time he coached me. By the end of the season, my behavior was entirely different. He never pleaded with me to do something, or do it better. He simply gave me a choice: "You either do it or you don't."

When football season rolled around, I tried out for quarterback. Coach Vaughters already had someone picked for the position—a big guy from Chester, Pennsylvania—but I wanted the position anyway.

"You don't really want to play quarterback," he told me. "You just want it because it's a star position."

I tried to convince him otherwise, but to no avail. Finally he decided to teach me a lesson. He put me in, but, without me knowing, told the offensive line to let the defense through. They pounded me over and over and over. Coach Vaughters and his assistant laughed at me from the sidelines, and every time I got knocked on my ass, he yelled, "Give him back the ball, give him back the ball." I was crying under my helmet, but I wouldn't quit. He must have respected my stubbornness, though, because I made the team. The big guy from Chester was the quarterback, just as Coach Vaughters had planned, but I got to be a fullback.

When Coach Vaughters posted the list of guys he had picked for his basketball team, my name wasn't on it. I knew I was a pretty good player, so in gym class that day, I asked him why he hadn't put me on the team. "Because you can't play," he said.

"Try me," I said. "You've never seen me play."

He had me shoot from all different angles. I had had a lot of practice on and off the streets. I made every shot, even with Vaughters watching me, and so he put me on the team. I wasn't a starter, but I could live with it.

Coach Vaughters holds a special place in my memory because he found a way to get past my defenses when no one else could. If he had said "Carl, I love you," or "Carl, we need you," I would have shut him out. Emotionally, I was very difficult to get along with at that time. In order to preserve my reputation, I had to appear big and important. It wasn't safe to let anyone to get too close, but deep down I needed people to be close to. Coach Vaughters challenged me. He knew there was something behind my tough exterior, but he also knew better than to encourage me openly or to directly approach that hidden part.

The only time he gave me anything close to a compliment was during the baseball season. We were playing an all-white school. Their remarkable pitcher had a wicked curve ball, could throw real fast, and was striking everyone out. I went up to bat and hit the ball straight up the middle. No one could believe it. Coach Vaughters came up to me and said, "You had that look in your eye. You smashed it right up the middle. That's the kind of person you are." We lost the game, but I was proud that he had singled me out for praise.

Coach Vaughters introduced me to parts of myself that I actually liked. Playing for him at Glen Mills, I got an inkling of other standards of success besides the old one I was still trying to live up to—the look on my mother's face. I could find self-worth from successfully hitting the ball or even just showing the coach I could play. I realized that success could mean meeting an internal challenge or personal test, independent of what anybody thought. From that point—at least when I remembered to—I tried to gauge my accomplishments more by what I had learned or achieved than by the result.

Glen Mills was unusual in that our teams went out into the community to play against regular students. As ambassadors, we were expected to be on our best behavior, but the constant awareness that we were different from the other teams, because we were locked up, was so intimidating that it often affected how we played.

It was the same when we visited black people's homes in and around Philadelphia. As at BCC, we had been introduced to successful black men and women, community leaders, and businesspeople. Now we had to dress up, wearing ties that made us look and feel uncomfortable. The Glen Mills administration was trying to show us a life other than the one we had been living, but in spite of their good intentions, I felt unworthy to be around these people. In our hearts, none of us believed we would ever have a shot at life in Germantown or the other middle- and upper-class communities that surrounded Philadelphia.

In spite of all the positive things that happened to me at Glen Mills, I still wanted to get out of there and go back to the streets, where I could run my own life. You needed 128 points to get out. For good behavior, you could earn a maximum of 21 points a month. But you also lost points for bad behavior, like getting into fights or trying to skip out or being insubordinate. I had 45 points at one point, then got in trouble and dropped back to 30. Then I had a good stretch and made it up to 62 points without really thinking about it. It helped to be back up, because I could count my points and plan when I would leave. It was good motivation. Guys who had 92 points knew they could go home in two months, and they were careful not to lose any. Once you had your 128 points, you were out of there, whether your family wanted you back or not.

Glen Mills, like the other detention centers, taught me how to follow rules, but it didn't prepare me at all to go out and lead a moral, nonviolent life. It didn't change the way I viewed the world. If anything, I got tougher there, developed a bigger reputation, and became even more hardened to the violence I saw and committed.

I returned to 13th and South with an enhanced reputation, as one of a select group who had made it through Glen Mills. I was proud that people thought I was tough and cool. But for the first time in my life, I didn't like being on the streets. I can still remember how depressed I felt, standing on a corner that I used to feel like I owned—knowing I had no money, nowhere to go, nothing to do—and thinking, "I can't wait to go back to jail." At Glen Mills I had made a lot of noise about wanting to be back on the streets, but the only environment I really felt comfortable in was jail. There I was a shot, a somebody, and people respected me.

My problem wasn't with Glen Mills, or YDC, or YSC, or BCC; my problem was with me. I was still convinced that the cycle of running and taking and jail was my destiny. All the young toughs from Philly at Glen Mills had thought the same thing. All products of the same mold, it never occurred to us to aspire to anything else.

Four

CAMP HILL

I had been out of Glen Mills only a month or so when Stoney came to me with the news. "They got Fish," she told me. A bunch of guys from 15th and Clymer had come down on our turf, put a gun to his head, and blown his brains out. He was fifteen years old.

I was devastated. Fish was like my other half. I couldn't understand how the guys from 15th and Clymer had had the nerve to come right onto our turf. It made me feel vulnerable.

The news left me numb. I remember punching a wall, but I could barely feel the pain it caused. When the numbness faded, I was consumed with rage, and I vowed revenge. There was no escaping the violence now. Someone would have to pay for Fish's death.

————

Not long after Fish was killed, I was arrested for strong-arm robbery. A bunch of us had been down on the corner, looking to get somebody for what had been done to Fish, when some poor guy came walking down the sidewalk. I don't even think we knew him, but that didn't matter; we would have lashed out at anyone. We grabbed him and beat him up real decent. Right before we ran, I grabbed his watch.

The police were after us before we could get off the street. They chased us down and threw us up against a wall. Because of my record, I was sent to the State Correctional Institution at Camp Hill—the same place where Uncle Haywood had served time for rape (long before he raped Stoney) and where another uncle had received the death penalty.

The judge, who was a woman, asked my mother, "Mrs. Upchurch, what do you think we should do with him?"

"I don't care what you do with him," she replied. "I know I can't control him."

The judge warned her, "We may have to send him away to a longer place of stay."

"Do what you want with him," my mother answered.

I was so hurt by what my mother had said that I hardly heard the judge's next statement—"We recommend that he be sent to the State Correctional Institution at Camp Hill for an indeterminate amount of time." When I went back to my holding cell, I didn't cry as I had during my previous sentence hearings. Rather, I was irritated by the other kids who were crying. Nothing could touch me now. I yelled at them to shut up.

In November 1965, at the age of fifteen, I reported to Camp Hill. Both adults and juveniles were at this penitentiary. At all the other detention centers, I'd been called Carl or Upchurch. At Camp Hill I was known by an official number—G9451.

There were no green fields, rolling hills, or well-kept cottages here. Instead, we were surrounded by gun towers and electric bars. I was assigned to a cell with armed guards standing outside. Camp Hill had a reputation for being racist. The old-timers referred to it as White Hill, because everything there was white—the guards, the teachers, the warden. Even the lieutenants' hats were white.

Camp Hill was divided into nine wards, some for adults and some for teenagers. I was put in a ward with other guys who were fifteen, sixteen, and seventeen. I already knew a lot of them; we had gone through gang wars and other lockups together. We would reminisce— "Remember what you did in West Chester?" "Remember what happened at YSC?" It must have sounded like returning to school after summer vacation.

At Camp Hill, if you weren't serious about your reputation and didn't command respect, people fucked around with you big-time. You had to be tough and able to stand up for yourself, or else you had to be in a gang and have somebody else stand up for you. Luckily, I was both. My reputation, built on the streets and at other facilities, preceded me. Although I still had to prove myself when I got there, people knew who I was, things I had done, and that I was from 13th and South. No one took advantage of me and I was known as a stand-up person. I also had proven myself as an athlete, which gave me additional props. People started recruiting me as soon as I arrived. I was somebody.

As at Glen Mills, whenever someone new arrived, particularly someone with a reputation, he had to prove himself by boxing the guys who were already holding check. They ran gym lines here too—we'd line up for gym, and eight or so of the toughest guys in the cell block would fight the new guy. If the guy could hold up, everybody would know he was down, and he would hold some check. A guy who could really take a beating but wasn't all that tough could be an associate. People would know he was all right and he wouldn't get messed with, but he wouldn't have the authority of a shot. A guy who got beat into the ground was nothing but a chump. Guys who couldn't hold their own had to take all kinds of shit—get beat up, slashed, even fucked.

I was put in H Ward, which was called the nut ward for some reason. Everyone who was in there was a little strange, but no more than anybody else. Most of us were urban blacks from Philadelphia. Some were from Chester and Altoona. When I arrived on the ward, a guy named Lamont came over and said, "Hey new boy, where you from?" I told him. "You want to box?" he asked. I figured I could take him, so I said, "Yeah."

When we were finished, about eight other guys were waiting for me. We fought for about forty-five minutes, and I beat them all. I immediately became one of the shots in my block. People knew better than to mess with me. I was known as someone who would fight at the drop of a hat. I liked to fight, I was good at it, and I walked around thinking I owned the world. Lots of my cornerboys came through while I was at Camp Hill: Henry, Chuckie, Thomas, Vernon, Lynn, and Cabbage. Since I was already holding check, they came in under my protection.

There were plenty of guys at Camp Hill from 15th and Clymer, and my cornerboys and I kicked their asses every chance we got, each time taking revenge for Fish's death. Whenever we read in the paper about an incident involving 13th and South and 15th and Clymer, we made them pay.

We were especially vicious after we read that three guys from 15th and Clymer had shot Butch. The newspaper report said they had walked down Kater Street and held a gun to his back and fired. The bullet hit his spine. Butch crawled to the corner, where some of our guys got help. He survived, but had trouble walking afterward, and eventually one of his legs had to be amputated. Although I was away at Camp Hill, I was outraged that the guys from 15th and Clymer had had the nerve to pull this again, especially after Fish. Those three guys knew Butch was our runner, and they shot him and ran. That was a violation of the biggest kind, and I wanted revenge.

Each cell block at Camp Hill had four tiers with twenty-five cells in each tier, holding a total of a hundred convicts. Eight to nine shots controlled each cell block, just like the toughs on a city block or the shots in the cottages at Glen Mills. Whenever things got out of control on the block, the shots were notified. As a shot, I kept people in line and fought to protect my cornerboys.

One time I was eating in the back of the kitchen, when a prominent member of the 49th and Hoops gang came in and told me he didn't think I had any right to be holding check: "Who you think you are? If you run gym lines on my cornerboy, you can run 'em on me." He swung at me, and we fought it out right there in the kitchen. I had on rubber galoshes over my shoes because of the wet kitchen floor, and they made me slide all over the place. He caught me across the eye once; it wasn't a great punch, but it scraped the surface. Still, I gave as good as I got and we fought to a draw.

The positive reinforcement that came from being able to kick somebody's ass built my self-confidence. I was respectful of guys who had better reputations than I did, but not afraid. I never backed down. If we fought to a draw, I'd be the real winner because my reputation wasn't as big. If I beat somebody's ass, my rep would improve. The more I fought, the tougher I became.

Camp Hill had a lot of shops for us to work in: a tailor shop, a masonry shop, a woodcarving shop, and an electrical shop. I didn't want anything to do with the shops. I guess we were supposed to learn a trade there, but the system didn't seem to produce anything significant. Most of the projects that guys worked on in these shops were trivial. The guys who worked in the tailor's shop, say, would add an extra stripe around the collar of their uniform. I didn't respect the process, and I sure didn't know of anyone who had become a tailor or a mason after Camp Hill.

Compulsory education didn't exist, so I didn't go to school either. What I did was work in the powerhouse. The whole place ran on coal that had to be shoveled into a furnace twenty-four hours a day. We worked eight-hour shifts for twenty-five cents an hour—earning two whole dollars a day. I used most of the money to buy cigarettes, soap, and writing materials. The rest I gambled; we also played for soap, toothpaste, and cigarettes.

I worked the third shift, which meant I slept while most everyone else was working. I'd go down to the powerhouse at midnight and shovel coal into the early hours of the morning. Powerhouse workers were allowed outside their cells when nobody else was, which gave us a certain prestige. We also received extra clothes because we got much dirtier than everyone else. I liked doing physical work, staying busy, and having some responsibility.

Even though I didn't take classes at Camp Hill, I completed the

GED I had started at Glen Mills. The notice they posted about the GED test said it would take five days to administer, which translated into five days off from work. I'd be a fool not to jump at that deal, I figured, so I signed up with no intention of trying to pass. Each test-taker was given a different section of the test at a different time. It just so happened that the first section I got was literature. If I'd gotten the math section first, I probably would have blown the whole test off, but I liked literature, and I could answer a fair number of the questions. That boosted my confidence. Then I got the science and social studies sections, both of which required reading and answering questions. They didn't seem too hard either, so I kept going. When I got to the grammar section, the questions were like "What's wrong with this sentence?" I didn't know anything about dangling participles or run-on sentences, but because I'd read a lot, I could mostly tell which sentences were right and which were wrong. When the results were posted, everyone, including me, was surprised that I received a high score. At first I thought it was somebody else's score, but no, I had really passed. At the age of sixteen, I was officially a high school graduate.

While I was at Camp Hill, I read all the newspapers I could get my hands on, from front to back. Some of the guys had newspapers sent to them from their hometowns, like Erie and Scranton. When they were finished with them and left them for trash, I took them into my cell and read them too.

As had happened at YDC, BCC, and Glen Mills, one person at Camp Hill made a lasting impression on me: Mr. Winters, a day-shift guard on my block. He was a strict disciplinarian, but he was fair, and people respected him for being a decent guard and a good person. I liked him, but of course I didn't allow myself to get close to him. Looking back, though, I think he appreciated how I handled things on our block. As a shot, I kept people in line and kept things quiet, and I was known for being tough but not an asshole.

There was one guy on our block called Tank. Once when we were lining up to go to a movie, Tank started giving me a hard time. He didn't want to stay in line, so I said, "Come on Tank, man, get back in line."

"Fuck you," he said. "You ain't the police," meaning I wasn't a guard.

"Get the fuck in line!" I told him. He didn't budge.

Mr. Winters said, "Y'all fight it out." So I kicked Tank's ass real good and told him to get the fuck in line. Winters would act as if he didn't like it when I handled things this way, but when it came down to it, he let me do it the way I wanted a lot of the time.

The football and baseball teams at Camp Hill were dynamite, but we only played intraprison games because there weren't any other institutions or high schools in the area to compete against. Sports was one way the prisoners built their reputations. Hitting the ball over the fence made you somebody. But no one slid into the base unless they had to. Someone would have asked, "What the hell are you sliding for? Who are you trying to impress?"

While I was at Camp Hill, I had minimal contact with my family. Occasionally I wrote to Gomere, but no one except Stoney ever came to visit. My mother sometimes dropped Stoney off without coming in herself. To say that she wrote or sent money even once a year would probably be an exaggeration.

Stoney graduated from high school while I was away. My relationship with her grew even stronger while I was at Camp Hill. She always sent me birthday cards and wrote long, thoughtful letters that allowed me to get to know her better and keep up with what was going on in the family. She loved to read and write, and her letters opened me up to a new way of thinking. She was a more thorough thinker than I was. She impressed me with the power of her ideas yet wrote to me as if she assumed I understood her thinking. She became my teacher. She questioned me insightfully and incisively, which prompted me to think for myself. When a letter from her arrived, I always squeezed the envelope to see how thick it was, then put it away to cherish it when I had time to sit down and go through it line by line. Thanks to Stoney, a new part of me began to open up. Her writings were magical.

Stoney also knew a lot about issues I was still grappling with. She'd recommend books to me, and I would check them out of the prison library. Once I'd read them, we talked about them in our letters. We wrote about Irving Wallace's *The Word* and about *Five Smooth Stones,* a book that addresses racial issues in the South. I could never have shown this part of me to anyone else, especially at Camp Hill. I somehow felt that sharing even a line from Stoney's letters or from a book she'd recommended would make the magic of it all disappear.

The other reason I didn't share any of what Stoney and I talked about was that I knew there were no props awarded at Camp Hill for intellectual development. I didn't even tell Snake and Moses, whom I hung out with sometimes, though I knew they had been to school. They knew stuff and I found them interesting, but the other guys gave me shit for spending time with them. They'd say, "Hey Carl, why you hanging with them fuckin' nuts?" I didn't think they were nuts, and I valued their friendship, but I kept my secret life to myself. What was happening to me inside, slowly and quietly, was important, but it had no place at Camp Hill.

I wrote to Stoney every chance I got, and it was great to be able to spend a whole evening writing to her. I would take a shower, go back to my cell, and sit down to share a few hours with my sister. Camp Hill is forever associated in my mind with really getting to know her.

The whole two years I was at Camp Hill, I was anxious to leave, even though I had absolutely no plans for what I would do when I got out. I would have a lot of war stories to tell, I knew. I was bigger, stronger, healthier, and more mature. My reputation had grown, and the guys on the streets would know that I'd made it through the pen as a stand-up guy. I had been in with the big boys and had not only survived but prevailed.

On a blistering afternoon in July 1967, I was released. I boarded a bus for Philadelphia, sweating in a brown wool prison-issue suit. With sixty dollars in my pocket, I thought I was ready for anything. But the first thing I saw when I stepped off the bus at 17th and Market was a girl walking toward me in a miniskirt. Except for girls in bathing suits, I had never seen that much bare leg in my life. I couldn't stop staring at her.

She looked right through me, and the power and control I had felt on the bus only moments before vanished. I'd thought I would be quite a catch—a bad-ass ex-con with a huge reputation—and here this woman had barely noticed me. I was nothing to her, completely invisible, and I was once again confronted by a world I wasn't a part of. When I caught the local bus home, I felt very small.

Once I got back on my own streets, I hoped, I'd recapture the feeling of being big and tough that I'd had in the penitentiary. It didn't happen. The world had changed a lot while I was at Camp Hill. The Vietnam War, the Southern Christian Leadership Conference, the Student Nonviolent Coordinating Committee, Martin Luther King, Jr., and the Congress of Racial Equality now dominated the news. I had read about those things in prison, but I was unprepared for how much they had changed society.

People had big Afros now and no longer conked their hair to make it straight. The airwaves were filled with war news and political talk. I may have kicked ass and been a shot in the pen, but outside I was nothing.

I went right back to the streets, looking for the closest environment to Camp Hill I could find. The only way I knew how to evaluate myself was through street activity—how tough I was, how clever I was, how much I could steal, how well I could maneuver. Any other standard of measurement felt oppressive and alienating.

———

While I was at Camp Hill, my family had moved to 5335 Webster Street, in West Philadelphia. "Gee, the family's moving up," I thought when I first saw the neighborhood. It was much more respectable than South Street. People didn't call each other motherfuckers, and nobody shot anyone or beat anyone up in the street. At night people just sat on their porches, laughing and joking. My mother was still working steadily at Metal Masters and had married a man named Frank Lonon. He worked as a longshoreman at the pier and was some kind of manager. They had purchased a house and a car, neither of which we ever had had before.

The people in this neighborhood were completely different from people I had known on South Street. The girls were neat and clean, with polished fingernails and nice clothes. The guys weren't rough; they wore clothes that kids today would call "fresh"—the newest sneakers, the latest jackets, and brand-name jeans. Everyone said "Yes ma'am" and "May I?" and "Please" and "Thank you." The kids went to dances and high school games on weekends, and nobody hung out on the corners or chased each other down. They were interested in normal teenage stuff. I was a teenager too, but these kids made me feel like a space alien.

Even so, I was instantly popular—everybody liked me and sought me out for games and dances and parties. The ex-con who didn't fit in was suddenly Mr. Personality. People were intrigued by me. I must have done some pretty serious things to get to Camp Hill, they figured. My hard edge must have made me seem mysterious to them. They liked it that I had the courage to do crazy things. When we went to dances or parties, I didn't wait around and hope girls would talk to me, like most guys did. Instead, I'd walk straight up to a girl, stand about an inch away from her face, and say, "Hi. How you doing? My name is Spoon. You want to dance or what?" Because my approach was unconventional, most of them said yes.

I spent the summer hanging out with the neighborhood kids my age. Then, early one September night, they all headed home. "Where the hell are you going?" I called after them. "School's tomorrow," they said. Going to bed early because of school the next day was totally foreign to me. They were serious about their education.

At seventeen, I was still high school age, but I had already earned my GED. Secretly, I might have liked going to West Philadelphia High and playing sports, even going to classes. But I stayed home and called what they were doing "sucker shit." I didn't like being different, though. Every day, I couldn't wait for school to be over so I could hang out with my new friends.

I didn't work during the day while they were in school. I just ran around stealing and doing the kind of stuff I'd always done. I went back to my old haunts in Center City and South Philly. When I got bored with stealing, I did stick-ups at movie houses and bus stations, usually getting away with $100 or $200 a pop. The other kids knew I was doing something because I always had a lot of cash, but that was part of my mystique. Even though they whispered behind my back "How does he get his money?" they didn't really want to know.

My new friends in West Philly had mothers and fathers who were teachers and lawyers and counselors. When I was with them, I felt like an ordinary high school student, except that I didn't go to school. Sometimes I even felt comfortable and relaxed in this environment. For the first time, I didn't have to act tough.

In other ways, though, I still felt awkward and out of place. Even though I knew this was my best shot ever at a normal life, I was still stealing and robbing. I'd spent five or six years incarcerated; I knew the police stations, the lineups, the jails. What I didn't know was how to live a crime-free life.

It seemed inevitable that I would end up back in prison or dead. I was floundering. I knew I had to do something just to save my life. So I joined the army.

Five

FORT MCCLELLAN

The bus that delivered us to Fort Bragg was filled with eighteen-and nineteen-year-old kids. I was only seventeen, but they still looked like kids to me. Sergeant Jones, our DI, greeted us as we got off the bus.

"You fucking jerks, where do you think you're at? This ain't no big city. You're gonna learn in the army!"

The rest of the kids were terrified, but I was instantly in familiar territory. The language was what I'd heard all my life. Its intent to intimidate, to be overtly abusive, was a style I could deal with in my sleep.

As I stood next to those terrified recruits, I knew that here was a standard I could measure up to. Sergeant Jones was the neighborhood in a starched uniform.

I enlisted in the army the first opportunity I had, just a few weeks short of my eighteenth birthday. When it came time to report, I rode the Amtrak down to Fayetteville, North Carolina. On the train I felt like two different people. My street side was jaded and cynical, far older than my eighteen years. My other side was full of eager anticipation, excited about going into the military. I sensed I was crossing a threshold into something new, that it would be an opportunity to do something constructive.

Facing the prospect of a fresh start, I felt good about myself. As the train headed south, I was determined to leave Philadelphia behind mentally as well as physically. I had never been into heavy drinking or doing lots of drugs, and as soon as I enlisted, I quit both. I was in good shape, with the body of an athlete. The confidence I'd felt coming home from Camp Hill was back, and I made up my mind not to let it disappear this time. Visions of me performing heroic military deeds floated through my mind, and I was convinced that something positive was going to happen to me for a change.

Since basic training was an achievement-oriented situation, I thought, "I'm going to like this." First thing, they wanted to see how well you could shoot. No problem—I was classified "expert" on the M-14 rifle. Then we had the obstacle course and the monkey bars. I loved it all, even getting up at five in the morning. My company was filled with eighteen-year-olds; they were mostly babies compared with me. At night in the barracks we'd play cards for money; those fresh-faced kids kept me in spending money the whole time I was at Fort Bragg.

After basic, I went home for Christmas. My military uniform was a big hit in the neighborhood, and everybody wanted to see PFC Carl Upchurch. It felt like a movie about a guy coming home from the service. The buzz went up and down the street: "Spoon's home! Spoon's home!"

I was on top of the world. Money, legitimate and illegitimate, bulged in my pockets, and everybody thought I was cool just for being in the army. Even though I had been in the service for only a short time, I was convinced I knew the whole military inside and out. Everybody listened to my stories with rapt attention. The Vietnam War was beginning to rage, and people figured I was on my way over there, so I was a potential hero. In fact, as far as most were concerned, Fort Bragg was the closest thing to Vietnam. At the end of my leave, I returned to Fort Bragg filled with pride and confidence.

I was a good army trainee. I improved my skill at firing weapons and breezed through the physical regimen, passing both with flying colors. Sergeant Jones figured me out along with everybody else in his company. One night, when we had to stay out in the cold, he said to me, "Carl, you never like to be forced to do anything, do you? You do much better when I present you with a challenge."

"Yeah, that's right, that's right," I said.

It was similar to what Coach Vaughters used to say. Sergeant Jones was the taskmaster I seemed always to need to be motivated to achieve. I learned a lot from him during those eight weeks we got our bodies in shape and learned to march and shoot.

When I graduated from basic, they sent me to the Advanced Infantry Training (AIT) school at Fort Jackson, South Carolina. AIT was the first school I'd ever liked. I discovered there that when I put my mind to it, I could understand new material quickly, articulate ideas well, and present myself in a military fashion. And because I came to AIT with a positive frame of mind—happy with myself and my circumstances, possessed of a steady paycheck and plenty of money that I hadn't had to steal—it helped me learn to appreciate the side of myself that valued pride and strength of character.

AIT stands out in my mind for another reason too: Barbara Jean Toatley. She worked at the Wade Hampton Hotel. One night I went there for dinner with some guys from New York. I looked up from my shrimp cocktail to see two nice-looking girls peering out at me from behind the kitchen door. When they finally got up enough nerve to come out and introduce themselves, I learned that one was named Barbara Jean, and the other was her sister, Loretta.

Barbara Jean and Loretta were from a good family—upstanding, churchgoing girls from a way of life I'd had no contact with. They were the first black women, other than Stoney, whom I looked at admiringly instead of lustfully or degradingly. I stayed at Fort Jackson for eight weeks and got to know Barbara Jean pretty well. I went to the Toatleys' house on Friday nights for fish fries. Other nights Barbara Jean and I would go to the Green Door or the Fontainebleau, or to Benedict College for dances. We listened to the music of Clarence Carter, James Brown, and Otis Redding. "Sittin' on the Dock of the Bay" was her favorite song, so she was devastated when Otis Redding died. When I met Barbara Jean, I was free from the constant bombardment of negativity in my earlier environments, and I was able to risk exploring the more sensitive areas of myself. I even opened up enough to admit that I wanted to be involved with her seriously. But the eight short weeks of AIT at Fort Jackson were up before we were ready to make any long-term commitment.

All of us were eager to learn what our next assignments would be. I couldn't believe it when I read the posting. My permanent duty assignment had nothing to do with marksmanship, my best skill. I had been classified as a clerk/typist, of all things, and was being transferred to post headquarters at Fort McClellan.

I learned how to type from scratch, and I got good enough to mostly get the job done. But I hated it. One steamy summer day I was sitting at my desk in one of those metal Quonset hut–type buildings trying to type a memo. I was sweating heavily and popping salt pills. I had to type the memo over and over because it was supposed to be error free. The harder I tried to do it correctly, the more mistakes I made, and the more my frustration mounted.

Finally I'd had enough—enough of the heat, the typing, and the stupid memo, and enough of being forced to do something I didn't want to do. So I went into the company commander's office and said, "Man, I don't want to do this no more."

"What do you mean?" he said in a bored, unfriendly commander-type voice.

I was so pissed off that I didn't even bother to show him the required deference. "I'm sitting here," I said, "sweating my ass off and chowing salt pills. I'm not doing this shit right. I don't even know what I'm supposed to be doing."

He stared at me, waiting for the "Sir." I stared right back. "You have to follow orders, soldier," he said in a robotlike voice.

"It doesn't make any sense, man!" I said. "I'm not doing it."

"I'll have to write you up," he said, still bored. "Uniform Code of Military Justice. You'll get an Article 15 for refusing the command."

I didn't care what he did to me; I just knew I wasn't typing that memo one more time. "Then just write it up and let me sign it. I'll go to the brig or whatever," I said, "but I'm not doing any more typing."

"Sit over there in the corner," he said. Then he picked up the phone, and I listened to his side of a long conversation.

"How about we make you a lifeguard?" he asked when he got off the phone. I stared at him in disbelief for so long that he asked again, "How would you like to be a lifeguard?"

Finally I said, "Yeah," even though I'd never had any lifeguard training. But this was the army. They'd made me a clerk; I figured they could make me a lifeguard.

He took me over to the pool to show me around. I was the only black there. When he was ready to leave, I figured I better tell him. "I can't swim," I said.

"What?" His voice cracked in the middle of the word. "You can't swim?"

"I can't swim," I repeated matter-of-factly. After all, he had asked me only if I wanted to be a lifeguard, not if I was qualified to be one.

He gave me a stare and finally said, "How would you like to be in the mailroom?"

I worked in the mailroom for a long time, putting the guys' mail in their boxes. There were three or four of us on duty there. It was fairly easy work, we got to listen to music all day, and we had a great time.

It was also a great opportunity to pick up extra cash. Whenever a registered letter or envelope with special postage came in, I stuffed it inside my shirt instead of putting it in the mailbox. Later, in the bathroom, I would open it up. Sometimes there would be a naked picture of the guy's wife. More often there would be money—twenty, thirty, forty dollars. I always trashed the letter and the pictures and took the cash.

Money orders and checks were of no use to me, so I threw them away too. I collected around seven or eight hundred dollars a week raiding the mail, and I spent it on diamond rings and rich living.

My mailroom scam was finished off the day a fat certified letter came in. I could tell there was a lot of cash in it, so I took it in the bathroom, took all the money out, then put it back together. The guy who picked it up was pretty sure it had been tampered with, and he raised a real stink. There had already been a lot of complaints about lost mail, and the authorities had to do something. All the evidence pointed to me, since I'd signed for all those registered letters. But they couldn't nail me because they'd never caught me in the act.

With time-honored army logic—fuck up, move up—they decided to change my assignment. The commander approached me and said, "Carl, we want to move you from the mailroom."

"But I like my job," I said.

"I know you do," he told me. "But we want to promote you to another position."

I went from private to specialist fourth class, and my earnings went from $137 a month to $264 a month. I was rolling in dough, with the new pay grade, the money I had stolen from the mailroom, and the money I won playing pool and poker. I felt like a kingpin.

My first assignment as a specialist fourth class was the small arms committee. The only problem was that I still had the MOS or duty assignment that classified me as a clerk, from my stint as a clerk/typist. An MOS is *the* identifying mark in the army, and until mine got changed, I couldn't get the raise that went with my "promotion" and I could be on the small arms committee only unofficially. This bugged me, so I began to work toward an infantry MOS. I never did get it.

On the small arms committee I finally got to use my expertise with weapons. I taught four different weapons systems to troops who were on their way to Vietnam: the .45 pistol, the M72 light antitank weapon (LAW), which had replaced the bazooka, the .50-caliber machine gun, and the M72 grenade launcher. Though I was proficient with all four weapons, I was an expert with the .50-caliber machine gun.

These guys' lives were going to depend on that gun, and it was my responsibility to teach them everything about its care and cleaning, cooling system, mounting—all the operational details. I had my spiel down pat:

> *Good morning, men. I am Specialist Upchurch of the small arms committee, and I will be your instructor for approximately the next thirty minutes. During this time I will attempt to familiarize you with the care and cleaning of the .50-caliber machine gun. Now as you all know, proper care and cleaning is essential with the .50-caliber, so I would like your undivided attention. Watch carefully as my assistant shows you how to . . .*

I was an efficient, totally military instructor, and I rose to the challenge of this job just as I had back in the bakery at Glen Mills and the powerhouse at Camp Hill. Besides, I liked showing off.

While I was teaching small arms, my own number came up several times. But each time I got ready to head for Fort Ord, California, the jumping-off place for Vietnam, my commander changed my orders. He kept me at McClellan by citing the military policy that in times of war you are assigned wherever you are most effective. Since I was very effectively teaching people how to handle their equipment, I ended up staying at McClellan while thousands of men went on to Vietnam.

One of my buddies at McClellan was a guy named Fleeger, another infantry instructor. Fleeger was from the South, and white, but race was never an issue between us. We were just two army shitheads—he was a white version of me—and we did crazy, goofy stuff both on and off the post. One day, we went down range to pick up grenades from the grenade launcher. We found some duds—grenades that hadn't exploded. They had to be disarmed by removing the explosive device, a little ball on the top of the grenade. Fleeger used a hammer on one that was stuck, and the grenade blew up in his hand, taking off four of his fingers. It was his ticket out of the army, and I never saw him again.

Every other Saturday all the instructors and their units would give a demonstration for the townspeople to show them how wonderful the military was. The small arms committee assigned me to demonstrate the M72 LAW, and I took great pride in doing so. I would stand silently on the stage, pointing out the front and rear sights and turning the gun every which way, while my commander said into a public address system, "Here in the hands of a well-trained rifleman, you see the M72 light antitank weapon, the LAW. This weapon has an effective range of . . ." It felt great to hear those words—"a well-trained rifleman"—and know they referred to me.

————

As the war trudged on, I spent my days teaching young soldiers how to use their guns, then watching them take off for Nam. But in the evenings, every time I picked up a newspaper or turned on the TV, I saw images of the black power and antiwar movements. At first they made me angry. Since the military was the best thing that had ever happened to me, I felt personally threatened by denunciations of the war. But no matter where we went, we couldn't get away from criticism of the American presence in Vietnam.

Black power was a concept I didn't understand. It had never occurred to me to question the way society was organized. Things were the way they were, that's all. The only connection between me and those guys on TV was that I had let my Afro grow a little longer, and it stuck out from under my helmet.

It was Jane Fonda who began to make me think. One night she was on *The Dick Cavett Show,* and they were arguing about the war. I wasn't paying much attention at first, but I got more and more interested in what she was saying so passionately about the antiwar movement. Finally, I was riveted to the screen. As Cavett played devil's advocate, Fonda's frustration and anger mounted. Americans weren't thinking about our most important issues or about the immorality and illogic of the war, she said. Soldiers were bombing babies. African-Americans were disproportionately represented in the army. Even before the show ended, I was thinking about the Vietnam War in a different way. Articulate and armed with staggering statistics, Fonda appealed to my intellect. Not only was I convinced by the logic of her analysis, I was enraptured by her passion. But I didn't get personally involved in the antiwar movement until the assassination of Martin Luther King.

On April 4, 1968, my world changed irrevocably. The enormity of grief in the days that followed King's murder got to me as nothing political had before. So many people from so many different backgrounds had believed in this man. I wondered what he had stood for.

Politics had never meant much to me. I'd been aware of H. Rap Brown, Stokely Carmichael, Eldridge Cleaver, and other leaders, but I didn't know much about them. After King died, I really listened when I saw them on the news, and I read the papers more carefully. The more I read, listened, and absorbed, the more suspicious I became about the military I had embraced so enthusiastically. I realized what my mission really was: teaching young men to kill. Gradually, I grew ashamed about participating in a war that perhaps was not morally correct.

My enthusiasm for the army faded quickly after King's death. And my .50-caliber presentations began to reflect my changed viewpoint.

Hey, good morning, men. Ya'll are about ready to go head out and really do some damage to some people in this world. My job is to show you how to do it better, how to kill people we call "gooks" and "slant-eyes."

Needless to say, the guys in charge were not impressed. Nor did they know quite what to do with me. The "crack-to-it" soldier with shined boots and precise military manner had become angry and uncooperative. My changed attitude wasn't enough to land me in the brig, but I was walking a thin line.

As I became politicized, I found myself more and more irritated by society's racism, vividly illustrated by the murders of Martin Luther King and Bobby Kennedy. I grew conscious of racist remarks that I'd previously ignored, conscious of the slander against my race in the speeches of Strom Thurmond and Jesse Helms. I saw George Wallace for what he was. And I finally recognized that African-Americans were fighting a war that old wealthy whites were orchestrating and that young wealthy whites were easily avoiding. As I saw the connection between the racial situation in this country and the immorality of the Vietnam War, I realized that by being in the military I was being used and manipulated to someone else's advantage.

My commander didn't interfere when my next set of orders for Vietnam came in. He just gave me full pay and thirty days' leave before I was to report to Fort Ord. Four months earlier I would have gone to Vietnam eagerly, but now I had no intention of reporting. It didn't matter that Nam would have brought me a promotion, along with the infantry MOS I'd wanted so badly. I didn't want anything to do with it.

When my leave started, I hitched a ride from South Carolina to Philadelphia with Lieutenant DeJohn. We drove 846 miles straight up US 1 in his big, black '68 Caddy. I never went back. I don't know if they looked for me or not. Nobody ever mentioned it until the next time I got locked up and a run of my fingerprints showed me listed as AWOL. By then, I didn't care.

I was nineteen years old when I returned to Philly. When my family figured out that I wasn't going back to the service, they weren't surprised. It was as if they expected me to screw up again. They were right; within four months I had started robbing banks.

It was a conscious job choice. My stash of army money was about to run out, I didn't want to sell dope, and I wasn't a pimp. My only civilian experience had been as a stick-up man, and I'd been pretty good at it. I made the decision while standing in line in a bank one day, waiting to cash in the savings bonds that had been taken out of my military pay every month. When I got up to the window and saw the drawer full of money, I said to myself, "That's it. I'm gonna rob this bank."

I didn't have a gun at that time, but getting one wasn't difficult. I'd owned one before, and all my buddies had them. Besides, my reputation was still strong, and I'd kept my contacts from South Philadelphia. I got a .25 automatic, went back to the bank, and robbed it. When that money ran out, I did it again. I'd go in with my pistol hidden and stand in line until my turn came. Then I'd reach under my jacket or sweater, pull the pistol out, and order the teller to clean out her cash drawer and the drawers on either side of her. Then I would run out of the bank. I robbed eight different banks that way. They had cameras, but they didn't catch me.

My family had no idea what I was doing, but they knew I was up to no good. Even when I'd show up with $18,000 in cash, they accepted the cash I handed around and asked no questions. It was easier, safer that way.

During my bank-robbing phase, I met Brenda Lawson. She was seventeen, still in high school, and very different from Barbara Jean, but I liked her a lot. We met totally by accident. A bunch of us were playing stickball one afternoon, and I hit a ball that landed on her front porch, where she was sitting. When I went to retrieve it, she looked at me and asked, "Is that all you do with your time?"

I looked at her—she was pregnant—and asked, "Is that all you do with yours?"

Brenda and I became friends even though she was pregnant by another guy. We'd sit on her front steps at night and talk; once we sat there from nine o'clock until seven the next morning, and then I walked her to school. We were both learning how to care about each other. After her baby was born, I acted as if I were the father. Brenda and I still sat and talked, and sometimes we took the baby, a little girl she named Nia, for walks. I used to forget that I wasn't Nia's dad, even though Mitchell, the guy who really was the father, was in and out of Brenda's life all the time.

During the time I was with Brenda, I organized a neighborhood bus trip to Atlantic City. Kids paid money to go, some of their parents fixed food, and I assigned someone to bring the marijuana. It was on that bus, on the way to Atlantic City, that Brenda asked me for the words to end her relationship with Mitchell. She was pleading for me to help her, to rescue her, but I honestly didn't know how. I never answered her question, and our friendship was never the same.

I continued robbing banks until January 1972. I never did get caught, but the FBI had a good idea that I was the man they were looking for in eight different stick-ups. They called my grandmother and told her they were going to shoot me down in the street if I didn't turn myself in. She believed it and called me, crying and begging me to turn myself in. I argued with her a little, but I finally agreed to do it.

In court, I pleaded guilty and was convicted of five of the eight robberies. I was sentenced under the provision of the Youth Corrections Act, signed by President Kennedy, that said that anyone younger than twenty-six at the time of conviction could be paroled after eight months to eight years. I got four sentences of eight years and one sentence of seven years; they all ran concurrently. The three robberies that were thrown out and the concurrent sentences were the bonuses I got for turning myself in and pleading guilty.

Since robbing banks is a federal crime, I was sentenced to the Federal Correctional Institution in Milan, Michigan. Before I knew it, I was back in jail, an environment more familiar to me than any other. This time I was a real terror.

Six

MILAN

I traveled from Philadelphia to Michigan in the back seat of a car, in handcuffs and leg shackles; two federal marshals were in the front. At Milan I settled into fulfilling what I thought was my destiny: being a criminal for the rest of my life. And I decided that if I was going to be a criminal, I might as well be a good one.

On a Saturday morning, about eight months after I arrived at Milan, Frank Lewis and I stabbed someone. This guy had dope in his cell, and we wanted it. He was asleep when we walked in. "Hey, man, get the fuck up!" Frank yelled. At first the guy denied he had any dope. Frank took a homemade knife and rammed it through the guy's foot, pinning it to the bed. The guy was screaming, "Don't kill me! Don't kill me!" Frank just leaned on the knife, holding it in place until the guy finally told us the dope was stashed in the ceiling light.

We both ended up in segregation, then were shipped out of Milan. I went first to Petersburg, then to Terre Haute, then to Atlanta, and finally to Lewisburg. At each place, I got progressively meaner.

Milan had had some pretty famous guests. Elijah Muhammad, the founder of the Nation of Islam, served time there for refusing to join the army during World War II. So did Joe Valachi, who spilled the Cosa Nostra's secrets in *The Valachi Papers*. I wanted Milan to remember me as the baddest, toughest guy they'd ever had to deal with.

My number was 28862-117. I lived in a large room filled with bunk beds, dormitory-style. As always, my first job was to take a long look around to see what I was dealing with.

This wasn't a local Pennsylvania crowd. There were guys here from Detroit, Pittsburgh, Milwaukee, and Indianapolis, but I figured they couldn't possibly be as tough as the guys back in Philadelphia. A lot of them didn't even have prior records. I brought my reputation with me, and I let everyone know I was a tough guy from a tough city.

Holding check was still important, and convicts jockeyed for position just as they had at Camp Hill, but because of my reputation I got respect without playing any of those games. I felt superior because I no longer had to struggle for prominence.

Milan had the usual shops that were supposed to teach rehabilitative skills—a masonry shop, a carpentry shop, an electrical shop, and an auto repair shop—and we were paid for our work. It seemed somewhat more productive than Camp Hill, but I still didn't want to do any of it. College-level courses were available, but they didn't interest me either.

Like a lot of other people, I preferred to spend my time "on idle," just sitting or lying on my bed, staring into space. I hung with a group of guys my age who had been all over the world and were international drug smugglers or jewel thieves. Their stories fascinated me. Lots of them had done bigger jobs than I had and had gotten away with a lot more money. Listening to them, I fell into the deadliest trap of prison life: wanting nothing more than to be a better criminal. I had had a lot of practice, after all, and I was already walking proof that prison life most often teaches convicts how to be better at whatever put them there rather than straightening them out.

It wasn't long before I started robbing people—stealing money and dope to sell. Frank Lewis became my walkie. We watched each other's back, no matter what. I respected him because he came from Brooklyn, which carried more prestige than almost any other place. All of New York, but especially Brooklyn and Harlem, is regarded as the playground for the meanest, the deadliest, the most dangerous of all hardcore criminals. Frank, for his part, respected my reputation. He and I started terrorizing the prison. Being on idle, it was easy for us to catch guys in the dormitory when no one else was around. If we suspected that a guy in a single room had marijuana or other drugs, we would barge right in. Working with Frank felt like being back on the street, sticking people up with a knife or strong-arming them.

After they locked us down every night, we'd get together in the back of the dorm, away from the guards, to smoke pot and listen to the radio all night long. Nobody bothered us as long as we were on our beds or in our areas when the guards came around to check every four or five hours.

I had no occasional moments of pride, no sense of achievement at Milan; the good parts of my time in the army might as well never have happened. I was contemptuous of the straight-arrows who just wanted to do their time and get out, refusing to participate in the stealing and the drug scene. Most of them had college degrees but had done something stupid that landed them in Milan; one guy was a basketball player from Marquette University who'd gotten caught bringing a pound of marijuana into the country.

The straight-arrows kept away from the rest of us, staying in their own little cliques. The bits and pieces of their conversations that I overheard reminded me of the letters Stoney and I had written while I was at Camp Hill. I was attracted to their conversation and their ideas, but at Milan I was neither able nor willing to deal with my small kernel of intellectual curiosity.

My attitude toward the straight-arrows was a classic case of conflicting feelings, a situation that was now all too familiar. I had made a conscious decision to turn my back on ever going straight, but I was attracted to their conversations in spite of myself. For their part, they didn't want anything to do with my criminal side, while my tough-guy buddies criticized me for hanging out with the squares.

My solution was to occasionally be accidentally-on-purpose near enough that I could eavesdrop on their discussions. I understood a little of what they said about the history of African-American literary development and African liberation movements; about Kwanzaa; about the subliminal seduction that Vance Packard talked about in *The Hidden Persuaders;* and about what it means to be an African-American male in this society. But a lot of it went over my head. And those moments were just a tiny piece of my time at Milan.

I still read newspapers, though. And in 1973 and 1974, black power, which had already gained a strong foothold in the general population, became a force inside the prisons, including Milan. I was intrigued by it, but accepting black power would have meant becoming a completely different person, taking the time to learn about my history and my African-American roots, and I wasn't yet prepared to give up the gangster life.

The Nation of Islam was active at Milan as well, as it continues to be in every American prison. A number of Black Muslims there were very serious and took a leadership role in the prison. They faithfully practiced their religion: they were very neat and clean, wouldn't eat pork, didn't smoke cigarettes, didn't curse, and never did dope. I was never tempted to join them. I didn't have the discipline to get up at seven o'clock to exercise, pray to Mecca, and march and drill. I wasn't interested in being clean shaven and hanging only with the Muslim brothers. However, when I was enraged about something, the Muslim doctrine that oppression comes from one source—the devil, the white man—became a very appealing concept. But the prospect of going to temple every Wednesday and Friday night and praying four times a day made me want to run out and smoke some weed.

The newspapers were filled with stories about Watergate. It captured my attention then because of the timing: I'd begun my Milan odyssey the same day H. R. Haldeman testified to Congress about his role in Watergate. On August 9, 1974, the day I was transferred from Milan to another prison, I watched Richard Nixon leave the White House. He had just resigned and was getting on a helicopter, waving good-bye to his staff.

I was outraged by Nixon. I was nothing more than a petty thief who had stolen a few thousand dollars, but he was a traitor whose crimes had torn the fabric of our democracy. I might have stolen money and done cocaine, but he had had his hands on the reins of government and arrogantly thumbed his nose at the Constitution. The sheer inequity of it all struck me forcibly: His crimes were far more threatening to the American way of life than mine, yet I had been sentenced to more time for eight bank robberies than Nixon and his cronies—all those white-collar political criminals—put together. I have since gained enough perspective to realize that whether we were jailed or pardoned, we were all guilty.

———

My stay at Milan came to an end after the guy Frank and I had stabbed ratted on us to the administration. They sent us to separate facilities to reduce the likelihood of more mayhem at the next place, so Frank went to Tallahassee, and I ended up in Petersburg, Virginia.

Within a month of my arrival at Petersburg, I got into a nasty fight. I was still in Receiving, not yet released into the general prison population, and I asked a white guy, a real redneck, for a cigarette. He just looked at me like I was dirt and went back to talking to his buddies. I had a very short fuse back then, and I took his lack of response as a racial slur, so I picked up a trash can and bashed him over the head with it. To my surprise, he didn't go down—in fact, he fought hard. But I busted him up pretty good. When the guards finally broke up the fight, the front of my white T-shirt was dripping in blood, mostly his. They took us out through a crowd of guys who were milling around to see what had happened. I heard one of them say, "Oh man, he [meaning me] really fucked up that other guy. He fucked him up bad."

I thought, "Yeah, that's right," and felt a surge of pride that I had ensured my reputation at Petersburg so quickly.

They took the redneck to the hospital; I headed for the segregation unit. After he got out of the hospital, the redneck didn't spend any time at all in solitary. That upset me because to me it didn't matter how the fight had started or who threw the first punch or did the most damage—we'd both been fighting and were equally guilty. But they took me to segregation and kept me there, while he went back into the general population.

I had heard that Petersburg was a lot more racist than Milan, and that incident proved it. In 1974 the state of Virginia had much more prejudice than I had experienced in either Pennsylvania or Michigan. The Petersburg guards were especially vicious racists. We'd hear "Hey, nigger!" and "Gorilla, do that!" all the time, and they'd tell us, "You ain't nothing now. You ain't up in those urban jungles now. You're down here with us."

I was in segregation at Petersburg for six months. When I wanted to talk to somebody, I had to yell to the other guys on the block. Mostly, I just slept. When I finally got out of segregation, I got tapped to play on the Petersburg basketball team. I was twenty-four years old and a very good player. Basketball was the one thing I liked about being there. I almost got to play against Moses Malone. He went to Petersburg High School, right in the neighborhood. We listened to his games on the radio, and his team won the state championship while I was there. Since we had a good team too, we finally asked if the high school team could come in and play us. Somehow the prison officials worked it out that we would play in an exhibition game. We were all very excited about it. But Moses was a senior and on his way to the University of Maryland, and his coaches decided they didn't want him to risk an injury playing on an outdoor cement court. He didn't even come to watch the game. They beat us, but only barely, and about a month afterward we heard that Moses was skipping college and going straight to the ABA.

Things weren't as intense at Petersburg as they'd been at Milan. Somehow the environment was different. Because of the racial climate and the hostility of the prison officials, blacks generally stuck together and worked together more. It was hard to rob someone who was defending you against racial attacks. But there were still conflicts. A lot of guys I'd known from Philadelphia were at Petersburg, and we used to fight guys from D.C. I still robbed people, though mostly whites. And I still got into hellacious fights.

About a month after I got out of segregation, I was sitting in the chow hall, when a guy across from me said something like, "Who the fuck do you think you are?" I picked up a metal food tray, came across the top of the table, and hit him in the side of the face with it. The guards had to forcibly remove me from the dining room. I went back to segregation and sat there while they arranged a transfer. For the next eight months I was out of segregation only when I was traveling between institutions. I went to Terre Haute, Indiana, then to Atlanta. Finally, the federal penitentiary in Lewisburg, Pennsylvania, agreed to take me, and put me straight into solitary. It turned out to be the biggest stroke of luck I had ever had.

Seven

LEWISBURG

The only emotion I knew how to express was rage. I spent days in solitary at Lewisburg lying on my bunk, silently raging at what I was convinced was an unjust legal system. It never occurred to me that I bore some responsibility for where I was.

I memorized every detail of that cell. It was mainly gray—the walls and floor were gray cement; the cot was gray metal; the table and chair were gray wood. My blanket was gray too. The sink and toilet were white, sort of, and my clothes were khaki. But even the tier was gray.

By pure accident, there was a book in my cell. One leg of the gray table was shorter than the other three, and someone had stuck a thin book beneath it. I had been in the cell for a couple of months before I even noticed it. My boredom had reached epic proportions, and I was going over the cell inch by inch, when it finally caught my eye. I pulled it out, excited to have found something to alleviate the monotony.

I turned it over and stared at the cover in disgust. It was Shakespeare's sonnets.

I didn't know much about Shakespeare, except *thee*'s and *thou*'s. He couldn't possibly have anything to say that was relevant to my life. I put the book back under the table leg. After three more days of staring at gray, I pulled it out again, muttering that Shakespeare was better than nothing.

I won't pretend that Shakespeare and I immediately connected. I must have read those damn sonnets twenty times before they started to make sense. Even then, comprehension came slowly—first a word, then a phrase, finally a whole poem. Those sonnets began to take hold of me, transported me out of the gray world into a world I had never, ever imagined.

I called him Bill instead of William; we were, after all, quite close. He introduced me to the beauty of language, and I developed a real respect for the precision of his words. For example, one sonnet talked about the *swarthy* color of this woman. *Swarthy*. The word spurred me to ask for a dictionary. Once I had looked it up, I realized that the sonnet was about a black woman, at least a dark woman; it changed the whole sonnet for me.

The side of me that had surfaced in my letter-writing with Stoney surfaced again. Looking back, it's easy to see the pattern that emerged over the years. I would get excited by the worlds Stoney was offering me, or by the learning opportunities I had in the army, only to fall back again and again into mindless violence. At the time the shifts just confused me. Over the years, though, the periods when I battled the world using my mind began to overshadow those when I battled it with violence. At Lewisburg I was still two people, one in my cell and another out in the prison, but the balance of power swung solidly to the positive for the first time in my life. It would swing back later, but what happened at Lewisburg was a big step toward getting where I am today.

I had almost always been contemptuous of intellect. That book of sonnets didn't just change my opinion—it quite literally changed my mind. I discovered the magic of learning, the thrill of going from not knowing to knowing. By struggling to understand Shakespeare, I came to see that ideas have a beauty all their own, beyond even the beauty of the words that frame them. The words too fascinated me. I couldn't just run over the ones I didn't know, ignoring them; I had to look them up, learn to live with them.

My real connection with Shakespeare started with a line in Sonnet 29: "Like to the lark at break of day arising." That sonnet, which became my favorite, was about me and my experiences, as if Bill had just sat down and looked into my heart. I read it more than any other, and before long I had it memorized.

> When in disgrace with Fortune and men's eyes,
> I all alone beweep my outcast state,
> And trouble deaf heaven with my bootless cries,
> And look upon myself and curse my fate,
> Wishing me like to one more rich in hope,
> Featur'd like him, like him with friends possess'd,
> Desiring this man's art, and that man's scope,
> With what I most enjoy contented least;
> Yet in these thoughts myself almost despising,
> Haply I think on thee, and then my state,
> Like to the lark at break of day arising
> From sullen earth, sings hymns at heaven's gate;
> For thy sweet love rememb'red such wealth brings
> That then I scorn to change my state with kings.

I didn't appreciate the magnitude of Shakespeare's poetry until much later, when I took college literature classes at Western State Penitentiary and learned about the structural rules of sonnets. When I realized that Shakespeare had had just fourteen carefully constructed lines to work with, I was stunned that he could produce something like Sonnet 29.

Lewisburg had a weird rule: Guys in segregation always got first pick at the library books, even though it was assumed that anybody bad enough to be in solitary wasn't going to be interested in reading. Every

Saturday afternoon, the prison chaplain came to our unit, bringing us anything we might have asked for, including books. I wanted to ask for something else to read, but I didn't have a clue where to start. At least I knew that Shakespeare had written other stuff besides the sonnets, so I requested anything else they had by him. I ended up with *The Complete Works* and started plowing my way through thirty-eight plays and some other poetry.

The chaplain kept up with what I was reading and was very supportive and encouraging. Each week he'd ask me how it was going, and finally one week I got up the nerve to answer him. We eventually talked about whatever play or poem I was reading, and those discussions invariably led to other books. If we were talking about Shakespeare's poetry, he would say I had to read a certain other poet. He encouraged me to list the books and authors that sounded interesting, so if I read a magazine article that referred to, say, T. S. Eliot, I'd put Eliot on my list.

Caught up in the first flush of literary exploration, I was pretty impressed with myself. In retrospect, it was lucky that I was in the cell alone. At that point in my life, I wouldn't have been able to resist flaunting my fledgling knowledge to guys who would have burst my bubble mercilessly.

There was no rhyme or reason to my reading. From Shakespeare, I moved on to the African-American writers of the 1920s, the Harlem Renaissance, then to some contemporary black authors. James Baldwin, speaking to me every bit as piercingly as Shakespeare, introduced me to my history. With uncompromising clarity Baldwin told the truth about the African-American experience, and *Another Country* swept me away.

My first contact with Maya Angelou was *I Know Why the Caged Bird Sings.* Her writing still touches me like no one else's, especially her later poem "And Still I Rise." I read *The Autobiography of Frederick Douglass* and *No Place to Be Somebody,* a play by Charles Gordone. Then I stumbled across Dudley Randall's poetic simplification of the philosophies of Booker T. Washington and W.E.B. Du Bois. I was especially struck by these two verses:

> It seems to me
> Said Booker T
> It shows an awful lot of cheek
> To study chemistry or Greek
> When Mr. Charlie needs a hand
> To hoe that cotton on his land.
> And when Miss Ann looks for a cook,
> Why stick your nose inside a book?
>
> I disagree
> Said W.E.B.
> For if I should have the drive to seek
> Knowledge of chemistry or Greek
> I'll do it. Miss Ann can look
> Elsewhere for hand or cook.

I had never heard of either man, and Randall's poem set me off on a new track. I learned that Washington's accommodating style of leadership emphasized the practical approach, urging our entire race to hoist themselves up by their bootstraps. W.E.B. Du Bois, by contrast, called for the development of an African-American elite. In fact, his entire Niagara Movement, the precursor of the NAACP, was dedicated to educating and shaping the small percentage of the black population—Du Bois called them the "talented tenth"—whom he thought capable of leadership. This small group would then serve as a filter for all subsequent African-American development. I was mesmerized by Du Bois's *The Souls of Black Folk,* one of the most significant, comprehensive, and scholarly chronicles of the African-American culture—who we were and what we were saying. Every other black author I have read, whether they acknowledge it or not, owes something to the scholarship of Du Bois, I believe, particularly those who comment on the social, political, and economic conditions of African-Americans.

It was exciting to learn. No matter what subject or author I asked for, the chaplain would find me the right book. Sometimes I felt like I'd been starving my whole life, and all of a sudden I'd come to a banquet where I could have as much as I wanted.

So I devoured. Nikki Giovanni affirmed my anger, but she also showed me that anger could be channeled in a spiritual direction rather than a violent one. Dostoyevsky had the words for my loneliness and isolation. And Mark Twain, in "The Mysterious Stranger," made me think, for the very first time, about what it means to kill, to maim, to destroy things, to be insensitive and uncaring, to be a savage—all the things I had been, had been proud to be, in my life up to that point. Twain laid the foundation for my subsequent understanding of how sickening it is to cling to violence as if it were decent or human or spiritual.

I asked the chaplain for everything he could find by Mark Twain. Among other things, I read about Tom Sawyer and Huck Finn, then about "The Man Who Corrupted Hadleyburg." At first, all I saw was Twain's humor, which I liked a lot. But as I read and reread his stories, I began to understand that he wasn't writing just to be funny; he was using humor for social criticism. Twain had somehow transcended his own origins as a white native of a slave state to fully understand what was happening in the South. I came to view the Civil War through his eyes, amazed that his sharp wit could make me laugh even as he laid bare the ugliness of slavery.

I had read enough of Mark Twain to be angry when I learned that a university professor from Michigan was railing against Twain and *Huck Finn* because of the word *nigger*. Without stopping to think that I was just fourth-grade Carl Upchurch and this guy was a college professor, I wrote him thirteen passionate pages in defense of Twain and the book. I said, "You turn to page so-and-so. . . . You look at Twain's other work. . . . You refer to his essay on this point. . . . You check this out, and then you tell me how you, with your learned letters, come to call this man a racist." There I was, in the most oppressive of environments, facing racism at every turn. And there was Twain, who spoke to my heart, made *me* less of a racist and allowed me to see past the racism around me. I couldn't let that experience be diminished by some guy just because he was black and had the letters *Ph.D.* after his name. He never answered my letter, but it sure made me feel good to write it.

From Twain I moved on to Stephen Crane. I read *The Red Badge of Courage* and a moving story called "The Open Boat." I remember thinking, "Oh my God, where have I been all these years?"

In that spirit I started devouring everything the prison library had to offer. Most of it was pretty heavy stuff—Sartre, Camus, Plato, even Machiavelli's *The Prince*—and I had to read each one several times before it sank in. I took to arguing out loud with the authors, unconcerned about my lack of total comprehension. Those one-sided arguments became a valuable learning tool for me, one I still use today.

For example, I might read a line and say, "That's bullshit, and I'll tell you why it's bullshit. What you're failing to take into consideration is that this is all from *your* cultural perspective, from *your* way of looking at things. There are other cultures that don't eat at a table. Since you've overlooked that, your whole premise is erroneous and not valid."

If I agreed with what I was reading, I'd stop and say, "Well put. How well stated that is." For example, when I first read that it is possible for a human being to be redeemed, I was so excited, I agreed out loud, then told the air why it was true. I would often stop in the middle of a page and talk for hours before going back to reading. Then when I shut the book for good, it was time for more reflection. "Naw, you missed it," I might say to the author. I remembered the books much better when I talked them out; after a debate I could actually see that page in my mind.

It fascinated me to figure out how an author came to his or her conclusion, even one that didn't feel right to me. "Oh, I see. You believe this because you're a forty-four-year-old white female, formerly married to a stockbroker who was never home. He robbed you of your artistic inclinations, kept you suppressed, and chained you to the stove and your three little ones. So you've concluded that this is the male understanding of the world, and you pursue these particular lines of liberation for yourself based on that experience. Since you came out of that situation, I can understand how you came to that conclusion about male behavior. However, if you had come out of a different set of circumstances, you might have been a different person in relation not only to yourself and to all males but to society." Some of my conclusions may have been totally off the mark, but I thrived on the mental exercise.

Everybody in segregation heard my solitary debates, of course. They thought I was weird, but then everybody's weird in prison. I was always hearing, "Upchurch, why don't you shut up, man?" or "There goes Upchurch again, out there talking." Eventually, they seemed to develop an interest when I read things aloud. On days when the block was too quiet, I'd hear, "Hey, Church, why don't you read something?" Two of their favorites were *A Message to the Blackman in America* by Elijah Muhammad and Maya Angelou's "And Still I Rise." And then there was the famous July 5 speech given by Frederick Douglass in 1852, in which he laid bare the plight of the American Negro:

> What, to the American slave, is your 4th of July? I answer: a day that reveals to him, more than all other days in the year, the gross injustice and cruelty to which he is the constant victim. To him, your celebration is a sham; your boasted liberty, an unholy license; your national greatness, swelling vanity; your sounds of rejoicing are empty and heartless, your denunciations of tyrants, brass fronted impudence; your shouts of liberty and equality, hollow mockery; your prayers and hymns, your sermons and thanksgivings, with all your religious parade, and solemnity, are, to him, mere bombast, fraud, de-

ception, impiety, and hypocrisy—a thin veil to cover up crimes which would disgrace a nation of savages. There is not a nation on the earth guilty of practices, more shocking and bloody, than are the people of these United States, at this very hour.

Go where you may, search where you will, roam through all the monarchies and despotisms of the old world, travel through South America, search out every abuse, and when you have found the last, lay your facts by the side of the everyday practices of this nation, and you will say with me, that, for revolting barbarity and shameless hypocrisy, America reigns without a rival.

My understanding of the American Revolution came through my engagement with the passion of Thomas Paine's early writings. I loved to argue with that guy; as far as I was concerned, he stood head and shoulders above the rest of the revolutionary war writers. At an absolute low point during the revolution, when no one else had the tools to rouse the troops, this one man sat down, put pen to paper, and, with his passionate commitment to a new day, rallied the colonists behind him. It was called *The American Crisis*:

> *These are the times that try men's souls: The summer soldier and the sunshine patriot will in this crisis shrink from the service of his country; but he that stands it NOW, deserves the love and thanks of men and women. Tyranny, like hell, is not easily conquered; yet we have this consolation with us, that the harder the conflict, the more glorious the triumph. What we obtain too cheap, we esteem too lightly: —'Tis dearness only that gives everything its value. Heaven knows how to put a proper price upon its goods; and it would be strange indeed, if so celestial an article as FREEDOM should not be highly rated.*

Paine, a man of the people, could communicate even with those who had no formal education, and my debates with him were never with his spirit or his heart or his character. Yet as progressive, as determined, as sincere, impassioned, and committed as he was, he had left America for France, just when America seemed to need him most for the hard work of building the democracy he envisioned. I objected to this at first, but eventually I came to understand him. I identified more with Paine than with Hamilton and certainly more than with Jefferson, who was eloquent and devoted to the cause of freedom but still owned slaves.

Victor Hugo's *Les Misérables* had a profound impact on me as well, because Jean Valjean was my mirror. After being sentenced to nineteen years in prison for stealing a loaf of bread, he was paroled and took refuge in the Bishop of Digne's home. Valjean repaid the bishop's kindness by stealing his silver candlesticks. The bishop, instead of turning him over to police, lied for him, telling the inspector, Javert, that he had given Valjean the candlesticks as a gift. Because of this unexpected kindness, the astonished Valjean vowed to start a new life. He eventually owned a factory and became mayor of his town, but the shadowy threat of Inspector Javert hung over him through it all.

This part of Hugo's magnificent book overwhelmed me with such sadness that I literally cried my way through it. I knew exactly how Valjean felt: No matter what, I would never be a saint; I would never be able to rid myself of the dark cloud of my past overshadowing me.

It's easy to see how Hugo and Jean Valjean blindsided me. Up to that time, I had been reading some of the most beautiful and noble ideas written by the world's greatest authors, people like Henry David Thoreau and Walt Whitman. These authors had told me of deep humanity, of love, of giving, of kindness, of fairness. I had had important conversations with them about what was just and what was unjust and how to be a moral person. I had learned from them how to do good in the world, how to be kind to people, and how to stand up to injustice. Day in and day out in solitary confinement, those authors gave me hope. Now here was Victor Hugo, telling me, "None of that matters, my friend. You will always be a criminal, and your conscience will pursue you forever."

When I got to the end of the novel, though, I realized that I had been too quick to judge. Yes, Javert had dogged Valjean's footsteps for years. But Valjean discovered the essence of himself during those same years. His life was not without blemish, but it was his own integrity, not the threat of Javert, that became the final arbiter. That outcome was important for me to know.

From reading *Les Misérables*, I understood I would always be the person who had committed those crimes. It is documented history and always will be. But I won't join those who judge me a criminal forever. Every day I must exonerate myself through my deeds according to the standards that *I* hold. My joy, my blessing, is not that other people forgive my crimes; it is the forgiveness inside me. If I do something to another person that I can't live with, I'm a criminal again. I can't look at my face in the mirror, knowing I did it. Valjean had a chance to get away when someone else was going to be put in prison for his crime, but he said, "I'm Jean Valjean. I'm the man you're looking for." He was willing to go back to jail because he had to be able to look himself in the eye and say "I'm the one." Those words saved me. If he could come clean and still be honorable, so could I.

My reading changed everything for me. I discovered that people I had never met knew exactly how I felt—so well that I could use their writings as reference points in my own life. Literature gave me a vocabulary I could use to express my deepest feelings and the insight to understand that my situation was universal. I escaped in a way far more satisfying than any tunnel under a prison wall, into a completely new world.

Another thing that changed dramatically as I read was how I viewed women. Early on I had learned to assess a woman body part by body part, totaling up her assets and defects, ultimately categorizing her as someone I could or could not have sex with. Needless to say, the feminist ideology taking form in the 1960s and early 1970s confused me. I read *The Feminine Mystique* by Betty Friedan, expecting it to be trash. Instead, I was astonished that such a simple proposition—that people should all be treated equally—could turn the world upside down and get so many people all riled up. After reading all about the American Revolution and the Constitution, I had assumed that, except for me, society was much more progressive in its thinking about equality for women. Yet most of the men, even some of the women, in the world were ready to shoot Friedan because of her simple proposition.

From Friedan, I went on to other feminists past and present: Elizabeth Cady Stanton, Susan B. Anthony, Germaine Greer, Kate Millett, Adrienne Rich, Gloria Steinem, and Marilyn French. There was a common thread in all their work, and I began to realize I wasn't the only one who had had to deal with oppression and injustice.

Applied to my own experience, these women's ideas helped me realize two things: first, that I am a person equal to any other person into whom God blew breath, and second, that standing up and proclaiming it would probably produce the same explosive reaction.

As I read further, I learned to synthesize complicated ideas. I learned to write a complete sentence, a complete paragraph, a complete essay. And as I tested my new ideas against my old rationalizations, I tried to figure out how to be a decent human being. The literature taught me how to look at myself. It told me that regardless of my condition, regardless of the circumstances I came from, I was a legitimate human being and a child of God. But I also learned that society considered me inferior because of my color—and considered any rights and privileges I have as a black man to be the gift of white men. I decided I couldn't respect a process that had to legislate me into being. I also decided I had a responsibility to stand up for people who hadn't yet learned to think of themselves as human beings.

My intense ideological "debates" with writers in my cell were the high points of my prison days. But the solitary conversations didn't provide enough of an outlet for my burgeoning intellect, so I wrote to my sister, to civil rights leaders, and to congressmen, expressing my feelings on my rights as a man and as a human being. I even wrote editorials I hoped would someday be printed.

Literature taught me about tenderness, and as I learned, I experienced tender moments of enjoying my own humanity. Ironically, it was in prison that I really understood what it means to be tender. Finally, *finally*, I had a label for the piece of me I knew was missing but had never been able to identify, that blackest of all the black holes in my soul, the one that was tender. I had survived for nearly twenty-seven years in a desert without it. Literature was my oasis.

One day the chaplain brought me a Bible. At first I couldn't get myself to read it because so many of the African-American scholars I had already read had awakened me to the concept that Christianity had played a major role in maintaining slavery. But when I finally looked at it, I found comfort in its pure intent and decided that it wasn't the Bible itself that had enslaved us, but the way corrupt souls had used it to make money on our backs. My own reading and rereading of its pages showed me a new kind of compassion, how we should ideally love each other, how to serve one another.

The Bible intimidated me a little, so I started out by memorizing the names of all the books: Genesis, Exodus, Leviticus, Numbers, Deuteronomy, Joshua, Judges, and so on. Once I had established this bit of "mastery," I dived in. I liked Job and the lamentations of Jeremiah. When Jeremiah challenged the scribes and the church officials not to be hypocritical, and when Job issued his plaintive cry to God, "Isn't this enough? Why me?" they told me I was not alone in my anguish.

When I needed inspiration, I read Matthew and Mark. And the Psalms gave me solace, especially the sweet music of David in the first psalm:

> *Blessed* is *the man that walketh not in the counsel of the*
>   *ungodly, nor standeth in the way of sinners, nor sitteth*
>   *in the seat of the scornful.*
> *But his delight* is *in the law of the Lord; and in his law doth*
>   *he meditate day and night.*

And he shall be like a tree planted by the rivers of water,
that bringeth forth his fruit in its season; his leaf also
shall not wither; and whatsoever he doeth shall prosper.
The ungodly are not so: but are like chaff which the wind
driveth away.
Therefore the ungodly shall not stand in the judgement, nor
sinners in the congregation of the righteous.
For the Lord knoweth the way of the righteous: but the way
of the ungodly shall perish.

I reveled also in Psalm 100:

Make a joyful noise to the Lord, all ye lands.
Serve the Lord with gladness: come before his presence with
singing.
Know ye that the Lord he is God: it is he that hath made
us, and not we ourselves; we are his people, and the
sheep of his pasture.
Enter into his gates with thanksgiving, and into his courts
with praise: be thankful unto him, and bless his name.
For the Lord is good; his mercy is everlasting; and his truth
endureth to all generations.

These beautiful words gave me a tender balance for the hard intellectual churning inside my head and helped me to further embrace it
all. The Bible gave me a generosity of spirit.

I emerged from solitary confinement into the general prison population an entirely different human being. Putting all my newly learned
virtues into practice, however, was a struggle. Every day I faced countless moments when it would have been far easier to revert to form. A
few months earlier, if a guy had said "Hey, Upchurch, fuck you man!"
I would have taken off his head, just as I had in the receiving area of
Petersburg and again in the dining room. Now I tried to look at him,
really look, and see the pain, frustration, and discomfort that had

caused him to lash out like that. On the basketball court, if I inadvertently pushed my elbow into someone's chest and knocked him down, I would reach down and give him a hand, saying, "Come on brother, let me help you up. I know you're mad, but let's keep it down. I respect you, and you respect me. Let's just play." And instead of having a full-blown fight on the court, we could go on with the game.

At Lewisburg, I finally realized that I could control my own destiny. With that discovery, I was able to begin the journey that eventually would lead me out of darkness.

PART TWO

Deniggerization

Eight

BREAK OF DAY

I still had to fight my way through Lewisburg, regardless of my new learning. One day I was stealing food from the kitchen to sell to the Italians on J Block, who had set up a kitchen for themselves. A brother from West Virginia challenged me when I was taking some eggs. His attitude and his words—"I'm gonna take you down, man"—had nothing to do with the eggs; he was challenging my rep, the only distinguishing mark I had in this jungle. He evidently didn't know that I was someone not to be fucked with.

I told him to meet me outside the kitchen so we could talk. Even though he had no way of knowing that I was hiding an eighteen-inch piece of lead pipe, it was naive of him to agree. I split his head open with the first blow and broke his jaw with the second. He tried to fight back, but I beat him half to death with that pipe, saying over and over again, "Don't you ever tell me what the fuck you're going to do!"

Later on, when I was thinking about the fight, I found myself looking at it in a new and surprising way. It wasn't my participation in a fight that surprised me—that was my knee-jerk reaction to everything. What surprised me was my feeling about it—shame. I had never felt shame before. It made me cry.

———

Through my reading, I had gotten a good look at my soul and my spirit. It felt like being reborn, taking on a life long denied them. But at least for the first few months, whenever I had to leave the books in my cell to go out into the general prison population, I was too often the same old "Church," using coping skills I had honed to criminal perfection. Everything I was trying to be had its roots in history. But so did everything I was trying not to be.

About two months after I was released from solitary, my old partner from Milan, Frank Lewis, was transferred to Lewisburg from Tallahassee, and my fledgling deniggerization process came to a screeching halt. Frank didn't trust my books. But he was a known quantity in a strange place, and it felt natural to revert to form, hanging out with him and doing the same things we had done in Milan. The rules were a little different because Lewisburg was a federal penitentiary. We had to be more careful about whom we confronted and how. The crowd was much tougher—men who wouldn't hesitate to kill us if we stuck them up—and we had to be prepared to give our lives, or take someone else's, at any time. The code we lived by meant that Frank and I had to uphold each other's honor and reputation. In a twisted kind of loyalty, he watched my back, and I watched his.

Frank never knew that whenever I went back to my cell, I went back to my books. This was my source of comfort and satisfaction, the arena of my personal struggle. I couldn't give them up, not even for Frank. I felt like a fraud.

It was a feeling I was coming to know well. I had felt it when I cried in my cell after beating up that guy from West Virginia, even though I had beaten him because I was supposed to according to the unwritten rules of reputation. But after that fight, I realized that no real achievement could be built on cheap props. That fight was pivotal in the development of my self-acceptance and my taking responsibility for my own actions. Not until years later would I find the word *niggerization* to identify my old negative feelings, my self-hatred, my repetitive self-destructive behavior. But that fight was the beginning of my denig-gerization.

I began to experience an intense inner conflict between my exciting new ideas and my old persona. Racked with self-doubt, I thought I might be only tricking myself into thinking I was college material. Maybe it was just another jailhouse delusion that a lot of us experience when we think about what we could be on the outside. Behind bars, it was easy to be a millionaire, or a college graduate.

I kept having to fight my recurring feeling that I would never be able to change. Since I still depended on my rep to keep me safe, I kept my ambitions and my reading pretty much a secret. But secrecy cut off any possibility of positive reinforcement from others. The result—I was constantly uncomfortable and off balance, simultaneously relieved and disappointed when people approached me in all the same old ways. They still confronted me, still had the same violent expectations of me, and any time I was under pressure to respond to some situation, I fell back on the responses I knew best—beating up someone.

At Lewisburg, my days consisted of working in the kitchen, hang-ing out on the tier, playing baseball and basketball, and reading. As I read, I started to understand that the chance being offered to me was the result of substantial numbers of African-Americans who had strug-gled throughout America's history to escape the bonds of niggeriza-tion. These writers, these educators, these organizers, some of whom had died long before I was even born, were now trying to engage me in their struggle. It was as if I had been born wearing strong boots with strong straps, but nothing could happen until I took the initiative to reach down and pull them up. My bootstraps are my tightly woven legacy from Harriet Tubman, Nat Turner, Sojourner Truth, Booker T. Washington, and W.E.B. Du Bois; from Martin and Malcolm and Medgar; and most important, from every nameless slave who fought this fight before me, and fights it now with me.

In 1976, at the suggestion of the chaplain, I read *The Autobiogra-phy of Malcolm X*. That book brought everything home to me. Here was a man who had already been through my struggles. Born Malcolm Little, he had rejected that "slave name" for Detroit Red, then grew past that hustling phase to become Malcolm X. His words gave me the courage to reach down and grab my bootstraps. He challenged my preoccupation with myself, telling me, "It's not enough to just fix yourself. What about your responsibility to your people?"

Of all the authors I had read, Malcolm's path most closely paralleled mine. I felt as if he were coming right into my cell and speaking to me.

"You are the one I'm talking to right now," he said. "First of all, you come from Africa. You are an African who lives in America. You are one with all other Africans who live in America. To be liberated, you must accept yourself. You must accept that you have a responsibility to your African-American brothers. You are a rebellious person, Carl. Learn to use your anger, your rebellious energy, in a better way, to stop your African-American brothers from emulating the white man, putting dope in their arms."

I didn't much like the responsibility that Malcolm was placing on my shoulders, and I challenged him on it. "How can I be responsible for people who want to kill people, who want to shoot dope, want to smuggle dope in from the streets? Don't they have to be responsible for themselves, just as I have to be responsible for myself?"

As always, arguing out loud helped clarify my thinking, and my inner conflict somehow lessened after I found Malcolm X. At last, I had something solid to stand on. All my suspicions about the causes of my own behavior and how I got where I was were somehow confirmed in his writings. His intellectual development had been African-American and spiritually centered, and it engendered in me a deeper appreciation of my existence in the "wilderness of North America." Malcolm's writings, and those of Louis E. Lomax, opened new emotional and intellectual vistas, allowing me to look deeper into my own past, into my own soul.

With Malcolm's help, I began sorting out the multidimensional influences that had corrupted me and taught me to function as a mindless, immoral, impulsive entity. The violence in my life—the shootings, the fights, the stabbings, the drug abuse, the hedonism, the disrespect for others—all of it, according to Malcolm, was rooted in self-hatred, generated by the niggerization process experienced by every African-American who lives through these circumstances. On Malcolm's horizon I saw the possibility of extricating myself from feelings of worthlessness and despair, self-denunciation and disrespect, emotional self-loathing and purposeful self-denial.

Another piece of the puzzle fell into place when I read about "two-ness," as described by W. E. B. Du Bois: "One feels his two-ness—an American, a Negro, two souls, two thoughts, two unreconciled strivings, two warring ideals in one dark body." I felt Du Bois's ambivalence, I felt those combative factions. On one side was my American understanding of who I was, derived from European writers and thinkers. On the other side was a seemingly endless parade of African-American artists, writers, poets, scholars, and social activists, each of whose individual history shed light on my own journey of self-discovery. The burden of my deliverance suddenly became shared by an entire history.

In Pascoe G. Hill's *Fifty Days on Board a Slave Vessel*, a recollection of the "middle passage" hit me like nothing I had read before. The description of men and women like myself, packed tightly in rows, urinating and defecating and dying on each other, immobilized me with anger and washed me in tears. The brutality of their journey made my own journey seem insignificant by comparison. Their misery captured me, bound me to them all the way down to my soul. Almost overnight, it seemed a sacrilege to continue my self-inflicted hatred, my self-centered ways.

Such strong feelings inevitably surfaced in my everyday discussions and reactions. One hot summer day I was sitting on the old wooden bleachers at the baseball field, watching two other convict teams play. Someone mentioned the Negro ball leagues, and I said, "Listen, up until 1947 they had all-white leagues and the Negro leagues. So you can't really count Ty Cobb's record or the record of any of the white players before then, because they didn't play against the best players of their time. They weren't playing in the Major Leagues—they were playing in the all-white leagues. Major League baseball records shouldn't start until 1947, when Jackie Robinson came into the league."

I went on and on about it, talking and giving statistics, not even noticing the strange looks I was getting from people sitting around me. When I was finally finished, a white guy dismissed everything I had said with a casual, "Man, that's bullshit." And one of the black guys asked me suspiciously, "How do you know all that stuff?" "Because I read it," I answered. They were totally unimpressed.

That was the first time I had dared publicly to articulate a position on a theory that I was struggling to understand. The response I got that day didn't exactly make me eager to display my newfound knowledge again. After all, I was used to being an authority because everyone knew Carl Upchurch; I definitely wasn't used to people responding to anything I said with suspicion or sarcasm. I was reluctant to lose the status I had fought so hard to gain in prison after prison, and I became less vocal about my studies.

Frederick Douglass's *Narrative,* to David Walker's *Appeal,* to Martin R. Delaney's *The Origin of the Races and Color* left me obsessed with the notion that I was part of a history bigger than my thieving, drug-infested behavior or the nigger mentality I had grown up with. I could hardly contain my excitement at discovering Zora Neale Hurston, Richard Wright, and Ralph Ellison, authors who culturally and spiritually liberated me and people like me from mental slavery.

Each and every syllable was exciting, fresh, and uplifting, much as Victor Hugo and Shakespeare had been. The critical difference was that these writers were significantly more potent, more spiritual, more personal to me. Discovering that we were all embarked upon a historic struggle for freedom presented a challenge to me, a challenge that carried with it a healing quality. I too was a part of Vincent Harding's enormous river—the whole of African-American experience. Only an emotionally and psychologically healthy person could hope to participate in this challenge, Harding said, and those who healed or joined the path of those healers before him had an opportunity to actually stand up in the great tradition of the African-American spirit and proclaim, "I am somebody!"

But my emotional conflict continued. I had always been involved in the prison drug trade, for example, and I got a cut of every load of drugs. Drugs were smuggled into prison by several different methods. Lots of guards were involved; they would just bring drugs in their lunch pails and sell them to us. Some guy's girlfriend might hide drugs in her mouth or even in her vagina. A visitor who brought someone a joint would just tuck it in his Afro. Virtually everyone was a user, and everyone had a supplier. The chain was strong. My reading tempted me to get out of the drug trade, but I would have had to sacrifice my rep to do it. Even though I understood that I no longer *had* to be a part of this circle of ignorance—selling dope, snorting dope, and beating people up—I wasn't yet strong enough to risk my rep.

My struggle was epitomized by a fight in the yard one day between the bikers and the Muslims. One of the Muslims had overheard a biker mouthing off to his buddies, saying, "There goes one of them no-pork niggers." The Muslim told his own buddies, and they came across the yard, ten or fifteen strong. Each side was saying the same thing: "We're gonna finally kill these motherfuckers, man. We're gonna take these motherfuckers off the count."

Up to this point I had been uninvolved, since I couldn't see that anything had happened worth killing someone over. But before I knew it, I found myself standing between the two groups, saying, "Why don't ya'll chill? Why don't ya'll cool it, man?"

The two adversaries turned on me at the same time. "What the fuck you talkin' about, nigger?" they yelled. "Who you talkin' about? You on their side, my brother?" they asked me simultaneously. "You a fuckin' Tom?"

Tempers soared. Both sides were armed with knives and baseball bats. They were ready to slash each other—to death if necessary. I was in way over my head. Then the leader of the Muslims took a step toward the bikers. Looking their leader right in the eye, he told his own men, "All these motherfuckers should die." A big, burly biker wearing a bandanna responded, "Bring it," and the tension inched up another notch. I backed out, saying "If this is what ya'll want to do, ya'll got it. Ya'll go ahead and kill each other. Ya'll got it." In the ensuing brawl two Muslims were stabbed; one of the bikers was killed later that evening.

I learned a valuable lesson that day—you can't just superimpose the wisdom of another time and place on a given situation. But it threw me into confusion and conflict. I had to deal with the kill-or-be-killed realities of my present to survive, yet I was struggling to be a live-and-let-live person. It was increasingly difficult to do both at the same time.

In April 1976 I was shocked to learn I had been granted parole. I wasn't exactly a model prisoner, but at Lewisburg I'd been a little more cagey than at Milan, and I hadn't gotten caught as often. And when I heard "Mr. Upchurch, we recommend that you be paroled on July 29, 1976," I wasn't about to talk them out of it. During the next couple of months, I behaved well enough to work my sentence down even more, and in June I was allowed to go to a halfway house to wait for the July parole date.

Parole was a disaster. My first mistake was to choose a halfway house in south Jersey, near Philadelphia. I could have gone somewhere else for this fresh start, but I wanted to go home. Even though my family, except for Stoney, had virtually ignored me the entire time I'd been in prison and in the army, they were all I had. I needed the emotional connection, especially to my mother. Unbelievably, I was still striving for her approval.

My second mistake was to go back to the streets of Philly, picking up with the friends and contacts I had known before Milan. We had to be out of the halfway house by seven or eight in the morning, depending on which shift we were on, and we had to be back no later than midnight. I was supposed to be looking for a job, but I bought marijuana and just hung out and smoked all day, every day.

I didn't have a clue how to deal with being back on the streets. In my cell at Lewisburg, I had had the solitude to study and think and picture a new life for myself. Once on the outside, however, I couldn't figure out how to live. Everyone else had their own lives; no one cared about mine. No one ever stopped to say, "Carl, can we assist you? Are you having trouble readjusting?" It was a barren atmosphere, and within three weeks of my preparole release, I had reverted to my criminal ways.

After all, robbery was my profession. I needed cash to begin my "new" life, so I hooked up with my brother-in-law, Robo, to get it. He drove me to Wills Eye Hospital in Philadelphia. While he waited in the car, I went in, found the accounting department, pulled out a pistol I'd bought on the street, and took $490 in cash.

I should have known better than to mess with my past pattern of my old successes. I had never worked with anyone else, never had a getaway car. I just did the stick-up and headed for the subway, losing myself among a myriad of other faces. But this time the cops caught up to us a block from the hospital; that short chase ended abruptly when my brother-in-law swerved to miss some little girls playing Double Dutch in the street, ran his car up on the curb, and stalled it. I got four more years for the hospital job, which I served at Western State Penitentiary. (I once jokingly said I should have gotten eight—that robbery was such bad style.) Then I had to go to Memphis to serve out the remaining two years of my original sentence.

I went into Western with a different attitude from those I'd had at other institutions. Through my reading I had learned enough to know that trading six years of my life for a lousy $490 was a bad deal, but just reading about new ideas wasn't enough to break the vicious cycle I had been in for over twenty years. Unless I took some deliberate steps to change, I would keep upping the ante with bigger crimes and getting longer sentences until I ended up dead. I knew there were alternatives; I just hadn't figured out how to get at them. So I promised myself that

Western would be my fresh start. I wouldn't do drugs, sell drugs, or fight; I wouldn't strive to be the biggest bad-ass guy on the block. I was determined to find a new way to live or die trying.

Western gave me the choice of working or going to school. The penitentiary had a deal with the University of Pittsburgh that offered prisoners an entire degree program. When they asked me what I wanted to major in, I picked psychology, thinking it would let me spend long hours absorbed in self-reflection, trying to figure out why I was the way I was. In retrospect, I made a conscious decision to stop being a nigger—to cleanse my thoughts, my feelings, and my actions.

College classes were not what I had expected. I was used to reading and studying on my own, and I wanted to think and to explore, to challenge and be challenged. Even in this new subject area, I was pretty arrogant. I was all ready to debate with the professors, to show off my knowledge. But most of the teachers expected us to sit in class, take notes, and spit the information back on a test. It was frustrating and unsatisfying.

A few teachers used a better process of learning. They asked hard questions and pushed me in new directions, suggesting extra readings that weren't on the syllabus. Without them, I might have continued to think I knew everything.

One of my favorite professors was Martha Connamacher, who taught chemistry and physics. Martha was a serene woman who also helped me think through some of the religious and spiritual questions I was grappling with at that time. Our relationship did not immediately start out on friendly terms. One day we were talking about religion. Martha was a Quaker. I told her that religion was phony, that black people get the short end of God's stick, and that there is no evidence to support the existence of a creator. I questioned how a thinking person could ever believe in something like the virgin birth.

She replied to my attacks in a calm and self-assured manner. When I called the Virgin Mary a white woman, using a derogatory tone, Martha simply said, "Carl, you actually don't understand the part of the world where Mary was born and where she lived." Then she challenged me to read whatever I could find about the Middle East.

Even though Martha was white, she became a kind of surrogate mother for me, helping to free me from my dead-end quest for my real mother's approval. I respected her very, very much. Her strong belief in God was palpable. She was the walking picture of faith. At first I thought it impossible that she could really be as good a person as she seemed to be, so I challenged her over and over. She never lost patience with me, though. She talked endlessly with me, helping me examine my beliefs. Through those discussions I found out more about her faith and began to further develop my own. Martha's influence is still with me today.

———

It was at Western that all the reading, all the thinking, finally started to have meaning outside my head. I had previously used my reputation to maintain my status as a tough guy. Now I used it to ask for—and get—respect for my efforts. I acted like the person I wanted to be. It felt pretty uncomfortable, but I stuck with it, gaining confidence one day at a time. And because I needed to change not just myself but to create a different environment to live in, I tried to get other convicts interested in ideas too.

I still read everything I could get my hands on, but my interests had turned to nonfiction. I pored over Bertrand Russell, who laid out philosophical debates in language I could understand. His theory about the truthful presentation of self impressed me—it emphasized treating each other with mutual respect and caring, with humanity, and with decency.

Frantz Fanon was a psychiatrist, whose writing about the Algerian revolution in *The Wretched of the Earth* demonstrated how people react to oppression and repression. Even though he used the Algerians to document his findings, Fanon's words transcended national barriers to touch my own psychological and emotional condition as a niggerized

American. He delineated how easily the colonized internalize the perspective of the colonizer, resulting in a divided self that sees and evaluates itself only through others' eyes. In other words, the colonized emulate their oppressors. The only way out of this cycle is to create a synthesis of the two perspectives.

Fanon's theory built on Du Bois's concept of "two-ness"—the difficulty of merging Americanism with Africanism to present a coherent spirit. But such coherence, Du Bois had argued, must be achieved to gain spiritual and psychological control.

At Western I developed opinions on some key moral and ethical issues that have remained with me ever since, such as that hypocrisy and the compromising of one's cultural values are debilitating to the human spirit. African-American males, living in degrading and devastating conditions of oppression, must either diminish the impact of those conditions or succumb to them. According to the moral code I began developing, every day I must look for routes by which I can navigate through the morass of compromise and hypocrisy without sacrificing my integrity. Should I sell out, opting to say and do the things the dominant culture prefers, making myself malleable and marketable and agreeable? Or should I be like Paul Robeson, who refused to use his celebrity to further the niggerization of his people and whose activist spirit forbade him to compromise his principles? Sadly, the "moral" route always brings unpopular repercussions; Robeson ended up penniless, in the relative obscurity of a West Philadelphia ghetto.

As a child growing up on South Street, I was sucked into destructive habits, forced to concentrate on surviving. I was convinced that I had nothing to offer and no choices to make. At Western I saw more clearly who and what I was, and began to understand what that meant.

Nine

STARTING OVER

I left Western and went on to the Memphis Federal Correctional Institution to serve out the rest of my original sentence for the bank robberies. When that was finished two years later, I was thirty-one years old and had been in prison for nearly ten years straight, except for a few weeks running around Philadelphia and living at the halfway house in New Jersey. I was ready to get out and start living.

———

I kept in touch with Martha Connamacher while I was at Memphis. She would send me books she thought might interest me to further my education. After four years in a university atmosphere, I was particularly interested in the field of education, so she sent me books by authors like Ann Phillips and Jonathan Kozol. I was getting very selective about what I read. Solitary reflections on a line by Elizabeth Barrett Browning weren't enough for me anymore. The classics still had a place in my heart because of what they had done for me at the lowest ebb in my life, but I had lost interest in reading them. I wanted to join the debate about who African-American people are in the American context. To do so, I had to learn from present-day social, political, and educational thinkers, men and women who had drawn their literary heritage from the same authors I had. I pushed myself to read current social and political writers.

I was more interested in the African-American response to Reagan than in Reagan himself. The fact that "trickle-down" was nothing more than "trickle-up" was obvious even to me. But more and more conservative blacks were becoming visible. I was impressed by Thomas Sowell, a courageous and thoughtful black conservative activist whose voice had barely been acknowledged before Reagan. Although I disagreed with him on many issues, his unwavering message was a reassuring constant amid the clamor of traditional civil rights voices that adapted themselves to the political agenda of the moment almost overnight. Disgusted, I knew such shifts were based on their own self-interest in protecting their bureaucracies and maintaining their livelihoods rather than serving the oppressed people for whom they ostensibly spoke.

After Sowell, I read Shelby Steele, a black author who was just finding his voice during the Reagan years. He probably wasn't a conservative then, but he is clearly in that camp now—against affirmative action, even though he's a product of it, and part of the Clarence Thomas, pull-yourself-up-by-the-bootstraps-and-rise-above-your-circumstances school of thinking. Like many other black conservatives, he came out of a tidy middle-class home with no comprehension of the experience of the urban poor. Steele became a political darling by taking positions that were unpopular with blacks but were very appealing to the dominant white culture.

As I plowed through the books Martha sent me, I became more and more convinced that there was no monolith of African-American thought. No single voice speaks for all African-Americans, even though professional Negroes like Jesse Jackson would have us think otherwise.

———

When I was released from Memphis, no halfway house awaited me. I was a free man and once again I had to choose where to go. My last experience on the outside showed me that I could easily revert to my old behavior patterns. In short, if I went back to South Philly, I would go right back to being a nigger, and what was developing inside me would never have a chance to take shape. I'd had plenty of time to think about this, and I didn't want to screw it up this time. So I was determined to avoid all contacts from my criminal past.

I called Martha to tell her I was getting out. She evidently sensed some hesitation in my voice, because she asked, "What are you concerned about?"

"I'm nervous about going back to Philadelphia," I answered. "From South Philly to North Philly to West Philly, I'm known. The gangsters and the killers are just waiting for me to come back out on the streets." Then this wonderful woman, already more of a mother to me than my own had ever been, held out a lifeline: "How'd you like to work here on the farm?"

Martha and Bob Connamacher had bought a farm outside Pittsburgh to get their children, Richard, six, and Harold, thirteen, away from the city environment. They had two black sons, Demetrius and William, whom they had adopted nearly ten years earlier, when the boys were just eleven and twenty-three months old. One day Martha and Bob had found the two babies unattended in an apartment they owned in the Homewood section of Pittsburgh. The mother had been gone for two days. The Connamachers waged a long and costly legal battle to adopt the two boys and get them out of that environment.

When I was released from Memphis, Demetrius and William were twelve and thirteen years old, and Martha and Bob were having trouble with them. Martha asked me to live and work on the farm because she thought it would help all of us: I would be totally removed from the negative influence of Philadelphia, and Demetrius and William might have a positive role model. Easing myself back into society instead of being thrust back in appealed to me, so I jumped at Martha's offer, even though I had to admit to being more than a little leery about living on a farm. Martha didn't know exactly what she wanted me to accomplish with her sons, but she trusted me to try to reach them. She knew

I'd had a difficult time when I was growing up and thought that some-how they might be able to identify with me.

Once I'd arrived at the farm and was settled in, I helped with the chores and spent time with Demetrius and William. We'd talk or just hang out; sometimes we'd go to baseball games together. The boys were underachieving at school in a little town called Fox Chapel—a cliquish, wealthy, arrogant place, about 99 percent white. I could empathize with their dislike of school but still tried to get them to take more of an interest. I discovered that I had good natural instincts about how to deal with the boys, and I think they liked me; at least, their actions said to me, "I need you. You're okay. I accept you." I can't say for sure how effective I was with them, but I felt very close to them both.

One day in 1993, long after I left the farm, I got a call from William. "Carl, they can't find Demetrius." "Don't worry," I told him. "Demetrius always did like to run away for a few days. He'll be around." A few days later, William called to tell me that they had fished Demetrius's body out of the river. I don't know what losing a child feels like, but losing Demetrius hit me hard. The news that he was dead devastated me. But William and I are still connected, and the work I do with teenagers today is partly based on my experiences with him and Demetrius.

———

Back when I was at Lewisburg challenging Martha to prove the existence of God, she had given me a pamphlet about the Quaker religion. She was very committed to being a Quaker, but I was suspicious of all Christianity because of what I perceived to be its contribution to the current condition of African-Americans. The pamphlet opened up a whole new set of discussions. Then Martha sent me the book *The Journal of George Fox,* written by the founder of Quakerism. It was the last book I read at Lewisburg, and after the Bible it had the most powerful impact on my spirituality.

The Quaker philosophy is based on nonviolence. I knew of it in connection with Martin Luther King, Jr., but it came alive for me when I read Fox's *Journal*. Fox's struggle reveals unparalleled commitment, not just to his faith as such but to living his faith. He traveled throughout the English countryside, forsaking his family, to share his beliefs with others. Trying to intimidate him, officials of the Church of England locked him away in prison towers, but he stood fast and would not be turned away from the central Quaker philosophy: to speak truth to power. Few in history exemplify the consequences of doing that better than George Fox. He was well respected by his followers because day by day he remained committed to the ideas of Jesus Christ. His journal is still one of the most impressive and inspiring works I have ever read on the question of faith.

In July, after I'd been at the Connamachers' farm for about a month, they took me to the Friends' General Conference, an annual meeting for Quakers, held at Swarthmore College. We stayed three days, living in the dorms. On the second day, I was asked to speak, which astonished me. I had never spoken in public before, but Martha said, "You've lived an extraordinary life—just tell them about it." And I did.

That conference was my first introduction to the Society of Friends on a grand scale. It was religion the likes of which I had never seen, and the Friends' purity of purpose impressed me. Quakers believe there is a piece of God in every one of us, and that everyone is valuable. This was exactly the reverse of what I'd learned at my mother's knee and while incarcerated, but I believed it to be true. And believing it, I knew I must learn to accept a wide range of people. Protecting another person, then, would be the same as protecting God and doing his work. Reading of the "light within," of being still and waiting for God's voice, it reinforced my own idea of God—that in solitude, in the most peaceful moments, God will provide answers. And when I look back at the authors who made the biggest impression on me, I see that every one had a connection to this philosophy, whether they were Quakers or not. In short, I had bought into Quaker ideals long before I had heard of the Quaker faith.

Another quality of the Friends that I appreciate is that they do their best without seeking recognition for it. I remember once seeing an old paper, published back in 1962, about Martin Luther King, Jr. At the bottom of the page, in really small letters, it said "Printed by the American Friends Service Committee, AFSC." The Friends have many ways to remind us that we're servants of God, meant to serve the people around us, not to focus on ourselves. Too many leaders, whether in business or politics, lose track of that when they reach the top of their professions and think only of attention and publicity.

While I was at the conference at Swarthmore, I saw a brochure about the School of Religion at Earlham, a Quaker college in Indiana. The brochure impressed me, and I spent long hours with Martha and Bob discussing whether it was the right place for me. Finally I applied, was accepted, and at the end of August, just two months after being released from Memphis, I was on the Earlham campus, beginning seminary studies.

It was my intention to get a masters of divinity in the two-year program—a year of coursework, followed by a year of theological reflection. After that, I could choose to go on to another program, or I could declare my degree completed. My vision was to develop Quaker churches in urban areas, bringing this unique faith to African-Americans who might otherwise never hear of it. It was a wildly idealistic vision.

Everything went well at first. The classes were demanding, but I rose to the challenge. All my professors expected rigorous demonstrations of detailed knowledge. When I wrote a paper, I knew I couldn't fudge on either the scholarship or the format. If I was assigned a book chapter or a poem to analyze, I felt obligated to offer a thorough and challenging critique. It didn't matter if the perspective I chose was far out in left field, as long as I was able to support it and argue it from a scholarly vantage point. Earlham's educational standards demanded precision of thinking at every level, and that training has served me well. To this day, whenever I am formulating a new idea or postulating a fresh position, I ask myself if it would fly at Earlham.

I quickly discovered that I was the only African-American enrolled in the School of Religion. It gave me a lonely feeling, especially on Tuesdays during the so-called common hour, when everyone came together to eat and socialize. There wasn't anything common about that hour at all to me; it was decidedly uncommon, not welcoming in any way. I found myself sitting with young students from upper-middle-class families and eating spinach quiche, of all things. I felt like an object of curiosity. People would invite me to their tables and try to act as if I were truly a part of the community, but it was obvious they weren't used to being around blacks. I felt they just wanted me to entertain them with anecdotes about my life in prison.

Feelings of loneliness and alienation can be overcome. What I couldn't overcome was the total lack of connection between the school and the African-American community. I soon concluded that I was a token at Earlham, admitted largely because the administration had a quota to fill. I felt on display all the time, and I resented it.

To put it bluntly, Earlham and I never fit. Neither of us got what we expected. They had wanted a malleable symbol; they got a loud, kind of arrogant ex-con who was looking for a principle by which to redeem himself. I went there seeking an institutional version of the spirit I had found in *The Journal of George Fox;* I got philosophies distorted by countless institutional accommodations that bore precious little relation to Fox's.

My disaffection with Earlham deepened during an independent study project with Professor Steve Butler. I was to write a reflective piece on any subject I wanted, so I chose South Africa. I did the research. I read Lyle Tatum's *South Africa: Challenge and Hope* and Bishop Desmond Tutu's *Crying in the Wilderness.* I went to Earlham's financial office and reviewed the college's investment portfolio against the United Nations' list of companies that continued to do business with South Africa. I wrote to Congressman Stephen Solarz of New York, asking for information. His data confirmed what I had found: Earlham had $41 million invested in companies that did business in South Africa. The rigorous habits of scholarship I had acquired served me well now; before I spoke out, I made sure I had all my academic ducks in a row. I talked to people I respected on campus, including Professor Peter Suber in the philosophy department. "You're absolutely right," he told me. "There's a long history of that kind of activity at this school."

I brought it up during a session of my pastoral counseling course. This class always started with the professor asking, "What bothers you today?" One day I responded by saying, "What bothers me is that this institution is unethical, and I'm a student here. I am very distraught." Then I explained exactly what bothered me. The instructor didn't respond during class, but later she caught up with me and said, "You're right. We do this, but we have to in order to survive as an institution. You have to accept it as part of the world."

I kept getting the same message, over and over: "We think it's a terrible, awful thing, but what can we do?" Those investments were subsidizing the faculty's paychecks, and they were implicitly asking me to join their gang. "Keep your mouth shut and get your degree. Once you leave here, you can go out and really make some noise." It was a crazy argument. If a woman is being raped, am I supposed to stand silently by? Should I go away, study criminology, then come back and put all the rapists away? It was an immoral way to think, and I was extremely troubled.

I felt that Earlham had let me down. Here I was, just out of prison, thinking that *I* somehow needed to be scrubbed and cleansed in order to become good enough for a place built on the spiritual legacy of George Fox. When Earlham didn't live up to my ideals, I became upset, fearful that there was no place to find salvation. Feeling completely alone and threatened, I lashed out.

At all-college worship, a weekly Sunday service at Earlham, I stood up and told the truth, not only about the South African investments but about what I saw as a 12 percent quota that existed for black admissions to the college. A few students knew a little about South Africa, but most had no awareness of the issues; I had to do a lot of educating. So I talked about Sharpeville and Soweto and the tragedies that occurred there; I introduced the students to Nelson Mandela, who had then been in jail for nearly thirty years.

I was braced for a racial backlash, but the next morning I was inundated with flowers, notes, and phone calls from lots of students and faculty members. Letters giving me every possible affirmation were slipped underneath the door to my room. "You're wonderful." "Don't stop what you're doing." "You're courageous." I couldn't walk to and from my classes without being stopped and asked about what I had said.

I was interviewed by other schools, by newspapers, and on local radio and TV. Everyone wanted to find out about this black guy, fresh out of prison, who was making all the noise. I was loud and passionate in my condemnation. Earlham wasn't supposed to be like Ohio State or Pittsburgh; it was supposed to have a separate destiny. It had carved out a special niche for itself in American higher education, then violated that sanctity in the most hypocritical way—presenting a public Quaker face while privately sacrificing its values for money.

Soon I had my own talk show on the college radio station. I formed an antiapartheid action coalition, wrote articles in Earlham's daily newspaper, and generally got lots of media coverage. On January 19, when we had a basketball game against Bluffton College (I was an assistant coach), I called a boycott to draw attention to Earlham's hypocrisy. Coach Avis opposed me; he felt the boycott would only punish the team. Most of the players didn't even know what South Africa was all about or why we were protesting, but all of the six or seven black students on the team decided to join the boycott. After the Bluffton game, all the black players went back to the team—except Andy Williams, the best ballplayer and most popular kid on campus. This superior athlete and 4.0 student chose to align himself with me, an endorsement that gave me even more credibility.

It's all too easy to believe cards and letters and phone calls telling you how wonderful you are. I thoroughly enjoyed my celebrity. It seemed as if every female student who saw me in person or on television called me up. The consequences of such adulation are obvious, and I took advantage of every opportunity, engaging in countless casual sexual encounters. I soon discovered, however, that my power, the courage of my convictions, was undermined by transitory pleasure. The sight of three or four girls in the front row could easily sidetrack me, especially since I knew they weren't there to learn about Earlham's South African involvement, and my intensity would diminish in visions of sexual pleasure.

It finally dawned on me that I was an incredible hypocrite, casting moral judgment on Earlham while behaving immorally myself. The excessive adulation had given me as false a sense of myself as the excessive scorn of my childhood. When I see an entertainer or an athlete receiving a lot of popularity and acclaim, I sometimes say a silent prayer for him or her. I experienced only a smidgen of such celebrity but found it totally overwhelming. It fed the diseased and undeveloped sides of me and warped my best intentions.

Of course, not everybody loved me. Some administrators and professors urged me to quit agitating and focus on getting my degree: "Carl, you've come so far. Don't blow it now. Get your degree, and you'll own the world." This logic never made sense to me. Own what world? So what if I'm a "Son of Earlham"—the African-American token who made good. Exactly what would I own? A share of the poison that I'm otherwise trying to exorcise from my soul? Should I swallow that poison for a piece of paper? They missed the point; getting the piece of paper itself had nothing to do with the redemption I sought.

We can rationalize almost any behavior if enough people condone it, but the final arbiter has to be ourselves and how we feel. We must possess some usable truth, truth that can help us wake up and be excited about who we are, not who someone else thinks we are. Usable truth is fashioned out of our own moral development, independent of what everybody else is doing or saying. It helps us be close to God inside ourselves—not try to be God or walk in God's shoes, just be close.

On the whole, my feelings about Earlham put me on the horns of a dilemma. After all, these people had taken me in when almost no one else would and at the age of thirty-two, just three months after I had completed a ten-year stint in prison. Their campus had given me my first real chance to stand up and do something positive with my life. I coached basketball, got good grades, and had the company of many attractive women. It should have been heaven for someone who had been away from the world for ten years. But it turned into hell. In an atmosphere where sound moral choices should have come easily, I consciously made immoral ones. By February, five months after my arrival, I was waging an all-out war against the institution; people who had supported me at the beginning were calling me an ingrate.

Once again, Martha Connamacher was my touchstone. She never said, "Why don't you just shut up and get your degree?" even when I called her at three in the morning to talk for hours, examining the issues and working toward a moral conclusion. In the end, I decided to leave Earlham at the end of the school year. My nine months there had felt like nine years. I feared that if I stayed another year, I might fall off an even bigger moral cliff and never recover.

I walked away from Earlham knowing that I had learned all I could and that I had made a difference in my short term there. The school agreed to enroll a South African student and promised to monitor its investments, doing some creative investing in companies that didn't do business in South Africa. It's probably the most I could have hoped for.

I went back to the Connamachers' farm and spent the next year in reflection. I thought social work might be what I wanted, and I entered graduate school at the University of Pittsburgh in the fall of 1984. But within a year I had dropped out of that program as well. I didn't have the same problems at Pitt that I had had at Earlham; I had purposely chosen a large school so that I could remain anonymous and not be the only African-American in the program. But compared with Earlham, the faculty at Pittsburgh didn't seem to take academic work seriously. Their main aim was to prepare people for jobs in social work, not to explore the problems plaguing our society. Nor did the faculty keep up with emerging social issues. AIDS was just becoming prevalent the year I was there. I read about it everywhere, but my professors dismissed it, saying, "It's a homosexual disease." I didn't know any different, so I didn't argue with them, but I did know that there were homosexuals everywhere, which meant the disease's social impact would be enormous. They acted as if the topic weren't even worthy of class discussion, focusing instead on irrelevant topics like the history of social agencies and the background of the dole in England. It seemed like the curriculum was written fifty or sixty years ago and no matter what changed in society, it was set. Crime and violence and misery and child molestation and unwed mothers and single-parent families and poverty-stricken households and spousal abuse and spiraling penitentiary numbers were rampant—just not on the syllabus. I didn't have the stomach for another huge fight, so I withdrew.

Shortly after I left Pittsburgh, I got a job through the American Friends Service Committee as a mental health worker at St. Gabriel's School for Boys in Phoenixville, outside Philadelphia. Because I was determined to stay away from my old neighborhood, I boarded with a Methodist family in Germantown, sleeping on the hard floor in the study. The woman ran a day-care center and made it clear to me that I wasn't allowed to go there: "Carl, I hope you understand. The parents don't know you." I was offended, but I was so nervous about being anywhere near Philadelphia that I kept my mouth shut so I could keep living there.

St. Gabe's had hoped that I could somehow work miracles with these youngsters because of my background, which was nonsense. In practice, I was a glorified prison guard. They offered no long-term comprehensive program for developing kids; they just released them when their time was up, setting them up for the old prison-parole-prison cycle. I was seeing again what I'd first noticed at Memphis—nothing had changed in the lives of inner-city kids since my own childhood, thirty years ago. I couldn't fix it, but I couldn't stay there and watch it either. So I left after three months, returning to the Connamachers' farm in western Pennsylvania.

The following July, I woke up one morning to find several shotguns pointed at my head. Local law enforcement, including the sheriff, had arrived to arrest me in connection with a nationally publicized incident in Philadelphia. On May 13, 1985, Wilson Goode, then mayor of Philadelphia, authorized the National Guard to drop a bomb on a row house in an effort to forcibly remove members of a primarily black religious group called MOVE. The bomb ignited a huge fire that killed most of the group members, including a number of children, and dispossessed many of the neighborhood citizens.

The cops picked me up to try to establish a past connection with MOVE, but since the only thing MOVE and I had in common was Philadelphia, they couldn't come up with any charges. When they arrested me, though, they had planted some syringes on me so they would have a back-up charge if the MOVE connection failed. The drug charge too was dismissed.

Still the cops didn't want to let me go. They were frustrated with the investigation, embarrassed by the national outcry, and looking for a scapegoat. They finally came up with "parole violation" to pin on me. Technically, it was true. I had been paroled to the Connamacher farm outside Pittsburgh, and I was not permitted to leave that area. Philadelphia was out of bounds. I had gone there twice, once for the St. Gabe's interview, then again when I started working at St. Gabe's. Finding gainful employment and staying straight were apparently irrelevant to the case, though, and I was sentenced to prison—three months for each movement to and from Philadelphia, a total of twelve months. Because I sat in jail for two extra months waiting around and being processed, I actually served a total of fourteen months.

They first sent me back to Western. The place was unbelievably overcrowded now, with two people routinely assigned to cells designed for one. Several people I had known there the last time were still serving out sentences there. I didn't stay at Western long since it was a maximum-security facility and I was in for only parole violation. Within three months I was sent to Greensburg, Pennsylvania, where I stayed until my release in August 1986.

The first three days I was back in prison, I was in complete shock, stunned by the injustice of what had happened to me. I had always accepted responsibility for my behavior, always been willing to walk into a courtroom and say, "Yes, I did that," and take my punishment. This seemed so unfair. Instead of looking through barbed wire at the hot summer sun on the fields, I should have been working on the Connamachers' farm. It seemed crazy for me to be locked up.

But after the initial shock and anger wore off, I decided to make the best use of the time I had to spend there. I began a period of cleansing, determined to become strong enough to stay on course until I could complete the job of deniggerizing myself. I had none of the old penitentiary demeanor about me at all. I treated the other prisoners as my brothers and let them know that I cared about what happened to them. "Hey man, how are you doing?" "What are you doing for yourself while you're in here?" "When's your court case?"

I finally accepted that everything in my life had been part of a pattern of growth and development. Nothing else can explain how, in the face of so many opportunities for me to fail, even to die, I have been so successful, so guided, so protected. It comforts me to think of my life in those terms, to see new signs every day that I am building on past experience. And every time I think I've finally discovered why I was put on this earth, I realize I am only being prepared for something else. Everything in my life, good and bad, has worked that way. Greensburg was no exception.

Ten

PROGRESSIVE PRISONERS' MOVEMENT

When I first moved to Ohio, I had a lot of blue pamphlets printed up and handed them out to everyone. The pamphlet told everything about my past—the crimes I had committed, how many times I had been incarcerated, when I had violated parole and been returned to prison. I even put a picture of myself on the back. It was the most liberating thing I had ever done.

I had reached a point in my life where I needed to be publicly proud of who I was, not hide from it. The mask I had worn up to that point—the one that was supposed to protect me from the hurts of the world—was actually holding me back from a fuller life. Like Jean Valjean in Les Misérables, I found the courage to take it off.

That symbolic act was a turning point. The energy required to keep up my facade could now be redirected to more positive ends.

At Greensburg I thought about what to do next. I was ready to take control of my own destiny and determined not to let this setback be the end of the line. Once I had ruled out all the things I *didn't* want to be, one choice stood out above all others: to dedicate my life to service to others. The problem was, I didn't know how. I had to take what I had learned about myself at Earlham and at Pitt and figure out where my unique talents could be best used.

I wasn't completely ready to give up on higher education, so I applied to Ohio State University in Columbus to try *its* graduate program in social work. I chose Ohio State for three reasons: it had recently adopted a policy on South Africa that I admired; I still wanted to avoid the small-campus atmosphere I had encountered at Earlham, and Ohio State is about as large as you can get; and most important, I was beginning to nurture a lingering relationship with Andrea Santoni, whom I'd met at Earlham and who lived in Newark, Ohio, only about forty miles east of Ohio State. Andrea had stood out among the beautiful women at Earlham because of her unique ability to see through hype. She believed in me, saw more deeply into my soul than anyone ever had, and recognized my barely discernible promise. Whenever I criticized myself for weaknesses, she focused on my strengths.

I had stayed in close touch with Andrea when I went back to the Connamachers'. When she learned I had been arrested, she was shocked and disappointed. She had no idea why I was back in jail, but the district attorney's office in Philadelphia sent her a letter trying to persuade her to get me to say I had been involved in MOVE. The parole board would go lightly on me if I "admitted" my involvement, they implied. Andrea came to Pittsburgh to talk to me about it face-to-face, and she believed me when I swore I knew absolutely nothing about the group. Although I ended up in jail anyway, for fourteen months Andrea's support was unwavering. Her belief in me, so empowering at Earlham, was even more so at Greensburg, and she continues to be the single most important force in my life.

In 1986 I moved to Newark to be with Andrea and started graduate school at Ohio State, commuting back and forth to Columbus several times each week. This time it took only two quarters for me to figure out that Ohio State wasn't going to supply the missing piece either. My experiences with higher education certainly did result in learning, but 95 percent of that learning didn't come from a course syllabus. I decided that a college degree was a bad trade for me and that I would give away no more of my life just to add some initials to my name.

I have a very healthy respect for education, but I question schools that present themselves as a litmus test for success. There are other, nonacademic ways of looking at personal and social problems, and leaving academia may make us more creative in finding solutions to them.

I had selected social work as a major both at Ohio State and Pittsburgh because of a vague idea that I might become a prison warden. It didn't take me long, though, to realize that a warden has virtually no one-on-one contact with prisoners, much less the chance to have an impact on them. The more I read about prisons and wardens, the more clearly I saw that wardens are trapped. They can't take a real interest in any of the convicts because they're really politicians, constantly having to adjust prison policy to suit the state and federal officials who oversee their funding. I didn't want to serve in that kind of capacity.

Still, I did enjoy studying the history and theory of the corrections system. But I had *been* in prison, while the professors who were "teaching" me about it knew only what they had read. At first, I didn't realize how little they knew about real prisoners in real prisons, but with each succeeding session, I was forced to conclude that much of what they said in their lectures wasn't true. I remained silent, partly because I was intimidated by the educational setting, but also because of my experience at Earlham, which had made me fear the notoriety that would surely result if I were to stand up and say, "Listen, man, you don't know what you're talking about. *I've been to prison.*" So even though I cringed at the falsehoods the professors taught, I kept quiet.

Moreover, it was unclear just what I would *do* with my degree, and these doubts prevented me from achieving the total immersion in my work necessary for a graduate degree. These are probably the real reasons I left school.

Some people, looking at my postgraduate academic record, have deduced that I am a quitter. It's only recently that I have been comfortable answering that charge. Here is what I say: I have indeed completed many projects over the years—the Progressive Prisoners' Movement, the Council for Urban Peace and Justice, and the gang summits, to name a few—projects that have had a major impact on the lives of people in our inner cities and our penal institutions. Unfortunately, however, universities do not confer degrees for such projects.

After I left Ohio State, I again went into a reflective trance, this time staring at the walls of the apartment Andrea and I shared in Newark instead of at the Connamachers' sheep and goats. Andrea willingly supported both of us while I read and thought and struggled, for nearly eight months, to sort out my thinking and decide what course I should pursue.

During that time, we lived close to Newark High School, and every day at 2:20 P.M. all the kids' cars would careen out of the parking lots and roar down the street. Sometimes I'd get up and watch them go by. Then the marching band would practice outside the school, and sometimes I'd walk up the block to watch them perfect their half-time show—trumpets and trombones flashing in the sun as the kids marched around, taking it all very seriously. The "normal" activities of a high school were exciting to me, since I'd never known them. And when winter came, I went to watch both the boys' and girls' basketball teams play in Newark and in Granville, a village just east of Newark.

Those basketball games were the only entertainment I allowed myself in my eight long months of self-debriefing. I examined the full scope and many dimensions of the prison situation—the death penalty, life sentences, overcrowding, inappropriate wages, prison brutality, oppressive conditions, preventive detention, and ineffective medical treatment, to name a few. Someone had to help these men, who had no support on the outside, so they would be able to withstand the temptation to return to crime when they left prison. Knowing that something had to be done, and that I was in a unique position to do it, the idea for the Progressive Prisoners' Movement (PPM) was born.

After Reagan was elected, the government instituted massive budget cuts that primarily hurt poor people. Some of the most devastating were the drastic cuts to Legal Aid. In response, prisoners began to take charge of their own destinies by organizing so that their voices could be heard. But they needed somebody on the outside to function as an advocate, because the major civil rights leaders—Jesse Jackson, Joseph Lowery, and others—were ignoring the central issues that impacted their lives, both in and out of prison. Unlike their predecessors, none of the current civil rights leaders had firsthand experience of the brutality and injustice of prison. As a result, they no longer participated in the national debates concerning prison brutality and other such causes that were brought to the forefront in the 1960s.

I wanted to work with prisoners to address injustice and to seek community and financial support for them. I started in an environment I knew well—Pennsylvania's maximum security prisons—circulating petitions to the prisoners and asking for signatures that would empower me to speak on their behalf. Then I broadened the scope by contacting activist organizations at prisons across the country. Before the year was up, I had signed up thousands of prisoners as PPM members. My vision was that our combined clout would sound a loud and spirited trumpet call to the nation. People from every walk of life—from inside and outside of prison; black, white, and Latino; Christian, Muslim, and Jew; male and female; rich and poor—would unite to let our voices ring out with a demand for justice.

I knew in my heart that I had finally found what I needed to do, and once I started talking about community and society and race and prison, everything came together. I received speaking invitations, visited prisons, and attended conferences. I was an unstoppable whirlwind of kinetic energy.

Anytime anybody would listen, I talked about the Progressive Prisoners' Movement. The ball really started to roll as my reputation spread by word of mouth. I traveled from coast to coast, talking to people all over the country; in my own county in Ohio, I don't think there's a single group I haven't spoken to at least once.

I started making some money here and there for my speeches and I used some of it to get a Progressive Prisoners' Movement logo designed. Once I had the logo, I designed a brochure and printed it on blue paper. It detailed my personal history and outlined some of my ideas about prisons and convicts.

> *I cannot forget those I served time with, nor can I deny the enormous weight of the responsibility I bear toward my brothers and sisters who are still behind bars. I want to unite them, to provide them with a constructive non-violent voice to speak up for their constitutional rights as prisoner-citizens. I want them to understand the direct link between being black and poor in America, the direct link between prisons and housing projects. I want to help break the cycle.*

I distributed the brochure to PPM members and asked them to pass copies of it along. Soon I was getting calls from all over the country, many inviting me to speak. Between coaching seventh-grade basketball in Granville and lecturing, I was now bringing in some income to augment Andrea's salary. It was a good feeling.

I spoke at prisons in Ohio and Pennsylvania and at colleges all over the country. Newspapers and magazines were interested in my story. A group in Atlanta invited me to speak at a conference on prisons, from which they were going to develop a book. When I was invited to Washington to sit on the National Commission on Crime and Justice, I contributed to a book of theirs as well.

I was a celebrity again, but not in the same way as at Earlham. I had now begun to understand the Quaker purity of purpose, and the depth of my commitment to the PPM, combined with a new maturity, allowed me to respond to the media attention with quiet dignity. That same commitment and maturity fueled my personal transformation, and a liberating spirit within me eagerly embraced new ideas. Since I was starting to do what I wanted to do with my life, I lost my defensiveness. And once the healthier parts of myself began to emerge, they reinforced my self-assurance. I felt as if I could accomplish anything.

Coaching helped me grow by enabling me to build a rapport with kids. In discovering what motivates young people and how to be a direct influence on them, I discovered more about myself. I would travel the country, pouring out my soul into every speech, then come back to the middle-school gym in Granville to fill myself up again. After every trip, that gym felt like a sanctuary, providing replenishment for my soul.

My pastor once told me that despite my enthusiasm for working with Granville seventh-graders, he didn't understand how I could reconcile my goals for PPM with coaching well-off kids from suburbia. His question surprised me. I would have thought he understood that we sometimes must do what we are called to do in unexpected places. I would have been willing to coach inner-city youth if someone had offered me a job there, but they didn't. This coaching job was in Granville, with white kids who didn't lack for comforts. My Quaker roots told me that everyone was important, worthy of time and appreciation, not just the poor and downtrodden.

Those twelve-year-olds were just as important as any prison convicts. Maybe I'm supersensitive, but I detected a hint of racism in the suggestion that "*our* kids are just fine; you should take your skills over *there* to work with kids everyone knows aren't okay." "Rich" kids need as much love and guidance as any inner-city children, and I cannot begin to separate the value of human beings based on what they have or don't have, or on who reared them, or who cursed and scorned them.

I had very ambivalent feelings about Granville itself. My expections, honed through years of niggerized influences, were obviously skewed. I came to this largely white college town expecting to find the village full of interesting, educated people. And I did meet and come to know some interesting people who eagerly discussed politics, philosophy, religion, and literature. But I also discovered a huge discrepancy between this real world and my former perception of it. Too much of the village's persona is based on "designer" values—the labels on your car or your clothes or your address. I had thought that "white" meant "educated," but not very many people had read Shakespeare or Mark Twain; not many were interested in current political debates over feminism or affirmative action. The tragedy here is that our children will inherit these values, or lack of them, from their parents.

My efforts to adapt to this strange environment did have some worthwhile consequences, however. Living in a community that was nearly all white put a positive pressure on me to hold myself accountable. It also helped insulate me from all of my negative influences, providing a calm backdrop against which I could wage my never-ceasing internal struggle.

———

Andrea and I were married in 1989, and our daughter, Mikayla, was born in 1990. When Andrea told me she was pregnant, I didn't experience the usual joy of a new father-to-be—I was petrified! I didn't want a child, had never wanted one. I was nervous about it, afraid that my feelings about my own childhood would bubble to the surface and scar my own child for life.

My fear of fatherhood stayed with me throughout Andrea's pregnancy, right up until the moment I saw tiny Mikayla enter the world. Then all of a sudden, everything was okay. My feelings for Mik were the biggest surprise in my life, and they told me that there had been a deeper regeneration of my spirit than I had ever thought possible. I would be a good father.

Eleven

BACK TO SCHOOL

I took a special assignment for part of one year at a middle school in Newark. One afternoon, a severely behaviorally impaired teenager attacked me. Screaming that I was a nigger, he pulled out a knife and tried to stab me.

The principal came to my aid, and together we subdued the kid and took him to the office. The principal called the cops, who asked me to press charges. When I looked at this kid, all I could see was myself, and I said, "No. We can't put this young boy in prison for being upset and angry."

My life had come full circle.

Watkins Memorial High School, east of Columbus, serves a largely rural area with few black residents. In 1990 a few students started to call themselves by some pretty ugly names—"Nazi" and "skinhead"—and overt racial troubles cropped up. The school's administrators decided to seek outside advice.

The Watkins principal networked his way through the county's social service agencies until someone told him I addressed those kinds of issues. He contacted me to ask if I could help. I drafted a proposal, explaining how I would work with the students and what I hoped to accomplish. The school system was satisfied enough to fund the program and assign a teacher to oversee it.

I could feel the tension as soon as I walked into the school. As I roamed the halls, I overheard things like "Watch out—they're gonna meet and carve up a few black guys tonight." Blind prejudice had been heated to the boiling point in the arrogant crucible of youth.

I began to earn their trust by talking to them out in the open—in the hallway or at the athletes' table in the lunchroom. Some of the kids recognized me because Granville had played basketball against them. I wanted other people to see me talking to them. They had to observe some friendly black-white interaction before they could learn to judge people on their merits, not their skin color. "Hey, I saw your name in the papers," I'd say. "You're pretty tall now. I remember that time I brought my basketball team here and we beat you. Now all of a sudden you guys can play." Gradually, through the athletes and the cheerleaders, I established some credibility, which gave me a base of operations.

I spoke to the English classes about how different cultures enrich all of our lives, using examples from literature and sports. I worked through the English classes because I was on familiar ground in there and was confident I could hold my own in discussions. I talked a lot about my own history, of course, to show them how destructive hate can be. It was slow going at first, and the questions they asked were pretty belligerent. But eventually I built up enough trust that a fair number of both white and black kids decided I was a person they could talk to. They were even able to talk to me together.

Once when we were pretty far along in the process, I took a group to Quest International headquarters in Granville. Quest's mission is to promote communication among adolescents. They took my group through a daylong series of workshops that empowered them to devise policies to make their school a better environment. When the kids themselves began to take an active part in addressing racial tensions, Watkins Memorial began to change. The tensions didn't disappear entirely, of course, but the threat of imminent violence was neutralized.

The year after I worked at Watkins, I was asked to do basically the same thing at Newark High School. Newark is a campus-style school with eleven buildings sprawled over a couple of acres, which makes it very easy for people to get on and off campus without being noticed. When I arrived, tension was high and teachers were nervous. There were rumors of strangers on campus and of kids carrying guns. "There's going to be a shooting today at three." "I think she has a gun in her purse." "He says he's going to kill somebody, and then there will be a retaliation."

Education had become secondary to fear. My first priority was to get everyone's attention off the potentially volatile environment and back to their studies. I used the same plan I had used at Watkins to establish my credibility—open conversations with individuals and small groups in the common areas, and group discussions in the English classes.

One of the books they read in ninth-grade English was *To Kill a Mockingbird*. During one discussion I asked the students why the black man in the book was put on trial.

"Because he was black," a lot of them said.

"But what other 'sin' did he commit?" I asked.

I usually wouldn't get much of an answer in the classroom, but later, in the hallways, they would come up to me and ask with hesitation, "That black dude—he got in trouble because he kissed a white girl, didn't he?"

I pushed them to think it out. "Why do you think that would be such a problem?" I asked. "I saw you kiss a white girl the other day. Some people may raise their eyebrows, but they aren't going to put you on trial for it."

They asked the very questions I wanted them to ask, the ones that would force them to think about a society in which just being black was a sin: "What about the time period?" "What about this man who came along and defended him?" "What about his children?" "What about that Boo Radley guy? Why was he in the story?"

The tenth-grade classes were reading *The Diary of Anne Frank,* and I used it to try and inspire the kids to be observers and chroniclers. "You don't have to have adult permission to write and observe and be in charge of your lives," I told them. "Thanks to Anne Frank, we have an understanding of what World War II was all about from a teenager's point of view. Even though she and many of the others in that attic perished, she left us a portrait of what her life was like. She showed us clearly how brutal and inhumane a culture can be." The students easily made the connections to the racial tension in their own school.

I passionately wanted those students to follow Anne Frank's lead— to take the responsibility to be chroniclers, to dare to be different, to break away from the gang and use their unique gifts to make everyone's life better.

I usually spent two consecutive days in the classroom. On the first day, I just wanted the students to relax and talk to me. After all, they didn't have a clue about who the hell this black guy was; they had just been told that a guest speaker would come in to talk to them. The teacher would introduce me with something like "Class, this is Mr. Upchurch. He has a very interesting background, and I think I'll just let him tell you about it himself."

I'd launch into my spiel, maybe cracking a joke but also trying to make everybody sit up a little straighter and pay attention. I'd never say "I'm Carl Upchurch, and I'm here to tell you about my past" and use my life story as an example of what their bad instincts might bring them. Instead, I tried to break down their skepticism and suspicion by telling them I *was* really glad to be in their class because I never had the opportunity to go to high school. That always got their attention; they instantly felt smarter than me. "Everybody goes to high school," they'd be thinking. "How'd he get away with that trick?"

I went on. "I never went to junior high either. The first time I was even *in* a junior high was when I coached basketball at Granville Middle School." Now even the skeptics wanted to know who the hell was talking such nonsense. By the time I told them I was in prison at eight years old, they were riveted.

Next I told them my purpose for being in the classroom. "I'm very excited to be here because it's an opportunity to talk about some of the things that moved me along in life, particularly education." They were amazed. Here I was, a person who had come from the bowels of society, speaking in front of their class as an authority.

I opened the discussion up to questions and answers, but I always laid down the ground rules first. They could ask me anything, I said. I would be offended only if they didn't ask about things they really wanted to know. For emphasis, I'd point my finger at my forehead. "This skin is not only brown. It's particularly thick because of everything that's been heaped on it," I told them. "I want this environment to be comfortable so you can ask questions. Please feel free to ask anything you want, because I like to hear how you think. I realize your opinions aren't always heard; in here they will be. We have a chance for dialogue, whether it's about race or sex or whatever the issues are."

The most commonly asked question was "What was it really like to be in prison?" I tried not to focus on the obvious, like being apart from family and friends and not being able to go anywhere. It was more important for them to understand what it's like to be locked in an environment where everything you are is constantly under attack—your sense of self, your dignity, your ability to see people in a humane context. I talked about how brutal the experience was and how every form of civil exchange goes out the window in the face of that brutality.

Although they were free to ask whatever they wanted, I used my answers to steer the discussion to the topic of violence—the reason I was in their classroom. Eventually they would ask, "Hey man, while you were in prison, did anybody come up and punch you out or pull a knife?"

I always took a long time to answer this one, because I wanted them to understand how I had come to believe that violence is futile. "At first, I *started* the fights. You couldn't survive without a good rep, and I didn't think about anything but building the best rep I could. Sometimes I had a buddy, sometimes I fought alone. But I always had a real short fuse, and I'd just as soon mess somebody up as look at him." Their eyes were huge.

Now I had to bring them around to the futility of violence without losing them. "See this scar? And this one? I collected scars like that for six years before it sank into my thick head that that was literally no way to live. If I hadn't changed, I know for sure I'd be dead now, instead of sitting here talking to you."

Somebody always said, "But Carl, what made you change?"

"Books," I said, and I proceeded to give them an abbreviated version of my literary salvation—how I found Shakespeare under the table leg, how I talked with Mark Twain, cried with Dostoyevsky, and soared with Maya Angelou. Through it all, my goal was to show them that even though I had a violent past, I no longer admired or even tolerated it.

But teenagers are a bloodthirsty lot, and they kept asking for the gory details: "How much money did you get when you robbed those banks?" "Tell us more about that fight in the kitchen." "Did your grandmother *really* shoot your grandfather?!" I would always answer honestly, because that was part of the trust-building. At the same time, though, I had to impress on them the futility of violence. I emphasized how fleeting the "rewards" of such behavior were—"I spent that forty bucks on dope, man, and the rush from it was gone before the guy was stitched up." "Every day I had to impress my cornerboys all over again, prove my manhood with some new outrage." "You had to have stuff to attract the women, but they'd forget they even knew you from one day to the next." "Nobody cared who you were; everything depended on what you had right now." I tried to make my point without preaching.

Sometimes we'd talk about how much money it takes to keep someone in jail for life. The question I got most often on that topic was "It must be pretty expensive to do that, huh?" My answer almost always surprised them. "I used to think so too," I said. "But keeping prisoners in jail until they die isn't nearly as expensive as what starts to happen once a death sentence is handed down. A cumbersome but very necessary death-row appeals system is in place, designed to protect a prisoner's rights. Because the great majority of prisoners on death row all over the country are poor and black, the appeals machinery is almost always funded by taxpayer money. It's not unusual for it to take years. Legal time, even public defenders' legal time, costs more than food and clothing and the few amenities given to lifers."

That discussion would naturally evolve into one about justice issues, which I most wanted them to think about, since violence and gang behavior are rooted in the issue of justice. Every time, somebody would ask, "Do you think it's right, man, for somebody to get the death penalty?"

I threw it right back. "What do *you* think? If somebody walked in here and killed one of you, what do you think should happen?"

Nearly everybody would say, "He should get the death penalty."

"Okay. That sounds pretty easy. But what if it were an accident? What if the guy didn't mean to kill anyone? Suppose he punched her in the face, and she fell off the chair and hit her head on the floor and died. Should he get the death penalty for that?" They changed course quickly, sure that nobody should get the death penalty for an accident.

I pounced. "Oh, so you're saying *you* want to decide who gets it and who doesn't."

"But what about somebody like Ted Bundy?" they would ask. "Didn't he deserve to die?"

"Okay," I answered. "Suppose, for the sake of argument, that Ted Bundy *does* deserve to die. Then how do you decide who deserves to live? Ted Bundy's crimes were heinous, and that's not a word we use very often. But if we kill *him*, where do we stop? If we're outraged by the murders Ted Bundy committed, we should be outraged by *every* murder, even if it has the seal of approval from the state." I liked to start them thinking about new ideas, so I always ended by telling them about a folk song that asks how long we have to keep killing people to show that killing people is wrong.

I was very direct and descriptive in these death-penalty debates. I described the smell of burning flesh in the gas chamber, and how the odor escapes through vents so the other convicts have to wear masks to keep from breathing it in. I told them what happens when human flesh is fried in an electric chair, to give them a new perspective. And I quoted statistics to back up my contention that the death penalty is an extension of our society's efforts to control a particular population, most frequently poor black people. "When was the last time you heard of somebody famous, somebody rich, being executed?" I asked. "When was the last time you heard of somebody being executed for murdering a black person? Maybe you don't agree with me that this is an operating principle of the state and federal governments, but I challenge you to take a serious look at who's sitting on death row. Then work back to what must be happening in the courts. You might just change your mind."

Certainly, many kids didn't agree with my views on the death penalty, but every time I got a group, or even a single student, to look at the issue with new eyes—to get past their raw emotions and argue rationally and intelligently with me—I felt I had accomplished something good.

We also had a lot of discussions on another justice issue—abortion. I never took a stand on this subject, just managed the debates so that everybody's opinion got a hearing. When they tried to pin me down, I'd respond, "Anybody who wakes up at six in the morning, makes a placard, and goes out to stand in front of a clinic to protect a life earns my respect for choosing to spend his or her time like that. Whether I agree with her position is not the issue; I am very appreciative to know a person who cares so deeply. But I also have strong feelings on the opposite side. I cannot possibly condemn a young woman for acknowledging that she is unable to provide a quality life for her child, that she can hardly support herself, and that she is in abusive circumstances, and for refusing to victimize a child by bringing it up in the same dire circumstances she grew up in." Absolute condemnation of either position amounts to emotional abortion, I felt, and I was no longer willing to do that to anyone.

Our abortion discussions were always spirited, and unlike the wild-eyed proponents on both sides of the national debate, the kids saw each other in a new and more respectful light after listening to and challenging each other's arguments in a setting in which everyone's opinions were validated.

No matter the subject, I kept relating it to issues raised in the literature they were reading. My history was only the hook to draw them in, never the issue itself, and the fact that I was an ex-con wasn't what decreased tension or eliminated gangs at any of the high schools where I consulted. Rather, the debates about justice, about how justice issues impact all of our lives, allowed at least some students to develop a better sense of self.

Although my presentations varied from school to school, the underlying message was always the same—the lessons I'd learned, which were the lessons I hoped they'd learn: "You have a right to your own body, and no one can violate that." "Anyone who says they have the answer to the world's problems should be challenged." "Everyone deserves justice." "Learning and growth are critical if you're going to stay alive in this world."

The kids had no reason to expect me to judge them any differently from the other adults in their lives. They had a preconceived notion of what my prejudices would be, whom I would favor, and what I would think. And as kids always do, they tested me. Someone would come up to me and say, "Man, I took a lot of drugs last night," then wait to see what sermon I would preach. When I said, "Drugs, huh? I bet you've got a bad headache this morning. So why are you taking all those drugs? I remember when I did that. I remember the scabs and the pus and the sores."

They would walk away knowing I accepted them—not approving of their behavior but also not judging them for it. At the same time they heard me saying clearly that I was through with that niggerizing nonsense. I told them I wasn't ever going to do that again, but I sure never said it in the way that the curriculum director and other official types had in mind when they brought me into the school. They thought I would preach "Go and sin no more," using my life as an example of the trouble the kids could get into as well as the redemption they could still find. Perhaps they expected some sort of Scared Straight program for potential offenders. Some administrators condemned me for my style, but my message came through plainly. I challenged the students to think about themselves and about issues in their lives in a broader context, and they rose to that challenge.

During my time at Watkins and Newark, my intuitions about kids were borne out: If we show enough confidence in them, if we allow them to make their own decisions, they will come to moral and decent conclusions. Kids who are encouraged to both think about and be responsible for what they do and say are more likely to make correct choices than kids who are forced to operate the way adults think they should. All they need is an opportunity to think through the entire range of possibilities. That was the basis of my approach, both in and out of the classroom. And every time some kid said "He's so cool," what they really meant was that they appreciated me for providing an environment in which they could explore the things they really cared about. If a girl whose parents hadn't graduated from high school really wanted to study and go to college, I gave her the encouragement she needed. If one of the athletes liked poetry, he didn't have to hide it from me, because I quoted poetry myself all the time.

My own experiences had taught me that a person's actions don't necessarily match what he or she is feeling. If I had had someone along the way who had listened to my concerns and validated what I was thinking and feeling, my life would have been quite different.

As the kids became more and more comfortable with my style, more confident that they could trust me, they began to seek me out on a casual basis outside class. I began to find out a lot more about them than just how well they could dribble a basketball or what they thought of their algebra teacher. They confided a wide range of concerns about typical teenage issues: grades, sports, parents, dating, sexuality, pregnancy, drugs, alcohol. Sometimes the conversations were pretty serious and pretty personal.

One young man shyly asked if he could tell me about his mother. He had heard me say over and over again, "Your body is your own. Don't give permission for anyone to touch it unless that's what *you* want." It turned out that she had been coming into his room at night and masturbating him, and he was desperate to find out if there were any way such behavior might be right or moral. I told him the truth: "No. Under *no* circumstances is what she's doing okay." I tried to be supportive by being very honest and direct.

In another instance, a young girl in the senior class came to me because her mother had recently been caught smoking cocaine. This girl was getting ready to go to a big university and was heavily involved in the Just Say No program. When she asked me what she should do, I gave her two pieces of advice. First, she shouldn't stop believing in who she was because of what her mother was doing; second, she should go to discuss the situation with a counselor.

I heard all too frequently about fathers who sexually abused their own daughters. When I look at my own daughter and I think about those fathers, I know I'd kill myself if I even felt the impulse to do anything like that to Mikayla. Most of the time, the mothers are totally oblivious to what's going on; sometimes, though, they simply choose to look the other way.

These young girls came to talk to me because they saw me as a person who could offer them support and advice, perhaps even protection. I had to call on everything I had to be open to them. These children were deeply scarred, and the damage they suffered was often permanent. I wish their fathers could have listened to these fourteen-, fifteen-, and sixteen-year-old girls and heard what they were doing to these souls entrusted to their care. Those girls loved and trusted their fathers, thought of them as gods on earth; the disparity between what a father should be and what their fathers actually were was tearing their guts out.

I felt I was really making a difference with the kids at Newark High School, relating well to both boys and girls, athletes and nonathletes, whites and blacks. But trouble started when the girls began to talk to me too much. Suddenly, some school administrators and parents decided it was unseemly for a black ex-con to be spending so much time with adolescent girls. Newark told me they had run out of money and couldn't afford for me to do any more classes. I've never believed it and am convinced that they wanted to get rid of me because I was becoming something of a hero to the kids.

From all the positive feedback they gave me, I knew the majority of students, teachers, and parents, however, appreciated my efforts. I went to many of the kids' homes, and I could tell that their parents respected what I was doing. A small percentage, however, said they didn't want their sons or daughters talking about the kinds of topics that came up when I visited school, like abortion and the death penalty; the truth was that they didn't want their children even *thinking* about those issues. Ironically, that very attitude convinced me that I was on the right road to helping the kids become responsible, thinking adults.

Which doesn't mean it didn't hurt. "Stay cool, Carl," I told myself. "Wake up, man. You know that black people make white people uncomfortable here in America. You know racism exists. You know the sexual inferiority that white men feel, and you run around talking to young white girls. You know the stereotypes that are assigned to you. You know that people think you're dumb."

I kept reminding myself of my old jail cells. To intellectualize from books was one thing. To be in the heat, where everything converges, has an entirely different feel. Still, it was only in the intensity of such a fire, I knew, that integrity could be forged.

Twelve

MARIA

The youngsters in South Central played in an atmosphere that was tense with constant fear and anxiety. They were unattended and neglected. Filth was everywhere. I watched in horror one day as a little boy picked up a piece of candy from the street and pulled maggots off it before popping it in his mouth.

The horrible poverty I witnessed when I visited L.A. in 1992 disgusted even me, who had spent much of my life destitute. These children broke my heart. They lacked the basic necessities of food, clothing, and shelter, and their struggle for survival was complicated even further by the widespread violence on their streets and the indifference of their neighborhoods and the rest of Los Angeles to their plight. In such an environment, it is no wonder that poverty and abuse are perpetuated for generation after generation.

It's bad enough to be poor and miserable. It's another thing entirely to see fear in the eyes of little children.

———

I grew up in a two-room flat with a mother who collected welfare checks for a living. The violence of fistfights and stabbings swirled around South Street in Philadelphia, but it was nothing in comparison to the continuous machine-gun fire that punctuated the air in South Central.

These images struck me indelibly. Young mothers sat in the projects with two and three babies but no husband in sight. Trash piled along the streets created a stench that competed with the noxious odor of dead animals rotting nearby. People were barricaded in little shantylike homes, while hundreds of unemployed young men just hung around in the streets, looking for trouble. The conditions in South Central brought tears to my eyes. The people trapped there were caught in a cycle of hopelessness and despair.

———

Rodney King—that name will be burned in America's consciousness forever. A man who normally wouldn't have been recognized for much of anything was the victim of vicious police brutality, recorded on videotape. I watched on television from Ohio as the verdict was read on April 29, 1992. I watched the Reginald Denny beating. I watched the National Guard patrolling the streets. I watched the burning. I watched the pillaging of neighborhood stores. Considering how dismal the situation was, I was surprised no one had seen the violence coming. People living in wretched conditions often react with violence and anger when they can no longer tolerate the injustice of their lives.

What bothered me more than the destruction was the reaction of the public officials who were supposedly addressing the problem. All of the current big shots—then-President George Bush, candidate Bill Clinton, Jesse Jackson, Joseph Lowery of the Southern Christian Leadership Conference, Congresswoman Maxine Waters, and others—trooped into South Central, shaking their heads and condemning the crisis. They pledged money and time and attention, did their requisite thirty-second sound bites, and headed for the next photo-op. Their reaction to South Central is a classic illustration of political ambivalence. Watching all the bigwigs parade in and out, the community of

South Central knew that after a few days everything would return to the status quo. A lot of words were spoken, but nothing would change.

The people most affected by the devastation, those living in the community, were not acknowledged, nor were they asked what they thought should be done. Yet none of the problems of South Central would be solved unless the people being blamed for the outburst could present their side of the story.

The more I watched those flames flicker on my television screen, the more aggravated and offended I became. I felt a strong pull to go to Los Angeles and talk to people there firsthand. I'd go as a private citizen and walk around those neighborhoods and talk to the people whose voices were not on the nightly newscasts.

Simultaneously, a group in South Central called Future In Action was talking about me. They had run across one of my old blue brochures from the Progressive Prisoners' Movement days, and in the wake of the uprising, they called me in Ohio to see if I could help. When I asked them about Future In Action, I learned that they were, unbelievably, Bloods and Crips, working together to sustain a truce they had managed to create. Hearing that made me even more determined to get to L.A.

The combination of my own salary as a middle-school basketball coach and a speaker on prison conditions and Andrea's salary as a social worker could not begin to support such a junket. So I went begging—to the American Baptist Churches–USA, to my own Granville Baptist congregation, and to St. Luke's Episcopal Church, also in Granville—asking them to donate money to send me on a fact-finding mission. Their combined generosity amounted to $2,200, which enabled me to spend thirty days in L.A. that June, just two months after the riots.

As soon as I arrived, I contacted the American Friends Service Committee. Through them, I met two Methodist ministers in Long Beach who let me sleep on their dining-room floor. I was lucky to have a home base, and I commuted back and forth to South Central, about forty-five minutes each way.

The key players of the truce were anxious to find ways to strengthen it. The more I met with them, the more determined I became to help them. Impressively, the truce was completely self-initiated; no one had come in and negotiated it for them. Clearly, the people most intimately involved in the problems of a community can best determine the solutions needed to deal with them. It was true in Ohio high schools, and it was true in South Central on an even bigger scale.

I wanted to know more about the voices coming from within the communities, especially about the guys who were responsible for the peace, to see if it could spread any further. "We want to take it to the UN," I was told by Daude Sherrill, a twenty-five-year-old ex-gangbanger who had helped establish the truce in the Jordan Downs housing project of L.A. "We want to speak in front of the United Nations." Daude's goal was to present the plight of South Central to the world community and ask them to declare his home a war zone, making peace a priority, just as in Somalia and Bosnia, Rwanda and Haiti. Unfortunately, no one at the UN wanted to listen to what he had to say because he didn't have an office, a reputation, or a set of letters after his name.

Daude was suspicious and apprehensive about meeting with me until he understood my own background; then we talked openly of our mutual concerns. He explained the truce and how only the collective will of the gangbangers enforced and maintained it. He stressed how important it was that gangbangers, not outsiders, had initiated it. When I asked why they did it, he replied simply, "Because we got tired of killing each other."

Kevin, a resident of Nickerson Gardens—Bloods territory—continued the story. "Before the riots, some of the brothers and Muslims from Watts wanted to get three major projects together—Nickerson Gardens, Jordan Downs, and Imperial Courts—to show we're all the same people striving for the same goals. We wanted them to come together and stop killing each other and inflicting mayhem on each other. We ironed out our differences and began to see slow change. But after the riots the truce just caught on everywhere. It's holding strong. Of course you still have Latinos involved in gang activity, but we have to take care of home first, and then maybe we can reach out to some of our Latino brothers."

Daude told me he was willing to forgo killing, gangbanging, and "slinging shit" (selling dope) so that he could serve his people in a positive way. He made it clear to me that even if I didn't have anything to give to his community's children or any way to help feed his community, he hoped that I could at least provide a public forum for him to speak. I asked him about the local ministers, such as those at the African Methodist Episcopal Church. His reply was blunt: "None of those phony motherfuckers speak for me."

Eventually Daude and two other ex-gangbangers agreed to accompany me to meet with officials representing a joint mission of the World Council of Churches and the National Council of Churches. Daude spoke eloquently to them of the suffering and hurt this community was experiencing—the same pain his grandparents experienced two generations ago. He emphasized the dire need for jobs and for a police department that served the entire community.

If a foreign enemy tried to impose the conditions in South Central onto the entire United States, if it took the lives of American citizens as lives are taken daily in our inner cities, we would retaliate instantly, and the war would be one of conscience, not aggression. A war *is* going on in South Central, but its victims are economically and spiritually impoverished people who no one seems to think are worth fighting for.

The 280 people who died in the South Central riots apparently were unimportant; we heard little about their lives or their deaths. The eight hundred lives that were lost in the Los Angeles area in 1992 received no media attention either. The economic impact of those deaths, especially when compared to the nine random carjacking deaths that occurred the same year in south Florida and so upset the state's tourist trade, was practically nil.

My goal in South Central was to find out who spoke for this community. During the day, tape recorder in hand, I'd wander the streets and go into neighborhood stores and bars. I tried to be casual, to not appear like a chronicler and an investigator. Sometimes my questioning made people uneasy—I was looking for specific thoughts on specific problems, not generalizations, and they weren't used to that. At night I'd go to the coffee houses in Long Beach and play a little chess.

I asked people I met how they felt about what was going on in the aftermath of the riots. "Who are you angry with?" The response was clear: The system was "fucking" them around.

I'd ask, "Do people like Jesse Jackson speak for you?"

"No, Jesse Jackson, nor any of them other niggers, don't speak for us. They're just exploiting us, 'pimping' the community." The angry feelings came out hard and fast.

"Why don't you talk for yourselves if no one is speaking for you?" I asked. Most believed there was no use in speaking out—they were already defeated. Others, though, had not given up and still longed to make their message heard.

One particular image from South Central is etched in my memory forever. I visited a nineteen-year-old Latina woman, Maria. She was very, very pretty. All of her features were dark, and her hair was very long and quite curly. If she had been brought up in another place, she could have easily been homecoming queen or Miss America. But circumstances had sentenced her to a much different life.

Maria had three children and no husband. There was no youthful twinkle, no girlish naïveté in her look. Like so many, she had become a mother at fifteen or sixteen. She herself no longer had a mother, and she didn't know her father. Her brothers were all in the penitentiary. She had no one but herself to depend on and had to endure the welfare system on her own. Couldn't I see what those pitiful circumstances were doing to her, she asked me plaintively. All her resentments poured out as respectfully as she possibly could manage—an avalanche of feelings, a verbal indictment of society.

At her home in East L.A., I asked her how she felt about her circumstances. Her eyes teared up as she tried to convey the pain, anguish, and torture of her daily existence. "Can't you see what this does to me?" she cried. "Look at the faces of my babies and tell me you can't see how this affects me." She had never been asked how she felt about her life, and she truly believed no one cared about her.

"Who represents your point of view?" I asked her.

"Nobody around here," she said, referring to the local politicians. "They're all liars and cheaters. None of them come around except when they want my vote."

As I listened to her, I heard an echo of things I had said earlier in my own life. It is common for someone in an oppressive situation to look at the rest of the world and believe that others have an unfair advantage. In that neighborhood, in a lot of neighborhoods, politicians come in and out, making big promises that are never carried out. It was no surprise Maria was jaded from so many false promises. Why should she believe the next person coming down the pike, including me?

Politicians and other so-called leaders have sold misery to whole communities. In Maria's face and in her circumstances, I saw the results of that kind of exploitation. As I talked with her, Maria's eyes roamed my face, trying to figure out which pigeonhole to put me in. Perhaps she hoped I could break the chain or stop the cycle to which she and her children were condemned. More likely, she expected I was the next cheater in the long line of merchants of misery out to exploit her. I felt a definite responsibility to her because of what she looked for in my face.

As we talked, she rocked her youngest back and forth. At one point I reached out and asked her if I could hold him. It was an instinctive move, especially with Mikayla just beyond infancy, but it immediately won her trust. I saw in her face what it meant to her: I valued her baby.

Maria's situation brought the plight of South Central home to me in a way nothing else did. Watching her kids play around her and fuss on her lap, I could see it all—pain, suffering, poverty, brutality, injustice, and hopelessness—all in that one little family. I had a sudden flashback to Philadelphia, thirty years ago, and felt a gut-wrenching combination of heartache and white-hot anger. I resolved to do whatever I could to take the fear out of those children's eyes.

The reality of Maria's situation is too stark for words to convey. She was filled with spirit and nuance and subtlety. But to society she is just another welfare mother gone bad, a dropout, a mother of three, and a drain on the welfare system—not a worthy human being.

Everywhere I went in South Central, I heard voices like Maria's. She was reflected in many talented and interesting people throughout the community—dynamic, caring human beings trapped by circumstances that stifled their potential, burying it under layers of anger, frustration, and hopelessness.

The South Central rebellion represents the failure of the politics of past generations. We need to unite at the grassroots level to articulate and support each other's struggle for justice. Just as the South Central residents joined hands to fight the fires and save their homes and businesses, together we need to take the initiative away from the politicians who got us in this jam. We must listen to people like Maria to find out what they need. We must ask Daude what *he* wants for his people, not just believe what so-called leaders tell us they need.

After thirty days of gathering impressions, taping conversations, and taking notes, I returned to Ohio. The first Sunday I was back, my minister asked me to give a report to the church on my trip. I was full of what I'd seen, and my anger came out in what I said. I broadsided the same church members who had helped fund my trip. I had appreciated their help before, but now I was enraged at how we were neglecting the Marias in our own neighborhoods to lavish care and concern on Marias in Third World countries.

"You sent forty thousand dollars' worth of medicine and funds to Nicaragua," I challenged them. "You drove a bus down there to try to help out. Yet people right here in central Ohio, in Newark, only five miles away from us, also desperately need medicine and funds. What are we saying to the world, to the people in South Central, when we turn our backs on them and go elsewhere?" Then I stormed out of the church.

A month later, I created a document about the South Central story. I sent it out to everybody I could think of—the organizations that had raised money to send me to L.A., peace-and-justice organizations. The most important point I made was that there was absolutely no peace-and-justice presence in South Central; the place was like a war zone. The article created a stir in the communities I criticized. To their credit, the peace-and-justice organizations recognized the truth of what I was saying. I was gratified by their response, but knew that if I didn't do something quickly to focus their enthusiasm, it would dissipate.

I must have appeared a little wild-eyed myself. I was consumed by the plight of South Central and communities like it all over the country. And for the first time in my life, I felt like I was in a position to make a difference on a grand scale.

Thirteen

COUNCIL FOR URBAN PEACE AND JUSTICE

I couldn't get the children out of my mind—their eyes haunted me from 2,500 miles away. No matter where I went or what I did, they were there. Watching. Waiting. Wondering if I, too, would fail them. Their desperate circumstances had narrowed their horizons to getting food and shelter, trying to stay alive one more day. I couldn't stand it that we allow such a barren lifescape to exist.

I desperately wanted to give those children a reason to smile. But I knew from living that life and from listening to Maria and others like her who were still living it that no help would come from outside the neighborhoods. As I searched for an answer, I became convinced that the best hope for those children was to stop the violence that surrounded them. That meant getting the gangs involved in constructive ways. To do that, they would have to agree to talk to each other and to work together to bring peace in their streets. I decided to try to bring them together in one place—to a summit of gang leaders from all over the country. Everyone thought I was crazy.

———

"I need an office," I told George Williamson, the minister at my church. The peace-and-justice people on the national level—the Fellowship of Reconciliation, the American Friends Service Committee, Pax Christi, and others—were all talking about Palestine and Israel and Bosnia. They weren't talking about South Central, as I thought they should be. I was setting up the Council for Urban Peace and Justice.

"We've got a space back here, by the choir room," George told me.

"I need a phone," I said.

"We'll get you a phone back there," he assured me. "What else?"

With an office and a phone I could get started. I moved all my files from home into my new office and officially established the Council for Urban Peace and Justice at the beginning of September 1992. Our mandate was to help bring peace to urban communities.

I put together an advisory board made up of local residents and church people. They thought I was dreaming some pretty big dreams, but because I was so passionate about the project, they gave me their support. I outlined what I wanted to accomplish and told them that to do so I intended to commit myself to the Council full time. I wanted to be paid a salary, have a staff member, and operate a full-fledged organization.

They said, "That's a fine idea, Carl, but we don't have any money yet."

"No, we don't have any money now," I said, "but we have to do this anyway. I'll get the money somehow."

To obtain financial support for the Council for Urban Peace and Justice, I had to specify a significant agenda. No one was going to jump up and pay me a salary simply because I had created it. So I asked myself over and over, what should this council do first?

Suddenly I knew. Sitting in my office at the First Baptist Church in Granville, I said, "What would happen if that truce in L.A. were brought together with fledgling urban peace movements in Minneapolis, in Chicago, in Boston? What would happen if everyone came together and announced a *national* truce, not just a neighborhood truce?" The council's first project would be to convince gang leaders in cities all over the United States—those already in truces and those who might be interested in joining—to create a national truce network.

By the time the words "gang summit" came out of my mouth, I was way beyond being talked out of the idea. I was convinced the idea could work. Nothing—not skepticism, not doubt, not even patronizing voices—could alter my course. All the pieces had come together in my mind and there was no turning back.

As I spread the word, the very magnitude of the idea turned some people off. "There goes Carl again," they'd say, rolling their eyes. But this was no daydream. I wasn't interested in debating the naysayers or being discouraged. I was ready to make it happen.

On September 9, 1992, I started working on the summit in earnest. My first task was easy: to set the date. I chose April 29, the one-year anniversary of the Rodney King verdict. Then the real work began.

We hit a snag ten minutes into the first planning meeting: How *does* one get in touch with gang leaders? You can't exactly look up Bloods or Crips in the phone book. I used some of the money that was trickling in to travel around, looking for and contacting gang leaders— not only from the Bloods and the Crips but from the Conservative Vice Lords, the Gangster's Disciples, the Black Gangster's Disciples, the Latin Kings, the Cobras, the Stones, and other gangs flourishing on the streets of our major cities.

I called Dr. Benjamin Chavis, who at the time worked for the United Church of Christ. I had met him in L.A. after the riots and knew he was interested in the gang problem. I told him what I was doing and asked for money. He said, "Carl, I can give you five thousand dollars now and another five thousand later." He finally committed a total of $25,000 to the summit.

Acting on faith, I sent out a one-page flier on the summit, giving the date and a description of four sessions: Challenges of Gaining Empowerment, New Visions for Urban America, Economic Justice, and Police Abuses and Brutality.

Then I called Spike Moss, who runs At-Risk Youth Services in Minneapolis. Spike was involved in negotiating a gang truce in that city and had formed an organization called United for Peace to bring rival gang members there together. "Spike, I'm doing a national gang summit," I told him. "I want to bring everybody from around the country together."

"You called the right person," he said. "I know this gang and this gang, and that leader and that leader. I'll fly you up to Minneapolis, and you can meet them and tell them what you want to do."

On November 14 I went to Minneapolis and for three days held clandestine meetings with gang leaders at one of the city's churches. Why were the meetings clandestine? These gang leaders were risking their lives by coming to see us. There was no predicting what rival gangs might do to them or even what their own gang members might do if they thought their leaders were somehow selling them out.

A hundred and fifty gang leaders from across the Midwest had jumped into vans and driven all night to be there—that's how much they wanted a sustainable peace. Spike Moss had done a tremendous job bringing them in; now I had to address them.

After Spike introduced me, I told the gang leaders about my plans for the summit. Their initial reaction was suspicious and defensive. "You're crazy, man." "You expect us to sit down in the same room with *them*?" "You gonna guarantee the safety of our brothers?" "How do you know we won't get crossed?"

That situation repeated itself many times in the course of all the face-to-face meetings that were necessary to set up the summit. I can't even remember how many times I heard "Man, Upchurch, fuck you. I'm tired of you. Who the fuck do you think you are. You don't represent no gang. You're independent. *We* represent gangs, and we don't even know who you are."

Because of my own history, their bluster didn't bother me. I understood what was at stake for all these young men and saw that their responses were actually veiled encouragement for me to do the right thing. Nevertheless, I had to be careful that my lack of intimidation wasn't misinterpreted as a sign of disrespect; that dynamic would have pulled us off track.

That first day in Minneapolis I spent building their trust in me. I used the same tactics I had used in the high schools, letting them see me, scars and all, and telling them about the choices I had made that had brought me here. It was hard work to bring them in one day to a state of mind that had taken me years to reach. But I kept hammering away at the same point: "You're going to die if it doesn't stop. Your little brothers and sisters are going to die. If you're lucky enough to live long enough, to have children of your own, *they're* going to die if it doesn't stop. But you, all of you together, can stop it. And that's what I'm asking you to do."

On the second day, they filled up the whole church. Once again I made my pitch about the summit, talking about what we could accomplish together. And finally they said, "We're down." If I could make it happen, they'd give me their support. The first major piece of the entire enterprise had clicked into place.

Once I had these major players involved, I needed to find a place to hold the summit. Fate intervened, as it has so often in my life. One day as I was walking through the church toward my office, George stopped me to ask what was happening with the Council. I told him about the summit. "Where are you going to hold it?" he asked.

"I'm thinking of somewhere in the center of the country, to make it accessible to everybody," I told him. "Maybe St. Louis. The problem is, I don't have a connection there yet."

George got excited, and when George gets excited, he's only slightly less wild-eyed than I am. "There's a guy who's part of the Baptist Peace Fellowship—Mac Charles Jones of the St. Stephen's Baptist Church in Kansas City, Missouri," he said. "You've got to call him. He'll help you."

I called him and introduced myself. "I'm with the Council for Urban Peace and Justice," I told him, "and I'm in the process of organizing a national gang summit. Kansas City is one of the cities we're considering, and I was interested in what kind of role you could play."

"Oh, my God," he said softly. "Say no more, just tell us what you need." He stopped me in my tracks. I had had a whole spiel ready but didn't need a word of it. "We already know it's necessary, and we want to be a part of it. You can have my church, my congregation—everything! Here's my home phone number and my secretary's home phone number. We'll do whatever we can."

I hung up and said a soft "Oh, my God" of my own. The second piece of the puzzle was in place.

Spike Moss and I traveled to Kansas City to meet Reverend Jones at the end of November. I had three pages of notes on how he and his church could help, along with lists of specific things we would need—meeting rooms, accommodations, food. I showed them to him, expecting a totally different "Oh, my God." All he said was "No problem. We can take care of that." Again, there was no need for the hard sell. All we had to do was get the bodies there; his congregation would take care of food, hotel rooms, transportation between the hotel and the summit, and places to hold the summit meetings.

The third piece of the puzzle—money—was the hardest. We needed enough to transport 150 gang leaders from all over the country to Kansas City. The commitment from Reverend Jones made it much easier for me to do fund-raising.

I made my pitch to churches and peace organizations and urban leaders all over the country. I attended peace conferences and made my pitch there too. This was exciting news for the peace-and-justice community, and lots of people called me to get involved. Before long, money was coming in from all over, and I had my 150 airline tickets in hand. When the media started calling for interviews, I knew the summit was becoming a reality.

Many volunteers put in long hours on the project. But one person involved in the early stages deserves the lion's share of the credit for pulling it all together—Jana Lowe. Jana's daughter, Seana, had been assisting me with some of the Council's work, and when it was time for her to go back to college, she suggested that her mother could take over. When Jana first came to see me, I wasn't sure she was right for the job. I made a stereotypical snap judgment based on her appearance—she looks like a typical, upper-middle-class white housewife. I wasn't at all convinced that she could understand what I was trying to accomplish, let alone mastermind the details of it.

As Jana and I labored through the months leading up to the summit, however, all my doubts were cast aside, and I grew ashamed of my initial judgment. She handled telephone calls to the White House, gang leaders, and the national media with the same finesse. She coordinated who would participate and where they were coming from. Most important, she was expert at handling *me* when things got hectic.

To say that I'm difficult in high-pressured situations is an understatement. Even the people who *like* me admit that I become demanding and sharp-tongued; I appear to be unappreciative, and I tend to place the same unrealistic expectations on others that I place on myself. Jana handled everything like a pro, and at the end of each day was still able to smile.

On February 4, 1993, we held a national press conference to announce the plans for the gang summit. A few gang members were flown to Washington, D.C., to participate in the event. We had decided to call it the Urban Peace and Justice Summit because it wasn't only gang members who would be attending. They would be joined by a number of urban activists—people who cared about the health and welfare of the poorer communities but were not themselves gang members. They were people such as Deborah, who heads the peace and justice committee of the World Council of Churches in Geneva, and Jim Wallis, from *Sojourners* magazine. Both made historic contributions.

To the media, I emphasized that the purpose of the summit was not to allow gang leaders to plot how to take over the country, but to listen to fresh voices from the hard streets of urban America. Our multifaceted mission was to address urban problems comprehensively and to assess ways to stop the cycle of economic and social violence. Even though gang members live in situations that nurture their antisocial behavior, we can't give up on them as human beings. Nor can we afford to ignore the causes of such economic disparity.

Our announcement in Washington generated even more media attention. Jana fielded lots of calls each day from television stations and newspapers; even the White House wanted to be updated. I became nervous that the summit might turn into a media event and that participants and the public at large would lose sight of what we were trying to accomplish.

Plenty of people weren't thrilled about the gang summit at all. I received a number of threats from Kansas City racists, who called it a "coon" summit. Other threats came from gang members not yet interested in peace, who thought I was presuming to speak on behalf of *all* gangs. I was told that my life would be in danger if I tried to pull it off.

In the midst of our Herculean efforts, I couldn't worry about threats. All my emotional, psychological, and intellectual resources were concentrated on making the summit successful. Dealing with fear, or even finding the time to sleep, wasn't a legitimate concern.

Locally, the summit was getting some bad publicity. Every time things got heated in Kansas City, one of our connections there would call me and say I had to go out there. I'd fly out, talk to the newspapers, go on local talk shows, visit schools, and meet with some of the people who said they felt disrespected. As I spent more time in their community, they began to understand the depth of my commitment and felt better about the summit.

Just as Kansas City was calming down, a rumor cropped up that inflamed the gang members who were involved. Someone claimed that I was actually a government plant, hired to bring gang leaders together so that pictures of them could be taken for the FBI. It was a real crisis, and I had to move quickly to quell the rumors and regain the gang members' trust. Without them, after all, there was no summit.

At last, the week of the summit arrived. On Monday, April 26, I flew into Kansas City with Vel Holmes, a neighbor in Newark whom I had asked to become my assistant in Kansas City. We got to the Howard Johnson's where everyone was staying, and Vel set up our office in a suite. The calls were already rolling in—Belgian television, the BBC, the CBC (from Canada), *USA Today*, CNN, and others. Everybody wanted an interview, and it was up to Vel to decide where and how I should spend my time.

To the national media, it seemed that I had just crawled out of the woodwork. I didn't have a long civil rights résumé, as most major African-American leaders did, and a lot of people were suspicious of me. I tried to put my background on the back burner because I was afraid the drama potential of my being an ex-con would take the attention off the summit and put it on me. I was determined not to let that happen. As it was, many of our adversaries were predicting that we would take over Kansas City, run guns and drugs in and out of town, and recruit new gang members.

I tried to project calm reassurance on the talk shows. I kept the focus on the meeting and kept the naysayers off balance. I refused to feed into any stereotype they might hold against me. Realizing they were no doubt expecting someone who was rough around the edges, I paid particular attention to the details of my presentation so I could not be cast in a poor light. I tried to allay fears by appearing reasonable but not overly serious. Occasionally I threw in a joke, even though the condition of our cities is nothing to laugh about. My vision for the summit, I emphasized, was that a working group of people would talk about solutions to urban problems and about a sustainable gang peace.

The fear-laden accusations made better headlines, though, and they appeared so frequently that my calm, rational demeanor finally got ruffled. It made me mad that the media, which could have helped create a more encouraging atmosphere for the summit, instead met us with suspicion, anxiety, and anger. I lashed out at the press. "I'm shocked by the irony of this. As long as we run up and down the streets shooting at each other, you don't care. But the minute we try to find a better way to relate to each other, we get fire and brimstone from the very people who criticize us for antisocial behavior." That statement was as openly angry as I got.

Even though I wasn't worried about the threats against me, others were, and I ended up with three bodyguards, two male and one female, who happened to be from the Nation of Islam. I also had a van and driver to get me from event to event, interview to interview. Wherever I spoke, I pointed out that not every gang member is automatically a criminal, and that not all crime is committed by gang members. Just before the summit, the Los Angeles police claimed that the truce in L.A. was useless: crime in L.A. had dropped *only* 2.6 percent since the truce was initiated. "The Los Angeles police should be ashamed," I admonished. "They're asking that a one-year-old truce eliminate all crime. No one at this summit is stupid enough to take that posture. What is being said here is that a kernel of hope is being generated. Don't expect overnight results.

"The summit is about more than just gang violence and truces," I continued. "It's about economics. If there are no jobs, if there's nothing to look to in the inner city, if there's no hope, then violence becomes an outgrowth of frustration. We know it's not going to be smooth sailing. You always anticipate hurdles when you try to bring people together under a peace initiative." It was unconscionable for the LAPD to disparage a peace initiative supported entirely by volunteers when salaried "keepers of the peace" passively stood by as frustration and the violence escalated.

On Tuesday afternoon I met with Keith Brown, a minister and director of Project NeighborHOOD, who held a reception for me. I was very nervous because a lot of prominent people who were working on behalf of the community attended, inspired by our hopes for the summit. Though I was outwardly comfortable and confident, inside I churned with anxiety because the magnitude of the task was just beginning to dawn on me. It helped when Keith proclaimed his unqualified support for the summit to the local press by saying, "This first Urban Peace and Justice Summit will bring the kind of peace that will enable us to reclaim our communities and make them alive and vibrant again." After Keith's endorsement, support for the summit grew.

An especially memorable message came from Hearts United, a grassroots Kansas City organization working to change community attitudes and behavior. Illustrating that not everyone in the city was fearful of our presence, a spokeswoman said, "These are hard-core, violent, destructive people defending themselves against what they consider injustice. Most of them get recognition only for their destructive acts. The gang summit is an opportunity to give them approval and respect for trying to create something positive. If we can receive them in an open way, maybe they can reveal formulas to us for resolving conflicts and living in peace on a global scale."

Amen.

Fourteen

THE SUMMIT

Gangs from twenty-six cities—cities as different in personality as Albuquerque and Boston, as geographically distant as San Francisco and Washington, D.C.—were represented at the summit. The diversity of those who attended was reflected in their dress. A few people, business types, showed up in suits and ties. Some gang members wore their colors: baseball caps, knit stocking caps, kufis, baggy jeans, sweatshirts—whatever identified them as part of their gang. Some shied away from showing their gang affiliation by wearing the Cross Colors brand of clothing. Together, they were what you would expect see any day on the streets of a large city.

At the beginning of the summit, they were skeptical but willing to listen. By the end, a miracle had taken place. At the final gathering, nearly everyone in the church rose, filed down the aisles, and went up to the chancel. They held hands and sang and prayed, while person after person gave a testimony or said a prayer. The huge church was filled to the rafters with blacks and whites and Latinos, gang members and church leaders and community leaders. They wept together and cheered together.

People raised their arms, their hands high in the air with the sum-

mit's new peace symbol—the index and middle finger held tightly to-
gether, a new version of the V-shaped peace sign of the 1960s. It
symbolized the need all of us have for peace, together—"One God, one
aim, one destiny."

————

THURSDAY, APRIL 29, 1993

After everyone was settled into their rooms, I gathered the organizers together for a final check of everything. We confirmed our
stance on the media presence: Except for the opening and concluding
press conferences, the summit would be closed to the press so that
participants could talk freely. We did set up a hospitality room for media
use, but their contact was generally limited to daily interviews with me.

Many of the ex–gang members at the summit had already begun
peace initiatives in their own cities. Sharif Willis, a Chicago native who
now resides in Minneapolis, had been minister of justice for the Conservative Vice Lords. After a lifetime of gangbanging, Sharif now walks
with a limp—his legs were strafed by machine-gun fire. Now he works
for peace, searching for ways to bring people together. Along with
Spike Moss, he co-founded United for Peace, a group of gang members
who work with local contractors to establish security measures in new
inner-city developments. It's a striking success that areas that were
once terrorized and vandalized by gang violence are now being protected by gangs.

Sharif was one of the speakers on the opening day of the summit.
"If we all come together, we can make a difference," he told the group.
"It's time for us to put our guns and pistols away and start loving each
other. This effort is far bigger than any one of us. This effort is about
all of us. The sons and daughters of this country are our sons and our
daughters. If *we* don't put forth the effort to try to make sure there's a
future for them, *nobody's* going to put forth the effort. There are no
big me's and little you's here. We are all in this together. We're going to
send forth a message when we leave here that's going to go all across

this country. We're tired, and we ain't going to take it no more because we're going to start to do something.

"We're going to start to work within our communities to try to promote peace," Sharif continued. "We're going to try to tell our brothers that it ain't about killing each other. It's about trying to do something for each other. We have been manipulated, indoctrinated to hate each other and to kill each other. That manipulation, that indoctrination—you people here are going to change that because you're going to bring about the truth. And with that truth we're going to set each other free. Remember, you're the ones who can make a difference. Each and every one of you. We're all in this together."

Sharif's call for peace was echoed by Nane Alejandrez of Santa Cruz, who said, "We are tired of seeing our mothers cry. We are tired of dying. We are tired of going to the penitentiary. We are tired of seeing our mothers, our wives, our daughters coming to visit us and guards touching them all over. We are tired. We are tired!"

Fred Williams, from Common Ground in Los Angeles, spoke of how hard the gangs had worked to hold the L.A. truce together. A former gang member, Fred had been convicted of a homicide early in his life and spent time in a penitentiary. Now he tries to keep the peace. He also has developed after-school programs and drop-out retrieval programs, which encourage present and former gang members to help younger gangbangers get back to school. Fred came to Kansas City with ten L.A. gang members involved in the truce to teach us how to spread peace.

Several months after the summit, before the second Rodney King verdict came down, I got a call from Ben Chavis one night asking if I could go to L.A. and await the verdict with him in the impoverished neighborhoods. Did I know someone we could stay with? Fred was the first person I called. Ben and I stayed with him from Monday until the verdict was announced on the following Friday. When we saw that the community was satisfied with the conviction of the two police officers, Ben and I departed—thanking Fred for his help.

Fred introduced me to another important player in the urban peace movement, a former L.A. gang member referred to only as Big Al. Probably in his thirties, he is now dedicated to serving his community in support of the peace movement.

Several years ago, Big Al stopped selling drugs, stopped the violence in which he was constantly involved. One night in a hotel room in L.A., I kidded him about always being broke and having to borrow money. "I'd rather be what I am today," Big Al told me, "than what I was with all that money, killing my own people."

Today Big Al serves gang members, old women, and children. He is the father figure missing in so many of our communities. Since the gang summit, he has participated in regional gang gatherings all over the country to bring peace to our cities.

At the opening session of the national summit, Big Al said, "We want this to work because we don't want our babies growing up to fill up those penitentiaries that they're building. It's time to look forward and stop looking back on your history. We came here to put this thing in effect because we know if it can work in L.A., it can be pushed throughout the world. To all these brothers here, we want to work with you—not because we're trapped but because we want to be friends."

The women who attended became an important part of the summit. It started with Marion Stamps, a fiftyish woman from the Tranquillity Marksman Organization in Chicago. Following the accidental shooting death of nine-year-old Dantrell Davis, Marion had been instrumental in arresting the violence at the Cabrini Green projects. Throughout the summit, Marion was bold and brash, aggressive but straightforward. "Women are dying," she told us. "And it's women who have to bury you eggheads." She emphasized that the sisters too are suffering, and that they would stand united with the gang members.

Then another woman, Najma Nazy'at, a Posse member from Boston, jumped up to speak. "Please, brothers," she protested, "stop saying that it's just about 'we mention the gangs, we mention the dying, we mention the jails, and we mention the *brothers*.' We're talking about not dividing ourselves. It's brothers and *sisters*. Peace." Later, Najma spoke eloquently about a different aspect of the problem. "Gangs have been made a scapegoat for all kinds of problems in society," she said. "The real issue we need to address is violence and aggression in our society, not just in a group of black people or Latino people."

Najma may have been the youngest woman involved in the summit. She had organized young children to protest racism in the schools in Boston. She insisted that young people speak for themselves, that they take responsibility for bettering their own lives.

Rodney Dailey, also from Boston, was a former gang member who had organized gang activities around the country and spent time in the penitentiary. But he had stepped back from all of that to form Gang Peace, which has had a positive influence in the Boston area. In one of Rodney's most effective efforts, a computer program helps Gang Peace work with local colleges to bring wayward inner-city youngsters back into the mainstream while at the same time promoting peace. In his speech to the summit he emphasized that a comprehensive, national approach, as opposed to an "East Coast" or "West Coast" approach, must be taken to the inner-city problems.

There were other dramatic moments during the opening event. Wallace "Gator" Bradley, a spokesperson for the Gangster's Disciples of Chicago, announced peace for all Gangster's Disciples across the country. It was a coming together of brown and black, of Latinos and African-Americans. "As long as we keep God before us, nothing can stop us," he said, echoing the feelings of everyone there.

Since the summit, Gator has become involved in Chicago politics, and every time I see him now, he's dressed in a suit. The clothes haven't changed his basic personality, though; he's still directed and compassionate. And even though he gets teased about never finding a camera he didn't like, Gator puts his life on the line twenty-four hours a day to hold the truce in Chicago.

In the opening session, each participant had a chance to say something publicly. "We would rather live than die," one young gang member said. "It's as simple as that."

———

The activists at the summit were dynamic young leaders, prepared to work in our urban centers. They were as intelligent, thoughtful, caring, compassionate, and committed as those who led us in the past. But they need support. They haven't been heard because no one has given them a chance to speak. Our first national Urban Peace and Justice Summit was intended to change that. It was important to have significant gang participation because only gang members can bring about a sustainable truce. They are the leaders of their communities, whether the hoary establishment—white or black—can accept it or not. It is impossible to speak on behalf of a community without including members of that community.

Bringing together these leaders to discuss the critical issues facing urban America gave more power and urgency to the situation. Whether someone is wearing a baseball cap or a kufi or a dashiki or a three-piece suit, he or she can still work to save urban America from disintegration.

As a new generation of national leaders started to emerge that night in 1993, I withdrew into the background. I had been the point person for the past eight months, shaping, then articulating, the plans for the summit. But I was the facilitator of this gathering, not its star. Sharif, Fred, Rodney, Nane, Gator—*they* were the peacemakers. They were the stars.

I didn't attempt to designate in advance who the leaders of the summit would be because I knew they would emerge out of the moment. Critics made more than one reference to the disorganization of the conference, and they were right on target. We had no committee chairmen, public relations firms, or fancy titles like "project director" or "summit coordinator." But we were all used to operating in the midst of chaos. Too much structure would have inhibited the very people we were trying to reach.

FRIDAY, APRIL 30, 1993

I woke up Friday morning scared because things had gone so well Thursday night. Tough gangsters from rival gangs all over the country had been in the same room—but there had been no anger, not even a hint of violence. I felt as if the other shoe were about to drop.

Friday was the first day we could accomplish a goal together as a group—establish a dialogue and take it into the community. I stood in the lobby, waiting for people to make an appearance for the first scheduled event of the day, breakfast with the mayor. My self-imposed job was to monitor everybody and make sure things went smoothly. "How you doing? What's up? How'd you sleep?" I asked as they came into the lobby. Throughout the weekend I arrived early and left late, striving to keep everything in balance, checking on everyone's temperament. I worked on very little sleep, but oddly enough I wasn't tired.

Kansas City's mayor, Emmanuel Cleaver II, also a Methodist minister, hosted a breakfast for all the summit participants at the Villa, a posh restaurant that frequently hosts fancy weddings, anniversaries, and parties for the wealthy and powerful of Kansas City. The press took great delight in the irony of gang members breakfasting amid rich marble columns in such a chic location.

After breakfast, Cleaver took everyone to the upscale Country Club Plaza Shopping Center and invited them to shop there. "It's not the peace lovers we need, but the peacemakers," he declared, "the ones who are willing to stick their necks out and take risks." The press chastised the mayor for the breakfast and the shopping trip, but he stuck to his position and eventually the jabs abated. The gang members, for their part, acknowledged that they were all the subject of constant media scrutiny and conducted themselves in a way that was above criticism.

The first session on Friday morning was at ten o'clock in All Souls Unitarian Church, and it was open to the public and the press. Reverend Jones and Reverend Sam Mann welcomed everyone to their city. Many of the leaders who had spoken the evening before talked again about what they hoped to accomplish at the summit.

Then Ben Chavis, newly elected head of the NAACP, addressed the group. "What brings us together is blood and lives," he said. "This is a sacred event. A spiritual bond has come between us. This is not a secret meeting. We don't have a hidden agenda. We have come forth to say to the world and to say to the people in our communities that brothers and sisters can come together across lines of race, across lines of language, across lines of culture and ethnicity, and we can make a difference.

"We are going to come together in a way this nation has never seen before," he continued. "We're not only going to come together, we're going to stay together, because the adhesion that brings us together is blood itself. That's why the establishment is so afraid of this summit. They know that if we stop killing each other, they know that if we turn to each other, this summit has the potential to change the course of American history." Chants of "Well" and "That's right!" flowed throughout Ben's speech; a standing ovation followed.

When it was my turn to speak, I made it clear that the summit was intended to confirm and expand a lasting truce. I spoke of economic development and political empowerment. "You've got some pretty dynamic brothers and sisters in this room, and the attention, lest we forget, is on economic justice, police brutality, generating new leadership. While Memphis and Selma are etched in our minds, we have some new dynamic leaders in this room. There's a whole lot more out there who represent the voices of their communities. When you ask the relevant questions, you will be able to see who really speaks for urban America."

The press was dubious. Someone asked gang leaders who already had truces to talk about how they were working. Fred Williams from L.A., Rodney Dailey from Boston, Gator Bradley from Chicago, Sharif Willis from Minneapolis, and Nane Alejandrez from Santa Cruz all testified about their work to maintain peace.

After that session I asked the media to leave. Most of the summit participants were soon available for interviews, however, as we spent the next several hours in Kansas City's neighborhoods. They talked to groups in churches, civic centers, high schools, and corrections facilities about how they had made a cumulative, conscious decision to turn their backs on gang violence and promote peace. Many gave vivid testimony about participating in drive-by shootings or hold-ups. They had risked their lives, their families, and their friends—and without exception they said it wasn't worth it. They urged kids to be responsible for their lives. These visits had a tremendous impact on the community. The media finally responded positively, and mothers and children welcomed the gang members. They could see we really cared about their neighborhoods.

President Clinton also commended our work that Friday, telling a reporter for the Kansas City newspaper that the summit had "enormous potential." If he had been asked to speak, he said, he would have told gang members, "There's a better way to live, and I'm doing my best to create more opportunities for you. You have to decide what kind of life you want to live—whether you want to have a long life, whether you want it to be full of conflict and danger, or whether you want to be able to make something of your life and have it come out differently." The president's acknowledgment helped allay some of the remaining skepticism and fear. His stamp of approval kept some of our harshest critics at bay.

On Friday evening the logistics committee hosted a community event. It started with a youth reception at Metropolitan Technical High School; then young men and women from the area put on a fashion show and a dance, did poetry readings, and shared rap music. It was a perfect ending to the day. The community event helped counteract some of the negative press. The interaction between the community members and the visitors established a positive spirit for the rest of the weekend.

That night a small group of us went for dinner at Maxine's, a nearby restaurant featuring some of the best food I've ever eaten. It was run by a feisty, independent black woman named Maxine, whose genuine hospitality was typical of what Kansas City's black community showed us. A terrific cook, Maxine fixed us a magnificent spread: fish, chicken, sweet potatoes, collard greens, rice, cornbread, and much more. We took over the restaurant, and she let us stay long after closing time. The air was electric as everyone shared their experiences and their hopes for the conference. As I sat and listened, I felt myself begin to relax a little. Though I still had many uncertainties about the rest of the weekend, I was starting to feel confident that the summit could be a success.

I was up until almost four o'clock that night, making sure everything was okay in the hotel. I talked to some of the press who were still hanging around while I dealt with glitches. Strangely, it was in the course of that Friday night that I came to understand how much prayer means to me. I realized that I was not big enough to carry all of this off by myself. Before I went to sleep that night, I got on my knees and prayed, "Help me just a little bit more. I'll carry it further if you can help me just a little bit more."

SATURDAY, MAY 1, 1993

Saturday morning began with a bang and a roar. The front page of the *Kansas City Star* sported a large full-color picture of seven tough-looking Kansas City Crips, wearing their colors and prominently holding guns. In the article they said they didn't support the gang summit and that they would never stop gangbanging. "Well, thank you, *Kansas City Star*," I thought. "What have we done to deserve this?"

Quickly I corralled Fred Williams, Big Al, and a gang member named Elementary, all of whom were affiliated with the Crips in L.A. I asked them to find those Kansas City brothers and bring them to St. Stephen's, where we were meeting that morning. While they searched, I kept the media at bay. When they found the young men, we learned they had been put up to it. They had been promised jobs if they brought their guns to a specific place to be turned in; instead, a *Star* reporter took their picture with their guns, while others coerced them into making those statements. We held a press conference, and the gang members publicly stated that the photo had been instigated by the writers of the article. They said they didn't really mean what they had been quoted as saying; then they apologized and joined the summit. The *Star* stood by their article and denied that coercion was used in obtaining the story.

During that uproar, the small-group sessions formed and were concentrating on the four areas I had identified: the challenges of gaining empowerment, new visions for urban America, economic justice, and police abuses and brutality. A fifth session, on women's issues, was spontaneously created by the sisters of the summit, led by Marian Stamps.

All the sessions were spirited and spiritual. They started and ended with a prayer; many included prayers in the course of business, especially when tempers flared. In fact, before people even went into the church to start the day's meetings, a Native American circle was held in the parking lot of St. Stephen's, where everyone held hands and asked for guidance. A variety of faiths were represented at the conference, and we found room for them all—Native Americans, Muslims, Jews, Hebrew Israelites, Ba'hai, and Christians—in a continuing balancing act. Jim Wallis of *Sojourners* commented that he'd covered numerous religious conferences, but he'd never prayed as much as he did during the gang summit.

Generally, I tried to keep the summit as open and as flexible as possible. I didn't allow speaker after speaker to talk endlessly; instead, I wanted the participants to discuss their experiences and decide on strategies. Facilitators emerged based on how the group discussions developed. Most people were pleased just to have an opportunity to talk and be listened to. Many had never had the luxury of a simple discussion about their experiences, and I saw gratitude in their eyes for this chance to do so.

The sessions were divided into two four-hour blocks, one in the morning and one in the afternoon. The goal of each session was to write a statement of general principles on which we all could agree; participants at subsequent regional summits would hammer out the finer points later. I walked from group to group, checking out how things were going, making sure nothing exploded into violence or unresolvable anger. Periodically, I would check on the press, who were not pleased about being shut out of the discussions.

While we were meeting that Saturday morning, supportive activities were going on in the Kansas City community. Carl Boyd, a radio talk-show host, moderated a town meeting called "We Are Family: We Are Listening," held at Metropolitan A.M.E. Zion Church. About 125 people attended. At one point they broke into small groups to discuss economic development, education, self-esteem, community involvement, and parenting skills. They recommended that youth centers be formed to help young people develop in these areas. The event was significant because it allowed community members who were getting caught up in the enthusiasm of the summit to show support for their brothers and sisters and to talk about how the violence of urban America had affected them. Like the summit participants, everyone in this group also felt that they had been heard.

By late Saturday afternoon, the pins and needles I had felt all week were fading. I was still seeing to details, but my anxiety that something untoward would happen dissipated.

When I returned to the hotel following the small-group sessions, Vel was waiting with at least twenty messages. *Good Morning America* had called, along with CNN, and a lot of others. We quickly figured out which were critical to respond to and which could be delegated to other organizers. I did a couple of phone interviews, then headed back to Saturday evening's event—a dinner and community rally at a church on the other side of town. There Mayor Cleaver met again with gang participants and about five hundred citizens from the Kansas City area. "I've been a member of a Little League baseball gang, a fraternity gang, a seminary gang, and a church gang," he said. "We have to let these gang members know that they can belong to another gang—the gang of people who love them."

Saturday night after dinner, I finally believed we were going to make it. We had gotten through most of the hard work, and only the final church service celebration on Sunday remained. I hadn't slept much since Thursday and was functioning on pure adrenaline. The feeling was much like running a race—years of training and preparation come down to making it to the finish line. I wasn't there yet, but I knew I was going to cross it.

SUNDAY, MAY 2, 1993

It was raining, but the weather didn't dampen anyone's spirits. The final event, a church service open to the public, was scheduled for 10:10 A.M. at St. Stephen's. The morning really started, though, with a three-quarter-mile march from St. Mark's to St. Stephen's. Nearly all the summit participants, as well as many local supporters, marched through the rain in their Sunday best, chanting "Stop the killing!" They paused at 11th and Paseo streets to pray for Pedro Rawls, a neighborhood child who had been beaten to death there a few years earlier. Pedro symbolized why we were all in Kansas City: to save our babies, to put an end to senseless violence.

I missed most of the march. I was stuck in a Kansas City television studio doing a live hook-up with *Good Morning America* in New York City. Ben Chavis was in their New York studio talking with them in person; I was the cut-in from Kansas City. I sped over to St. Stephen's as soon as the interview was finished, but it was almost ten o'clock before I got there.

As I came into the church, my eyes were drawn to a large banner across the sanctuary. It said simply "Let's fly to a better place." We had shown everyone that a better place did indeed exist, and we were giving them the tools to create it in their communities.

The service was long, with a host of speakers; all of it was moving. After the speeches, as Reverend Sam Mann got up to give his homily, African-American members of the congregation murmured, and I knew what they were wondering, "What's this white guy going to tell us?" Reverend Mann knew he would have to win them over. "I know y'all ain't never heard no white preacher talk like this," he said, laughing. "Get that shock off your face so we can go and preach a little bit!"

I had heard him speak before, so I knew what to expect. He has all the flavor and energy of the most inspired African-American Baptist preacher. Some folks said he couldn't really be a white man; others just watched and enjoyed. Only a few had problems getting past his white face. His text was from Revelations 7:9–12, which he "translated" something like this: "That crowd over there are strangers. They don't look like or act like or talk like us, but check it out—there's more of them than there are of us. And God's over there with them. That's weird, I thought God only recognized us. But there they are, standing up big as you please, talking to God. Hm, I guess if He thinks they're okay to be with, we must be missing something. Let's go on over there and get to know them."

Everyone got the point. Reverend Mann's unbridled enthusiasm, his message, and his unmatched delivery swept the congregation away. Most responded wholeheartedly, standing and clapping and calling out their approval. He was brilliant.

Reverend Mac Charles Jones, our local host, was the last scheduled speaker. His sermon about the prodigal son, from the fifteenth chapter of Luke, kept the crowd's excitement level high. The prodigal son, he said, was in a hog pen, so desperate and hungry that he would have eaten the hogs' food. He was like all of us, the reverend said. We have all lost our identities. All of us have fooled around in hog pens at some point in our lives because that's how our culture operates.

People are born again, Reverend Jones preached, not while they are in a church or a synagogue but while they are down and dirty in the hog pen. They gain new awareness only in life's hog pens—the barrios and the ghettos of our cities. He urged us all not to give up on our daughters and sons, and he reminded us that when the prodigal son came home, his parents gave him a party. They didn't curse him—they said, "Glory Hallelujah."

Jones confessed that he too used to be in a hog pen, running the streets, smoking dope, and looking over his shoulder. Most nights his parents didn't know if he would come home alive. But whatever condition a person finds himself in right now doesn't have to be the end of his life. Many more chapters are yet to be written; Reverend Jones said he was living testament to that.

After his sermon, the congregation sang "Amazing Grace." Then Reverend Jones issued an altar call: "I want to end this summit by saying that last night a brother called me in tears. He told me about a young brother who wanted to come out and work with this summit and stop doing violence to himself and others. I want to make an invitation to those of you who want to lay down your colors—for those of you who want to find another way. I want to invite you to come right now to the altar. I want you to know that from this day forward, a new thing is happening. You *can* do something else. This morning we are praying for a new community. Come to the altar, won't you? God is working now; it's time for us to begin. We've got to make those who come forward know that they've got a new family. We've got to bring them right into our hearts. We've got to help make a way."

At that moment, I might easily have stood up and tried to suck in whatever glory was available. But I knew there was nothing I could have added. The moment spoke for itself.

As I looked around, most faces were filled with tears—faces that only moments earlier had been hardened with gangster grimaces or worn indifference. These many different faces, along with their quivering shoulders and trembling gestures, made valiant attempts to steady themselves and maintain composure amidst the sea of emotion running through the congregation.

Throughout the entire church, individuals began to turn to one another seeking some form of confirmation in the arms and hands and tender touches of each other. The insecurity in me sought out the one expression that could confirm in my mind that this experience was somehow and in some way unreal. I found none. With each darting glance, my own resolve not to cry weakened.

There are few words that can capture the power of such a moment.

Standing at the rear of St. Stephens Baptist Church in Kansas City, Missouri, my assistant Vel Holmes turned to me and said, "God bless you, Carl." I experienced for one brief instant, a spirit at peace.

After the service I had to get to the final press conference, but I could barely move in the crush of people who kept stopping me to offer me warm words on the summit. I finally got the press conference started by asking the reporters not to be provocative or irresponsible in their questioning, then turned things over to the major players.

"Our vision is to expand the urban peace movement in order to stop the violence in our communities and increase our economic empowerment base," Fred Williams told them. "Our purpose is to assure self-determination and a safe passage through life for our present families and their future generations."

Then Rodney Dailey took the podium. "No amount of money in the world can replace the strength, intelligence, and love this summit has created," he said. "We present the following recommendations from our workshops." Then Rodney turned the microphone over to Prince Asiel Ben Israel, a minister who lives part of the time in Israel and part of the time in Chicago, to report on the economic goals from the workshops. "Economic development programs must address immediate needs for employment, housing, and social services. They must also provide for the long-term economic security of the community," he said. "Public assistance handouts do not contribute to the development of a stable and productive economic base for the community. We advocate the immediate establishment of half a million jobs for at-risk youth, to be allocated from the infrastructure budget for the rebuilding of America."

Sharif Willis then announced the recommendations from the session on police brutality: "We recommend the establishment of community-based citizens' patrols to protect the community from police abuse, through videotaping and more assertive actions." Many white people do not realize it, but black communities felt enormous relief when George Halliday's infamous tape of the Rodney King beating was played and replayed on televisions across America. They were overjoyed because they thought white America would finally know about the abuse and join with them to call for it to cease.

Sharif continued, "We recommend that President Clinton direct Attorney General Janet Reno to make public the status of fifteen thousand police-brutality cases. Because police brutality is so rampant, we recommend that President Clinton appoint an independent national commission comprised of people of color to oversee and monitor it. We also recommend the repeal of all antigang legislation and ordinances, both state and federal, including existing statutes in California, Minnesota, Oregon, and the city of Chicago, as well as the federal Weed and Seed program."

Blanca Martinez came to the mike to speak for the women of the summit. "We, the mothers, sisters, daughters, and girlfriends, women in organizations and street gangs, stand in unison to stop the violence. This violence is beyond street violence and police brutality. It includes domestic violence, rape, child abuse, and poverty. We are committed to work with our brothers in teaching our children how to replace self-destruction with commitment to life, family, education, and community empowerment."

Finally, Gator Bradley answered a question from the press about how we wanted white America to respond to the summit. "The white media regularly sensationalizes us to enhance their profits. That has to stop before white America can begin to realize that we too are Americans. We too are trying to help keep the families and the factories from leaving America. White America has no need to fear us. We need their support of what is represented here. But to support it, they first have to *see* it, fairly and factually. And that is up to you, the media. We're asking for your help."

By about four o'clock, when people were heading home, I let my exhilaration come out. The summit had been an unbelievable success, far beyond what we could have imagined. My biggest fear beforehand had been that people would start fighting in the lobby of the hotel or at the church. I could see the banner headlines in *The New York Times:*

"Gang Summit Erupts in Violence"! The reality was that not only had the summit been completely peaceful, but as the Kansas City chief of police had begrudgingly reported, crime in the city was significantly down during that weekend. Not one incident involving gang members occurred.

How were we able to avoid violence when it is so commonplace in many of those leaders' lives? A spirit was created at the summit that enabled everyone to realize they had a responsibility larger than their own individual agendas: to heal the devastation of our communities. Everyone seemed to know instinctively that it would be petty to quarrel. For many, the summit symbolized a last-ditch effort to bring about peace in their communities, which could be accomplished only if everyone rose above their personal grievances and worked together.

Our success wasn't just a matter of people putting their differences aside. In the course of fewer than three days, these people—gangsters and community activists alike—had actually started to like each other. A spirit of cooperation and even affection developed as they realized that they had more to bind them together than to tear them apart. In a unique coming-together, we each felt simultaneously like prodigal son and welcoming family. With that spirit, we were able to excel beyond all expectations.

I had first felt the spirit standing in the lobby of the Howard Johnson's on Thursday evening. Each person I greeted was a brother or a sister to me, no matter who they were or how they were dressed. The church and community members who picked the participants up at the airport also generated the spirit. Instead of arriving in an unknown place, these young prodigal sons and daughters were welcomed home.

The city, the mayor, the Reverends Mac Jones and Sam Mann, the congregations, the gang members, the activists, myself, Vel Holmes—we were all nourished and changed in a dramatic way by the experience. It was beautiful having everyone come together and embrace each other, especially at the altar call. I saw that peace wasn't a pipe dream; it was possible to refuse to be mired in the impossible. The cycle of carnage in the cities could be broken. We had hope.

Other people felt the spirit too. Marion Stamps told *Sojourners* magazine that the altar call made her feel like "God just came in and said, 'Hey, I'm telling you that what you're doing is important. Just keep doing what you're doing, and as long as you put me first, it's going to be all right. Don't worry about the nonbelievers. You just carry out my mission.'" We all knew we were involved in something bigger than ourselves, especially during the Sunday service. It was much bigger than the sum of our individual energies.

Sharif Willis, the Conservative Vice Lord from Minneapolis, also felt the spirit. "This opportunity was unparalleled," he told Jim Wallis. "Individuals who historically opposed each other sat down to dialogue and take some steps toward stopping the violence in their community. The spirit of that, and the honesty of that attempt, is something I never believed I'd be a part of, although I strive for it. Individuals recognized that the killing within our communities can no longer be tolerated, and the devastation we have wreaked must be rebuilt."

Sharif's sincerity moved us all. During one session he had stood up and openly wept. Passionately, he explained that the summit *must* work. He owed it to his community to work for peace, he said, because of the devastation he'd been responsible for in the past. I was shaken by the depth of his emotion. Before he spoke, participants had been contentious about which direction to take. Afterward they got back on course.

For all of us, the summit was much more than an opportunity to take on leadership roles. It was atonement.

AFTERMATH

I didn't leave Kansas City until Wednesday because I still had interviews to do and wrap-up details to complete. I sat down for a reflective session with Sam Mann, a kind of debriefing. Finally, I drove around Kansas City to take a close look at it now that the summit was over. I visited neighborhoods; I dropped into some African shops. It was like walking into an empty football stadium after the big game. I don't mean that I felt like a victor; this hadn't been a contest. I felt relief and joy that things had worked out well. We had completed only one round, and there were plenty of rounds left to go, but we had given ourselves a great start.

On the plane back to Ohio, my exhilaration dissipated into anticlimax. Vel, still riding high from Sunday's church service, didn't understand my mood. She tried to remind me that I had just done something worthwhile. At some level I knew she was right, but I was already looking ahead to what had to be done next. Part of me has never been able to fully accept and enjoy my own accomplishments. All the positive comments I got after the church service, saying, "Carl, you've just done something wonderful," made me uncomfortable. I've always been challenged by the journey itself. Actually, arriving at the journey's destination doesn't give me the same satisfaction.

In spite of how far I've come, a wounded piece of that little boy I used to be has never healed and can't accept praise. I have to fix it, so that I won't pass that on to my daughter.

———

Newark, Ohio, felt like another planet. The gulf between me and the white middle-class suburbanites around me had been there before, of course, but now I saw the full dimensions of the gap in understanding between our cultures. They simply didn't have the experiential "language" to grasp what had happened in Kansas City. I thought, "No wonder it's so hard to convince the politicians who spend our money that this is important. They truly don't have a clue!"

Even those who did have a clue couldn't comprehend the full magnitude of the summit because they weren't there. They hadn't experienced the emotions during the small-group sessions or on Sunday during the church service. They hadn't witnessed two rival gang members dropping their colors and hugging each other and pledging their lives to peace. They hadn't felt the spirit that began in tentative hope on Thursday night and grew to a climax of peace and reconciliation.

I expected the traditional civil rights leadership, feeling slighted for not being included at the summit, to take an offensive posture. Rather than working with us, they would try to compete against us and over-shadow our efforts. I expected all kinds of summits and conferences about urban America to be held by Negro leaders who had not been invited to Kansas City. The mainline churches and the peace-and-justice community would likely do the same thing. All over, people would come out of the woodwork to show they were involved, they were relevant, they were moving. And, to be fair, some of those efforts would indeed complement what we were doing.

But I also expected the summit to be ignored or trivialized by a powerful segment of American society. Lawmakers and policy shapers, I thought, would continue to focus their attention elsewhere, ignoring the potential solutions we offered even as they hammered out the details of some new kind of crime-fighting bill. These people worry me most because their $22 billion crime package has the power to bring our movement to a standstill by putting the new leaders in jail instead of listening to them, bringing them back into the mainstream of society.

People like that wish we would just go away. But we're not going anywhere. The energy of Kansas City continues to spread; we've met in other cities since then, and more meetings are planned. At least on this topic, I agree with President Clinton: There's a better way.

Fifteen

RIPPLES

*By the end of 1994, L.A. County had surpassed the UN's estab-
lished number of one thousand deaths per year, qualifying it as an
official war zone.*

At the Kansas City summit, I had addressed niggerization on a
large scale for the first time. I didn't use the word itself, but the sense
of it was there in every speech, every meeting. "Take a close look at
what you're doing to yourselves," I had said. "Your life doesn't have to
be this way."

The gang members latched onto the concept of deniggerization like
a lifeline because it explained so much about their lives, and at the
same time it held out hope for a better future. Once they understood
that they could *choose* to deniggerize themselves, the resulting sense of
empowerment was almost tangible. Suddenly, being a nigger didn't
have to be a life sentence. There are other ways to interact with society,
they saw. And even in those three short days we spent together, they
learned that those other ways do great things for the soul.

Hope is the defining word for the Kansas City summit. Some of us went there hoping to realize even a small piece of the dream. All of us left there filled with hope, inspired about the possibilities that beckoned. We set out to seed that hope all over the country, planning regional summits across the United States. Leaders were calling us, and some of the media were finally in touch. We moved out confidently, sure that we could convince people that their futures did not have to replicate their pasts.

In June 1993, a month after Kansas City, a regional gang summit met in Cleveland. It too was dedicated to stopping the killing, and the summit leader, Omar Ali-Bey, made a pledge to the gathered gang leaders: "This weekend will be one of the most important in the history of the city of Cleveland. The madness of our babies being killed in the streets, the madness of the drugs in our community, the madness of the violence—all of it will be dealt with."

Ben Chavis joined us again, declaring our initiatives to be "the most profound step taken by African-Americans in this century." And: "What is happening here cannot be underestimated. As a people, we can now turn our attention toward external discrimination plaguing us. Much of the forward progress we made during the sixties has been lost in two decades of self-destruction. That *will* change."

The next month found us in Minneapolis, where Sharif Willis and Spike Moss brought together gang members and peacemakers. On the first evening of the Minneapolis summit, Spike put the work that lay ahead of us in brilliant perspective. "It's easy tonight and this week, sitting here listening to everybody," he said. "But when you're back home, nigger, walking down the street, sitting by yourself, and that cocaine comes out and nobody's looking, or you're with that fine girl, chasing that pussy, and she wants to snort, that's when your true integrity will come. You are going to find out the easiest thing you did was stop the killing."

In every city where we met, we had to conduct a strong public-relations effort to allay community fears and suspicions naturally associated with gangs. But in Minneapolis the press was downright hostile. Even after six or seven warring groups had come together, stood up in the church, embraced each other, and pledged peace, the local press remained belligerent and suspicious about our efforts.

At first I didn't understand the intensity of the distrust and skepticism. But then I learned that Minneapolis, with a population of about 370,000, had an estimated 4,400 gang members, four times as many as just five years earlier. Back in 1985, gang violence had already reached a fever pitch when a young girl was shot in the head, supposedly for implicating the Gangster's Disciples in a gun-store burglary. The situation worsened through the late 1980s, when turf battles and drive-by shootings became more and more common.

Spike Moss, an outreach worker with a social services agency called City, Inc., had met Sharif Willis, newly out of jail, in 1990. Sharif grew up in Chicago, where he was known for using drugs and running guns, and he had been a Vice Lord since he was thirteen. He moved to Minnesota in 1982 and killed a man over a dice game in 1983. He began his work to curb gang violence during the course of a six-year stay in Minnesota's Stillwater Prison. When he got out, he was ripe to cooperate with Spike. Using his influence in the Vice Lords, he was able to persuade four gangs to agree to peace. Three local foundations paid his salary and supplied him with cellular phones, walkie-talkies, and beepers so that gang leaders could be reached easily if trouble erupted. The Red Cross even came in and taught some rudimentary first aid.

After Sharif negotiated the cease-fire, the rate of gang killings in Minneapolis dropped sharply. Whenever a riot threatened to break out, gang leaders worked at calming tensions. Construction sites they had formerly vandalized hired them for security, and United for Peace also helped them find jobs. Sharif, as president of United for Peace, promised the foundations supporting him that their money would not be used for drugs.

The organization proved its mettle on May 7, 1992, when a sixty-six-year-old man shot and wounded a youth who had been trespassing on his lawn. Rumors quickly spread that the older man was a cop, and more than six hundred people descended on his lawn, hurling bottles and rocks in protest. A Molotov cocktail was thrown at his house, and it burst into flames. The deputy police chief called Sharif, who alerted gang leaders by phone and walkie-talkie that their help was needed to calm the situation. With their assistance the fire trucks were able to get to the house, and people who had gathered in anger dispersed.

During the following summer, United for Peace performed numerous other services. They provided an escort service for senior citizens who needed to take their Social Security checks to the bank; they reprimanded gang members who painted graffiti on public buildings; they monitored shooting victims in hospital emergency rooms to prevent disturbances. Sharif had a weekly talk show, and the governor nominated Spike Moss for the Albert Schweitzer Humanitarian Award.

United for Peace came apart over a misunderstanding. On September 25 police officer Jerry Haaf was shot in the back four times, allegedly by four members of the Vice Lords, while he was in the Pizza Shack, a police hangout. One of the alleged assailants was a nephew of Sharif's; another was rumored to be A. C. Ford, the vice president of United for Peace. The police broke off all relations with the organization and implied that Sharif might have been involved. The governor withdrew Spike's nomination for the Schweitzer award, and the reputation of United for Peace never recovered. The murder remains unsolved.

The media turmoil we encountered in Minneapolis did not stop us from going on to other cities. In October 1993 we held yet another summit in Chicago, this one organized by Prince Asiel Ben Israel. Prince Asiel works day and night, in two countries, to bring about urban peace. He is a member of the Hebrew Israelite Nation, a group of African-Americans who left the United States in the 1960s due to political turmoil and made their home in Israel. He now spends half the year in Chicago, the other half in Israel. He is an honored, spiritual, passionately committed servant of the people.

For the Chicago summit, Prince Asiel brought together some of the best-known African-American leaders to support the efforts we had made thus far. He invited influential figureheads—Louis Farrakhan,

Jesse Jackson, Congressman Kweisi Mfume, and Ben Chavis—and presented them as a united part of the peace effort. His vision was a stroke of genius, but it made a lot of the old guard very angry. Still, it pushed the traditional black leadership to stand up and say they supported what we were doing.

On the first day of the Chicago summit, Prince Asiel filled a high school auditorium with gang members to tell them about the peace effort. As usual, people were leery about bringing gang members together in one place; but also as usual, there were no problems. After the first meeting Prince Asiel went out into some of the most violence-prone projects—Angel Gardens and Cabrini Green—to talk about the cease-fire and to preach peace.

We received a tremendous onslaught of criticism from the Chicago press—the *Sun-Times,* the *Defender,* the *Tribune;* even from syndicated columnist Mike Royko. Although it was documented that our efforts were actually beginning to stop the violence, that we really were advancing peace, that we had all kinds of concern for, and positive responses from, the community, the press virtually ignored those accomplishments in favor of bashing the gangs and former gang leaders involved. They seemed unable to make the transition from reporting on gang crime to reporting on gang attempts to control crime. And even though the level of violent crime began to drop in every city where we had held a gang summit, even though the crime rate declined while we were there, crime was not completely eliminated. As far as the press was concerned, that made us goats instead of heroes.

Gangs are not responsible for all the crime in America. The tabloid mentality of the media plays up the drug dealing and the drive-bys, fully aware that those kinds of crime, especially when committed by blacks, make Americans uncomfortable. But gangs don't run Congress. They don't create corrupt politicians. They aren't involved in the fiascos on Wall Street or the debacles of the savings and loan institutions. The fact is that much of America doesn't perceive illegal white-collar activity as crime.

One theme of my speech to the UN conference was that in virtually every urban area in the United States, the root cause of social problems is the economic disparity between the light-skinned and the dark-skinned. Somewhere in our collective psyche we have come to accept that distinction as a given. A person of color quickly discovers that this country has different rules for different-colored citizens.

I had taken Nane Alejandrez from Barrios Unidos with me to the UN, and he confirmed what I had said. We both emphasized that the country was brimming with potential urban peacemakers who need recognition and support if they were to be effective. "When I was growing up," I told the UN conference, "there was no one like Nane Alejandrez in my neighborhood. No one walked into our ghetto the way he now walks into the barrios to nurture the children. Little Carl Upchurch possibly could have avoided that ten-year sentence in federal prison if there had been a Nane in his life. So it's important to raise their voices. This is the last chance we have to keep this scourge of death from annihilating an entire generation of children."

The next regional summit was in Washington, D.C., in December 1993. By then the format had been refined, and we were holding the summits under the auspices of the National Council for Urban Peace and Justice. That fledgling organization that I had created in the back of the Baptist Church in Granville had sprouted wings. We set up a national headquarters in Pittsburgh, named Kahlid Raheem as national spokesperson and executive secretary, and established a board of directors. They elected me president, but Kahlid did the lion's share of the work.

While Nane and I were at the UN conference in November, a Lutheran minister from an inner-city San Antonio church approached me. Reverend Anne Helmke was ready to do something exciting with her church, and she wanted it to involve bringing peace into her city. Early in 1994 she contacted me again to ask what it would take to bring a summit to San Antonio. She had been talking up the idea all over the city and was getting strong support from the Chamber of Commerce, civic organizations, and businesses.

Primary elections were to be held in San Antonio that March, and the issue of a gang summit coincidentally became a political football in the district attorney's race. One of the candidates announced, without knowing that a summit was already in the works, that he would host one if he were elected. The other two candidates denounced him and the idea, stating that a summit would send the city's youth the message that joining a gang was the only way to get official attention.

Michael Harrington of Abiding Presence Lutheran Church, who was working with Anne to coordinate the San Antonio summit, responded to their attacks. "They say we're giving the gangs credibility," he said. "If it gives them credibility, good! They are the solution. The only way to achieve peace is to get them together, face to face, to begin talking." After much hesitation, the mayor of San Antonio declared April 4–10, 1994, a week of peace and reconciliation.

The words *gang* and *gang summit* frighten people. Michael said people continually asked him, "Why do we have to listen to them? Why do we have to recognize them?" He always answered, "They are already being recognized every time the nightly news reports a killing. Instead of giving them that kind of recurring notoriety, we're proposing to involve them in the community's problem with violence and ask them what constructive contributions they could make."

Unlike the Minneapolis and Chicago media, which had taken such an adversarial stance, San Antonio's press was supportive for the most part. The Sunday edition of the *Express-News* outlined our plans in a positive article, and Lynnell Burkett, a columnist, wrote several supportive articles. This kind of reporting helped dispel the ignorance that underlay community fears.

Throughout the event there were many separate mediation and reconciliation counseling sessions, with thirty rival gang leaders representing 1,800 gang members. They dropped their colors, sat down in small groups, and looked for ways to end the violence. Gangs from each neighborhood came up with goals and recommendations—weekend and afternoon programs, parks and recreation programs, neighborhood security, literacy programs, teacher training, tutoring, college recruitment, cultural sensitivity training for police, adequate pre- and postnatal care, a mayor/business coalition, and better housing.

I had complete trust that whatever the mediators and the gang members did would work because whenever they came out of those sessions, they shook hands and hugged each other. Sure enough, before the summit was over, four of the gangs from the west side of San Antonio had agreed to a truce. Afterward three more gangs completed peace agreements, while five others were in the process of doing so.

———

One afternoon after I returned from San Antonio, I sat in my office at the back of the church bathed in the light coming through a stained-glass window. It was hard to believe that it had been only a year since the national gang summit in Kansas City. We had planted the seeds of deniggerization in so many places, in so many people, and they had begun to form a core of concerned and able new leaders.

Ex-gangbangers. Ex-criminals. *Ex-niggers*.

PART THREE

Antiniggerization

Sixteen

EMPOWERMENT

People treat us the way we *allow* them to treat us. Thus, if we are to change, we must be the agents of change in our own lives. As I look at our country today through the lens of my own history, I believe there is finally a critical mass of members of the underclass who are no longer willing to be treated as invisible or disposable. They no longer believe that rescue is at hand; they no longer believe that society at large has a stake in improving their lives; and they are finally angry enough to ask the question that will rock the American social, political, and economic landscape:

- We know you're planning to spend $50 billion on new high-tech military gadgetry, but *what about us*?
- We know you're worried about getting reelected, so you're planning to spend $96 million on a project in your home state that has nothing to recommend it, but *what about us*?
- How can you justify sending troops and aid abroad without allocating any money to eradicate the conditions that perpetuate the hellish conditions here at home? *What about us?!*

Those prepared to ask this deceptively simple question are ready and eager, individually and collectively, to pull themselves up out of the urban rubble. Nothing can stop this impending groundswell. The only choice we have is whether we're going to be part of the solution or part of the problem.

In reality, no single group has created the desperate conditions of our inner cities. No single race can be charged with committing the whole array of economic, political, and social crimes perpetrated against the poor and their children. We are all at fault: we who preach peace and justice yet enjoy the bounty of exploitation and oppression; we who don't give our national crises the same priority we give international ones; we who barter away human rights for a slice of the power pie; and we, the poor, who, intentionally or not, help perpetuate our own condition by refusing to hold society accountable for what it does to us—and by refusing to hold ourselves accountable for what we *allow* it to do.

It is long past time for African-Americans to take their future into their own hands: to protest the slaughter of black males in urban settings, to be outraged at the unprecedented number of black children who live in poverty, to stem the exploding prison population and the epidemic of HIV among black men, and to acknowledge that the unbridled killing of poor people in America's death chambers is a national disgrace.

We can generalize forever about how "they" see us, treat us, and feel about us. Such grumbling may satisfy some conditioned reaction in us to be victims *and therefore not responsible*, but it does nothing to change our circumstances or improve our children's lives. The hard truth, as it relates to race *and* class, is that most people, black and white, who live outside of poor communities don't care about how poor people live as long they don't impinge on their lives. If we continue to wait for "them" to fix "us," it will never happen. We won't achieve equality until we respect ourselves, and we won't respect ourselves until we take responsibility for our lives.

There is a predictable pattern to the lives of most black inner-city boys. I say boys only because I was one, with no authority to give you a first-person account of the lives of black inner-city girls except to tell you that both begin in poverty, and both are surrounded by drugs, violence, and gangs. The pattern of young black urban males is that they are destined, for the most part, to grow up to be drug users and/or sellers, to become proficient with street weapons, and to end up either dead by age twenty-one or cycling through the criminal justice system, or both.

My formative years were spent on the streets. I used weapons and drugs, joined gangs, served time in prison. My life was a textbook example of the pattern—until I reached Western State Penitentiary. It was there, because of timing, maturity, and the people I met, that I was able to challenge those patterns and begin my recovery process.

I arrived at Western a cynical, angry smartass. My reputation was that of a dangerous man, and I played it for everything it was worth. I made weapons and collected scars and never thought beyond my own survival.

I started taking classes for the flimsiest of reasons: They got me out of other responsibilities. But as time passed, I found myself interested in what I was hearing in those classrooms. Looking back, it's clear that the opportunity to go to school came along just when I was ready to understand that education is a gift.

In my jail cell at Western, teased by self-discovery, I began to see the world in a new way. In the context of the stories, biographies, autobiographies, poetry, and history that I read, I began to evaluate my own life and my many shortcomings. I was challenged by a wide range of authors to examine the behaviors that had brought me to this place of despair. And eventually I glimpsed my humanity, small fragments of my connectedness to a wider universe of common decency. This connectedness served as a powerful reminder of the potential salvageability of self. It was in me at birth but was buried by poverty, racism, social inequities, anger, and hopelessness.

In solitary confinement I started consciously to re-create myself.

Twenty-five years later, I'm still trying to reconcile life's inevitable contradictions and be a better human being. This endless struggle transcends all social barriers, including race and class. Yet for people born into an environment rife with social disadvantages, the questions are monumental: How do we transcend and then transform such environments while simultaneously protecting the inalienable rights of those who, for whatever reason, are unable to protect themselves? How do we connect across those social gaps that segregate our efforts?

I believe these are the critical questions of our day. And I believe we accomplish precious little by consistently moaning about the inequities instead of taking actions to rectify them.

My goal, therefore, is to challenge Black America—especially *poor* Black America—to awaken to the possibilities that unfold once we take responsibility for our own lives. This is not to deny that society bears responsibility for our condition. It does. But first we must decide, one by one, that *we will not be victims any longer*. We will not be niggers any longer.

Change comes from within, and before we can change the world around us, we must change ourselves one by one. We must look in our mirrors and acknowledge our responsibility for our lives: "*I'm* the one carrying a gun." "*I'm* the one shooting dope into my arm." "*I'm* the one getting drunk every day." "*I'm* the one who dropped out of school." "*I'm* the one who would rather steal than work." "*I'm* the one who uses violence, or threats of violence, to make my way through the world." "*I'm* the one setting an example for the children around me." "*I'm* the one killing my brother." "*My* behavior contributes to my niggerization."

As African-Americans, we can neutralize niggerization by relying on ourselves, our ingenuity, our history, our church, our faith, and our intelligence. But we must do it together, as a people, rejecting the mantle of inferiority, settling for nothing less than total equality. There are too many young Carl Upchurches out there suffering from a sense of worthlessness. Too many of us are wasting vital moments of our future on self-destructive, abusive, pointless activities that are speeding us to our graves. Those of us who are already engaged in the lifelong process of recovering from this disease of self-hatred must take the lead if we are to eradicate the existence of a second-class citizenry mired in poverty and racial hatred.

Two things, at least, must happen to break the cycle. First, we who inflict the wounds must acknowledge our racial biases and our role in the all-too-frequent eruptions of overt violence. Second, the poor must use the lessons of history to empower themselves to demand that they be treated with the innate dignity to which they are entitled.

Social change has always bubbled up from the bottom. Those on top—the ones who have attained the power and grabbed the money—appear little inclined to change the status quo voluntarily. Change can't occur until the poor unite to articulate and support each other's struggle for justice—to refuse to tolerate *injustice*.

Education is one of the keys to our cultural empowerment. The time is upon us to seriously consider education—education of ourselves, education especially of our children and of those incarcerated—as an essential ingredient for lifting ourselves out of this morass.

The greatest gift an education gives is perspective. By now you should understand how remarkable it was for me to discover that someone, somewhere, was thinking as I thought, feeling what I felt, hurting as I hurt. Just knowing that was empowering. It validated me somehow, gave me a sense of self-worth—and the courage to persevere in the face of monumental obstacles.

We have to stop thinking of education as the simple accumulation of facts. Education is power. *That* is what we have to give to ourselves and our children. No less important, we have to give it to our brothers and sisters who are trapped in prisons because they've never learned they have the power to change their lives.

It's more complicated, though, than just preaching to our children to stay in school. Since we've passed our own attitudes on to our children, it's no wonder they believe that school is something they're stuck doing until the rest of life comes along. We, and they, need to rethink, reprogram, reposition these old attitudes. A broad spectrum of African-Americans have used education to deniggerize themselves— Malcolm X; Martin Luther King, Jr.; Maya Angelou; Carter G. Woodson; W.E.B. Du Bois; Cornel West; and many others. All these men and women hold the road map for change. They tell us in every way that education is essential to any movement toward freedom. Even in our most desperate hours—during slavery—we understood one fundamental truth: that we must become educated to make progress in this culture. Whether at Harvard or Howard, at Princeton or the penitentiary, education is our key.

Maya Angelou's words sent me the clearest message: "It doesn't matter what you read. Just read something." I live by that today. Our history, our journey toward freedom, our abilities to alleviate our burdens, all can be challenged with an education. And if there is one thing that we have consistently outlined, it is that without knowledge, without knowing, without learning, we're dead.

———

If we are courageous enough to make this huge change, to deniggerize ourselves, we will be unstoppable. Our self-loathing will become self-confidence, our despair will give way to determination. And our apathy, one of the most powerful enemies to our well-being, will be replaced by activism.

Collectively, we tend to ignore our societal problems, deluding ourselves that they don't even exist until, one after another, they blow up—sometimes literally—in our faces. Then we spring into action, taking great pride in our readiness to respond. But we focus our considerable expertise on returning the offending symptom to an ignorable state. Somehow we never get around to dealing with the underlying causes. Just look at what has, or has not, happened in L.A. since the 1992 riots. In spite of loud protestations from all the political interests who had something to gain by expressing concern, virtually no improvements—economic, social, political, or otherwise—have "trickled down" to South Central.

Why? Too few of us, both inside and outside neighborhoods like South Central, care enough to create the upheaval that would bring change. Too few of us are willing to risk what we have to help empower those who have nothing. Too few of us believe change is possible. That doesn't mean it won't happen. But those of us already in this tiny camp of believers have a moral obligation to take the lead. Any other course of action is vile cowardice.

The tools for crafting change are there for the taking. The most comprehensive of them is deniggerization, a complete change of attitude and action that will lead us to believe that we deserve better than we've gotten. With this tool we'll be ready to be agents of change, ready to assess our strengths and apply pressure where it will do the most good.

Economically, for example, our combined clout is far greater than we give ourselves credit for, especially when we use it in boycotts. It's a powerful card to play, the one that will most directly impact the economic system that keeps us at the bottom of the heap. The American economic system values only those who have acquired wealth and those who can impact its acquisition. We certainly do not have enough acquired wealth to be a potent influence. So we must impact the acquisition of individual and corporate wealth: by judiciously choosing where to buy food and clothing and furniture, by investing in black-owned banks and corporations, by buying bonds that fund redevelopment in our inner cities, by consciously supporting African-American artists and writers and athletes who have demonstrated their willingness to give something back to their communities.

The boycott has a long and glorious tradition in the history of civil disobedience. Martin Luther King, Jr., used it in Memphis and Montgomery; Jesse Jackson used it in Operation Push; Cesar Chavez used it. Louis Farrakhan uses it. It's long past time for us all to use it.

One of my personal goals is to see America, as a nation, abolish capital punishment. It's cruel, archaic, and totally ineffective as a deterrent to crime. Imposing and carrying out a death sentence has much more to do with satisfying the bloodlust of the "innocent" than with punishing the "guilty." I can tell you firsthand that prison is a living hell, whatever the length of the sentence and despite the few amenities that seem to so infuriate the general populace. The prospect of spending the rest of one's life behind bars constitutes a far greater punishment than death.

Blacks make up an outrageously disproportionate percentage of prisoners in America; we make up 12 percent of the general population but 49 percent of those incarcerated. We make up an even higher percentage of the death-row prisoners. And in the Southern Six—Georgia, Florida, Alabama, Mississippi, Louisiana, and Texas—blacks are executed at far greater rates than whites.

Protests call attention to the problem but have done nothing to remedy it. Candlelight vigils or "execution watches" outside prisons haven't worked either. I contend that our best weapon in the fight to make the Southern Six abolish capital punishment is economic. And that brings me back to boycotts.

How can we use boycotts to abolish capital punishment? By starting at the far end of a long line of dominoes. The most visible blacks in the country are athletes and entertainers. Wherever they perform, whether they're singing or dodging tackles or shooting a three-pointer that hits nothing but net, the vendors of everything from tickets to hot dogs to pennants to T-shirts pay taxes that eventually end up in state coffers. We can cooperate to boycott the Southern Six. We can ask our entertainers not to schedule concert dates there. We can boycott professional and collegiate athletic events there, refusing to buy tickets or team-logo sportswear. We can encourage our young student athletes, the ones that get offers of athletic scholarships from all over the country, to take their skills and their revenue-producing possibilities to other states.

All over the country, deniggerized blacks—and whites—can buy California produce instead of what's produced in Florida. We can buy carpeting made in Tennessee instead of Georgia. We can give up Vidalia onions and Georgia peaches and the Dallas Cowboys and Ole Miss. We can pass on Lone Star Beer and the Mardi Gras. We can put gas in our cars from companies not based in Texas. We can go to the beach in South Carolina and take our children to Disney*land* instead of Disney *World*. And on and on and on.

Boycotts will work. But *blacks-only* boycotts will take us only part of the way. We cannot reach our ultimate goals without support from the external world. All the social, economic, and political reforms I advocate ultimately require us to function as a cohesive community within a larger realm, working realistically with others to create change. If enough of us, regardless of the color of our skin, become conscientious consumers, if enough of us don't buy that small bottle of Louisiana hot sauce, there will be an eventual economic backlash. The manufacturers and the team owners and the college presidents and the Chambers of Commerce will put pressure on state legislators. And someday, executions in the Southern Six will be banned—because they will have become an economic albatross. It seems a ludicrous reason to abolish state-sanctioned killings, doesn't it? But philosophy is impotent in such settings.

———

Conditions that produce a racist, repressive climate confront us too often now, whether it be in the Southern Six, where we are all too often threatened with removal from the face of the earth, or in an inner-city ghetto, where we are all too often ignored. The current crop of politically elitist leaders is either unable or unwilling to challenge these conditions. It is time, then, for us to challenge *them*.

Politically, we are a force to be reckoned with. When we turn our attention to identifying and dismantling the structures designed to keep us where we are, the shock will be felt all the way to the top. But first, as always, we have to clean up our own act.

The nationwide contempt for the electoral process, especially among African-Americans, has dangerous implications. The juvenile exchanges that increasingly characterize our electoral process leave us not only misinformed but bitterly discouraged by the end of every campaign and little inclined to vote. It is hardly surprising therefore that the poor in this country mistrust politicians and the government apparatus they represent.

It is impossible, however, to discuss political apartheid without acknowledging that we bear some responsibility for its continued existence. Of all the spheres in which society would like us to play the victim, politics is the one where we do the most damage to ourselves. At every level of government, we continue to reelect representatives whose voting records clearly indicate their disdain for our welfare. In short, whether we've given up on the system or given up on ourselves, we do not hold our elected officials accountable for their actions.

Legally sanctioned racism is not new. Back in the days when election results were manipulated by the political power structure, we truly had no say in who our representatives were, at any level of government. Gerrymandering was a time-honored tradition, and the right to draw the precinct lines was highly prized. The system was designed to give blacks the vote without giving them any clout. To be sure, economic and social considerations came into the mix as well, but the system was founded with racist intentions.

Gerrymandering is now illegal. We are no longer confined to arbitrarily designed "centipede" districts that gave a huge number of black constituents one representative. Our fortunes, as least as far as proportional representation goes, should have improved. But within a few years of reluctantly relinquishing gerrymandering, the white establishment discovered that it didn't need it anyway. Why? We African-Americans have replaced the old legislated gerrymandering with "mental blocs," willingly doing to ourselves what the courts have forbidden anyone else to do to us. We vote black and we vote Democratic, no matter what.

Obviously, we cannot afford to make sweeping generalizations. The times, and our quest for equality and respect, require that we become thinking voters. We can no longer make our electoral decisions based strictly on political affiliation, religious affiliation, race, or gender. We must dig deeper, past the candidates' surface refinements—the nice clothes, the nice manners, and the sophisticated polish, which, after all, indicate nothing more than the presence of money and long hours of practice at fitting in—and ruthlessly expose their hypocrisy when they ask us to stand up and vote for them, then slink away and shut up. We must cast our votes for those whose stands on health care, jobs, housing, education, and crime indicate that they have our interests at heart. Once elected, purveyors of unkept promises and unrealized dreams must be held accountable, voted out of office, and replaced with men and women of higher integrity. Only in this way will we be able to make the political climate warmer to our needs.

Too many of us don't even vote at all. Our current pathetic showing at the polls each election day merely indicates our contempt for the electoral process. The fact is that *not* voting is self-censorship. *Not* voting is voluntarily giving up our voice. We cannot afford to "refuse to choose."

The marches, the vigils, and the protests that date from the abolitionist movement are very much in my mind as I advocate a more purposeful use of our electoral voice. Our ancestors took extraordinary and sometimes dangerous measures to correct injustice. They revolted on the slave ships and surreptitiously broke tools on southern plantations; in 1941 they threatened a march on Washington to open up the defense industry to black workers; and in 1948 A. Philip Randolph threatened a march that resulted in President Truman's Order Number 9981, ending segregation in the armed forces.

The Montgomery, Alabama, bus boycotts, the Freedom Rides of the 1960s, and the violence and rabble-rousing around civil rights issues forced the Interstate Commerce Commission to ban racial segregation on interstate carriers. The lunch counter sit-ins in Greensboro, North Carolina, challenged segregated public facilities. Two black protest marches in Selma in the early 1960s shook the conscience of America into reforming its horrendous treatment of African-American citizens.

Because these brave men and women stood up against injustice, the Voting Rights Act of 1965 was passed, and a whole host of other civil rights came into being: legal aid services for the poor, prohibition of discrimination in employment and housing, and federal prosecutions for those who were lynching African-American citizens, burning children in churches, and bombing educational institutions.

Thirty years later, we have made little or no use of that rich heritage. It's as if we somehow thought the Voting Rights Act was the end of the struggle. But the struggle has no end, and until we all recognize that, until we all begin to vote and vote carefully, we are doomed to keep repeating the old mistakes. We will do nothing to halt the succession of politicians who have no comprehension of who we are or what we need, who are disdainfully ignorant of the depth and breadth of pain that governs the daily lives of the underclass, who are hopelessly out of touch, ideologically indistinguishable, in their inhuman neglect of the downtrodden.

It's long past time we stopped using these "facts" as excuses for inaction. They should become reasons for action. Those who understand that the civil rights thrust in the United States has lost its focus are a widely divergent assembly. But we had better learn to work together. All of us who care about the direction of civil and human rights in this country, especially those who are in a position to lead the struggle into the twenty-first century, must begin immediately to be more imaginative and more deliberate as we move to face the challenges confronting us today.

Education. Economics. Politics. The tools of change are there for the taking.

Seventeen

AMERICAN APARTHEID

The four-hundred-year legacy of slavery is still with us. The process that once manufactured docile, obedient, self-loathing chattel continues to fester in our collective psyche. Freed from ball and chain, we are bound by a crippling slave mentality. We continue to be bought and sold by political and economic interests. Not only does this self-destructive mentality show itself in the unwed mother, the crack addict, and the gangbanger, it also lurks ominously in the behavior of the black elite that prides itself on having "made it."

One vital step toward empowering ourselves is to tell the truth about America's racial situation and the domestic policies that perpetuate it. The whips of the slave days may be gone, but they have been replaced by more sophisticated political and societal equivalents. And the intent is still for one class, one race, to control another. American apartheid is a fact that nobody dares to acknowledge out loud. We all know it's there, but we ignore it.

Remember our collective outrage about apartheid in South Africa? Although initially we were slow to respond to this blatant system of injustice, eventually we became deliberate, committed, and passionate in our resistance to the continued exploitation of black South Africans.

There was little division among us on whether it was wrong that 28 million blacks should be controlled by 4 million whites; we *knew* it was wrong. We asked our entertainers and athletes not to go there, we asked major corporations not to do business there, we supported the African National Congress's struggle for freedom, we demanded Nelson Mandela's release, and we expressed righteous indignation over the Sharpeville and Soweto massacres.

Our high school and college students exercised their considerable power in massive divestiture campaigns, not only against their schools but against companies doing business in South Africa. Students boycotted, protested, and held sit-ins and rallies. They invited ANC members to their campuses to address these issues. If an administration made no principled response, many students changed schools, exercising their economic power in another way. That same spirit, that same unity of purpose, must now be directed against the social, political, and economic apartheid that is crippling urban America.

Just as we are less honest than South Africa about our racism, we are also less honest about our social caste system. After hundreds of years the system is so firmly fixed in our minds that it has assumed a fact-of-life status. And we docilely, *slave*ishly, occupy our "place" in what we see as the grand scheme of things.

Where is our outrage? Why do we remain captives of this vertical paradigm? Why can we not see the social destruction wrought by a system whose every tenet values the individual at the expense of the community? It should be immediately apparent that such a system is not only absurd but threatens the future of our society. How can we possibly create a mutually supportive social structure when people think the only way to "better" themselves is to literally or figuratively step on someone else? It's long past time for us to take control, climb off the ladder, and refuse to play this particular game. It's a game that neither we nor our children will ever win.

The paradigm at work here says "If you have money, you must be smart; since you're rich *and* smart, you must deserve the power." Giant leaps of illogic have kept this myth alive for centuries. It's one that must be debunked if we are ever to have a socioeconomic climate that takes the new young black leadership seriously.

The thirty years since desegregation was legally mandated have produced little voluntary interracial bonding. Innumerable studies bear this out: integrated neighborhoods are rare; interracial marriages still raise eyebrows; blacks are certainly more numerous in the "professions" than they once were, but still fall far short of proportional representation; blacks in service jobs overwhelmingly outnumber whites; black neighborhoods are still in the worst parts of town, and still look like slums; HUD housing projects have a far higher percentage of black occupants than white; black men die younger; black women are more common than white women as single heads of household; and black children are far more likely to end up in jail.

The inherent racism and classism that conspire to keep African-Americans in their societal place—repressed—must be exposed and expunged. The scope of the change this requires is terrifying. *I know*. But we can't afford not to try.

Why not? Because our race is being decimated by the current social, economic, political, and educational policies of the United States. In 1980 there were fewer than 200,000 black maximum-security prisoners in America. Today there are nearly ten times that number—*two million black people* under the control of federal, state, and local authorities.

By the turn of the century, two-thirds of the United States prison population will be people of color. This obviously does not reflect the makeup of the population as a whole. Unless you are a white supremacist who believes that people of color are genetically predisposed to a life of crime, you cannot help but conclude that racial discrimination plays a role in the meting out of "justice." The blatant inequities in the criminal justice system, particularly in relation to the application of the death penalty, are the main reason African-Americans continue to distrust that system.

Statistics on crime do not show a similar increase during this period of prison expansion; in fact, the crime rate has fallen. We are putting more people in jail for fewer crimes. We are adding capacity at an incredible rate, either building new prisons or revamping old ones by turning gymnasiums into sleeping quarters or putting four people into cells meant for one. We cannot possibly incarcerate every person—every African-American, every Latino, every Native American, every Asian-American, even every white American—who feeds our fear of crime. But we're trying.

In addition to building more prisons, America has gotten tougher on the inmates. Jail, after all, is no place for "frills." Most Americans resent the basketball courts, the TV sets, the video games. Congress even decided that educational opportunities qualify as "frills," and as part of the 1995 crime bill, it did away with prisoners' access to Pell grants.

All of the new get-tough measures are mired in politics. Nowhere do we find any consideration of alternative approaches that have proven to be effective: job training and placement, curfews, drug treatment programs, counseling, community-service commitments, intensive supervision, and home confinement. Instituting this entire list of "correctional" services would be less costly than the average per diem for incarceration.

The 1995 crime bill has done nothing to lessen the pervasive black distrust of the criminal justice system. In fact, the philosophy behind the bill is entirely too reminiscent of Jim Crow and the Black Codes of 1865–66. While the bill included some minor victories for those of us who prefer reason to force, the final version, as signed into law by President Clinton, represented a clear-cut victory for those politicians who believe that *rehabilitation* and *crime prevention* are dirty words.

In its original form, the bill was intended as a comprehensive approach to crime and criminals. It originally included a Racial Justice Act to allow death-row convicts to challenge and perhaps overturn their convictions by proving that those convictions were racially motivated. Even though there is little argument that the death penalty is applied in a racist manner, pressure from constituents to be tough on crime prevailed, ensuring the inviolability of the rights of death-row inmates. The result? The Racial Justice Act, a simple way to check that the application of the death penalty would not be discriminatory was one of the first provisions to be "negotiated" out of the bill, after only a perfunctory discussion in Congress.

As always, politics played a huge role in deleting many of the original, more enlightened components of the bill. Meanwhile, in a clear demonstration that they are no longer the leaders the black community needs, the African-American establishment stood shoulder to shoulder with their traditional civil rights allies, black and white, and *never said a word.* They thereby gave tacit approval to this new kind of crime "prevention." I consider their behavior a flagrant abuse of the trust that we citizens place in them.

I cannot say it often enough: Race is an undeniable factor in our criminal justice system. Empirical and statistical research data provided by the Death Penalty Information Center show that this country executes its citizens based on three simple criteria: "What color are you?" "What color was your victim?" and "How much money do you have?" A sampling of the data reveals the bias:

- An African-American who takes the life of a white person and also has the burden of being poor is sixty-three times more likely to receive the death penalty than a white person who murders a black.

- While black people are 12 percent of this nation's population, they constitute a shocking 40 percent of the nearly three thousand inmates currently on death row.

- Since the Supreme Court reinstated the death penalty nearly twenty years ago, only one white person has been executed for killing a black—and he was already serving ten life sentences!

Our cynicism about the criminal "justice" system has caused us to lose sight of the fact that African-Americans, as a people, are entitled to equal treatment under the law. The resultant apathy is dangerous;

we cannot afford to let it dilute our collective outrage. And our leaders, who should be constantly reminding us that it is a mistake, have instead assumed a mental posture that brings to mind the slave days, like Uncle Toms, sycophant "darkies," fearful of speaking up for the cause of justice.

The federal government is not alone in its racist prescriptions for "justice." The states are getting in on the act too. In Ohio, for example, an amendment to the state constitution has removed the first level of state appeals, so that death-penalty cases, most of which involve poor black defendants, are now sent directly from the trial courts to the Ohio Supreme Court. Proponents of the amendment said the change was needed because the appeals process could take ten years or more to produce a definitive ruling. Obviously, that's an inordinate amount of time and resources to devote to a single criminal case. But easing overcrowded court schedules by limiting the legal recourse of people with no voice and no money is criminal behavior on the part of all of us.

Is there any hope in all this judicial maneuvering? Will any of it make us feel safer? The urban poor don't think so. They are astute enough to recognize that laws like the 1995 crime bill—laws that provide upward of sixty additional death-penalty provisions (including some for noncapital crimes), that prosecute children as adults, that have unconstitutional antigang provisions, that advocate a three-strikes-and-you're-out approach to felony convictions, that include mandatory minimum sentencing, boot camps, and antiloitering ordinances—not only overwhelmingly target the black poor but are a patently racist prescription for warehousing the underclass.

It should be clear by now that the conditions that many African-Americans and other people of color face are producing great human pain and suffering. The old paradigms upon which the American social structure is based are dangerously flawed. They don't address today's issues, and they offer no hope for improvement in the areas where improvement is desperately needed.

It should also be clear that those who created this structure are not inclined to change it. Change must come from outside the structure. We—who have everything to gain and nothing to lose, who have always thought of ourselves as having no power—are the only ones who can force this change.

My stint at Western took place when the concept of rehabilitative incarceration was still a guiding principle. We were encouraged to take advantage of a wide range of educational opportunities, from learning to read to finishing high school to earning a college degree. Legal aid services were available to us, and those who felt they had been unjustly imprisoned had some official recourse. We had drug counseling and federally funded programs that provided transportation for families on visiting days; my sister Stoney was able to see me regularly and helped me maintain my sense of family and of life outside prison.

Most prisons today offer fewer chances to positively influence the course of someone's life. Most "correctional" facilities have little or nothing to do with correcting. Rather, federal and state officials with the political power to set prison agendas proclaim jails at every level to be nothing more than holding tanks. The resultant punitive environment makes a clear statement: Rehabilitation is not the system's goal. "Frills" like learning to read or completing an education courtesy of a Pell grant are steadily being eliminated. Though effective rehabilitation is obviously unlikely in such a setting, the public nevertheless still expresses surprise that our prison system produces repeat offenders, and they continue to blame repeat behavior solely on prisoners themselves.

At Western, I came to the realization that if I wanted my life to be better, I would have to initiate change myself. No one was going to do it for me. If I just sat there on my bunk waiting for someone to come along and give me what I was sure I deserved (and resented not having), I realized I'd spend the rest of my life on that bunk or on another one just like it in some other prison, moving in and out of the system until I died.

I have spent the last twenty-five years working to break the pattern—studying, asking questions, learning how to solve problems without violence and how to motivate others to redirect their lives. It's true that the penal system today provides little incentive for self-improvement, but that is no excuse for prisoners not to assume responsibility for the quality of their lives—before, during, and after prison.

Today, although I have physically escaped from my past, I am still bound to it emotionally, unable to turn my back on the hundreds of thousands of children trapped in patterns like my former one. I cannot forget what it's like to be imprisoned, either in an inner city or in a correctional facility. And with all the authority vested in me by my own past, I can assure you that what passes today for urban and correctional policy will never break the pattern. These policies are not working; they never did work, and in fact, they are doing untold damage to those whose interests they should be promoting.

Almost every aspiring politician today has a "crime-fighting" speech. But listen carefully to what is being said, and you will see that what those politicians are really doing is playing to our *fear* of crime. The truth is, crime is fought with education and health care. Crime is fought by caring about every citizen. All of us who refuse to care, who refuse to take responsibility for the state in which we live, become accomplices in the systematic incarceration of poor black males.

———

The reality of American apartheid was painfully evident to me during the month I spent in L.A. in the wake of the Rodney King riots. I wasn't a visitor returning to a sanitized hotel room each day to recover from my exposure to this ghetto. I lived in South Central the whole thirty days, sleeping wherever someone offered me a bed or a couch or a corner of the floor. I told people my own story and listened to theirs. And as I came to know this forgotten area of the Southern California urban sprawl, the direction of my life was irrevocably altered.

The social geography of South Central is an ethnic and racial mix of African-Americans, Mexican-Americans, Chinese, Central Americans, whites, Filipinos, Koreans, and Samoans. There is some surface cordiality, but it masks a basic territorial tension.

The physical geography is visually deceptive. I was used to the vertical ghettos of the East and the Midwest: warehouselike tenements crowded up against each other with concrete as far as you can see in every direction. South Central is horizontal. It looks like a middle-class neighborhood—streets lined with palm trees. But the streets are also lined with garbage. The air carries the stench of filth and poverty, and the daytime sounds of blaring music are routinely replaced by night-time sounds of machine-gun fire.

The emotional geography had only one dimension: anger. It permeated virtually every conversation I had. In fact, many of the thoughts and feelings expressed to me by residents in and out of the gangs were driven by anger, not logic. Until we acknowledge that anger and their right to it, we will continue to miss the point of what they are saying.

Despair, hopelessness, frustration, and anger—suffering beyond most outsiders' understanding—are on the faces of all the residents of South Central. Even the youngest have hundred-year-old eyes, having seen too much, having nothing to look forward to, nothing to hope for. The fundamental goodness of humankind that many of us take for granted has been overshadowed by desolation: by substandard living conditions; multigenerational poverty; rampant drug use and abuse; open street-drug sales; inadequately clothed children; hazardous playing areas; disproportionate numbers of high school dropouts and teen mothers; local retail price gouging; gross idleness, particularly on the part of teens; and health hazards caused by the maggots, flies, dead animals, and garbage that litter the streets.

Where is our outrage?

Eighteen

LEADERSHIP

Black leaders made incredible gains for African-Americans during the early years of the civil rights struggle. They even persuaded President Richard Nixon to implement affirmative action policies, on the heels of Lyndon Johnson's efforts to expand federal employment to include people of all races. Law schools began encouraging African-American participation, both male and female. Congress permitted set-asides for the construction industry. The Fair Housing, Civil Rights, and Voting Rights acts became law. So did desegregation.

In theory, integration was a noble vision, entirely appropriate for its time. In practice, however, it had a cumulative negative effect on the black poor, siphoning off the best of us into the middle class, discarding the rest of us into urban ghettos. Too many blacks who took advantage of the opportunities presented by integration—the ones who got the most training and education—fled the cities for middle-class comfort in the suburbs. Most of them never looked back, never thought of returning to help those less fortunate than themselves, those for whom Martin Luther King, Jr., and Malcolm X expressed the most concern. The blacks who left called their exodus "moving up," but they were really moving out. Physically, emotionally, and psychologically, they severed their connection with the rest of the race, hoping that through education and affluence, they could live the white life.

So if not to the middle class, where do we look for leaders whom the voiceless underclass will trust? Even though he is one of the most identifiable black leaders in the United States today, I don't think Jesse Jackson is the voice of the underclass. His political skills, which have earned him a place in the second or third tier of the Washington power structure, have been honed to perfection over the last thirty-plus years, and he certainly deserves credit for championing the civil rights cause for nearly four decades. But the whole concept of civil rights has changed quite radically since the days of Martin Luther King. King's goal, in his own words, was that "one day . . . sons of former slaves and the sons of former slave-owners will be able to sit down together at the table of brotherhood. . . . With this faith we will be able to work together, to go to jail together, to stand up for freedom together."

Today the only African-Americans sitting down with "sons of former slave-owners" are a few elites who represent their own interests while pretending to represent all African-American interests. These few are responsible for the ideological coup d'état that has displaced Martin Luther King's vision, and they must be held accountable for the reckless course that Black America is now on.

Jackson, insofar as his public statements reflect his philosophies, doesn't seem to understand what this course is. "The rising tide of drugs and babies making babies and violence is cutting away our opportunity," he has said. On the surface, it's a simple injunction to "clean up your act!" But another, dangerously subtle message at work here effectively blames the powerless for their plight, reflecting stereotypical assumptions that African-Americans are self-indulgent predators, mindlessly engaging in self-destructive behaviors.

Jackson's vision of "civil rights" never takes issue with the premise that the existence of an intractable, overwhelmingly black underclass is a fact of life. His words, quoted in the preceding paragraph, send a chilling unspoken message to black people everywhere: If you learn to control your "innate" tendencies, some of you will be able to escape the ghetto life; for the rest of you, maybe things can be better for you *where you are,* but don't expect to ever get out of there. I keep wondering how Jackson could have become a leader of such stature without knowing that we can never have true equality as long as the goal is for "us" to become "them."

There is only one equality to be achieved—the equality of all, including those of us who have been convicted in the womb. If the African-American poor are to achieve any semblance of equality in this particular culture, it is precisely Jackson's sort of rhetoric, rhetoric that fosters the "us versus them" notion, that must be dismantled and discarded. To continue to encourage "us" to be more like "them" suggests three things: one, that they are better than us and therefore worthy of emulation; two, that there is nothing about myself, in my present condition, that I should value; and three, that I should feel no guilt at leaving others wallowing in the mire of poverty as I lift myself out. It is an immoral stance to insist that we need to look out for only ourselves, to see how far we can move as individuals, and it stands in diametric opposition to the notions of freedom, justice, and equality.

Jackson would claim he has dedicated his life to classic liberalism. But he displays little of it as he practices politics. The underclass blacks whom he most often defends with his words have seen virtually no action on his part that affects their day-to-day circumstances. Why? The plain truth seems to be that, in Jackson's eyes, the underclass has no value for his professional ambitions. Economically, they are non-players; politically, they are too divided to produce a block vote; socially, endorsing programs that would improve their lives is professional suicide. It is obviously more politically profitable for him to build his career by bringing goodies to his elite friends and associates.

If Jackson cannot speak for the underclass, how about the NAACP?

Since its founding in 1909 by a coalition of black activists and northern white liberals, including the distinguished Dr. W.E.B. Du Bois, the National Association for the Advancement of Colored People has overcome obstacle after obstacle and formidably challenged every social and institutional barrier to the political, social, and economic advancement of America's citizens of African heritage. The glorious and proud record of the NAACP marks it as the most effective and honored civil rights organization in the Western world. Not only have African-Americans benefited from its dramatic conquests—all of America has been legally, morally, and spiritually nourished by its existence.

But Du Bois's vision of a unified, collective purpose for the black community remains largely unrealized, and the NAACP's constituency is disintegrating. The urban young see it as irrelevant. African-American women are beginning to recognize the association's limited horizons with respect to issues of concern to them. Community activists nationwide are questioning the point of continued involvement. Young activists in and out of college and those of the underclass do not believe that the NAACP values their participation. The leadership squabbles that have recently embarrassed it serve only to reflect and perpetuate the growing schism between forces that can ill afford an antagonistic separation at such a crucial juncture in our nation's history.

From the beginning the goal of the NAACP was not to eliminate the underclass (though it certainly wasn't called that at the time) but to enable its members to escape it. The association's rhetoric would suggest that it is dedicated to the interests of all African-Americans. In practice, however, it focuses on issues like affirmative action and foundation funding, expending virtually no effort on prisons, health issues, unemployment, or urban violence. As long as the NAACP turns its back on poor blacks by calling on us to rise out of the cesspool rather than clean it up, it will continue to niggerize the majority of the "colored people" for whom Du Bois, at least, wanted advancement.

Even though Du Bois was one of the founders of the NAACP, he was generally underappreciated in his time. He had a sweeping vision for improving the lives of urban blacks, and in 1933, just before his departure from the NAACP, he convened the Second Amenia Conference, calling on African-American leaders from all over the country to join him in an effort to develop a "group economy" that would better serve the urban masses.

More than sixty years later, we have yet to realize fully Du Bois's vision of independent and self-reliant leadership of African-American people. For all his vision and positive contributions, he may have unwittingly created our most fearsome stumbling block to diversity in leadership. Convinced that he had come upon the only way to uplift his race, Du Bois promoted a theory that black leaders would come from the intellectual ten percent of the population. Thus, despite the best of intentions, he effectively instituted a mindset that, even today, keeps us from looking at other alternatives. As a consequence, African-American leaders see themselves as a black elite—in Du Bois's words, a "talented tenth"—who by definition do not relate to the underclass.

No leader or association of leaders mired in the past can be the voice of the underclass today. The brave old warriors of Memphis, Selma, Birmingham, and Montgomery—Wyatt Tee Walker, Joseph Lowery, and Jesse Jackson, to name a few—still dominate the leadership scene, prancing, posing, and preaching justice. They invoke the ghosts of Martin and Malcolm and Medgar, implying that their association with these slain giants is enough, in and of itself, to validate their credentials forever. We are reminded of every boycott, every arrest, every march, every sit-in.

At least one member of the Old Guard, however, has been able to apply Martin Luther King's dream to today's world: Dr. Benjamin F. Chavis, Jr. Because of Chavis, I had hope for the future of the NAACP for a brief moment recently. His appointment as executive director in 1993 was not without controversy, and he is increasingly at odds with the rest of the African-American power structure. He campaigned for the NAACP position, however, on a revolutionary platform:

We will make the NAACP a vibrant organization for all of our people, from African-American professionals on Wall Street to despairing and alienated masses in our inner cities, from the farmer on the land to the workers in the offices and factories, from our revered elders to our dynamic youth. We will succeed. Working together, we will bring forth an inspiring vision of a more just, compassionate and prosperous America, of a nation where all of its people, irrespective of race, class, gender, or ethnic background, can live lives of decency and dignity.

Once elected, Chavis set out to make his vision a reality. His broad-based strategy was founded on the realization that today's increasingly complex and dire state of affairs requires the intellectual and organizational resources of all of us, not just those of a self-selected African-American elite.

Consequently, Chavis reached out to Asians, Latinos, women, youth, ex-gang members, and the urban and rural poor. He trumpeted valiant calls for equal rights for gay people, the disabled, and the impoverished victims of environmental racism. He established a moral stance for the NAACP in South Africa and South Central. He walked the war-torn streets of Watts, Cabrini Green, Cleveland, and the Bronx, cajoling gang members to lay down their weapons. He reached out to leaders across the spectrum, urging President Clinton to back a jobs bill and stimulus package, and urging members of Congress to dispense with the racial biases inherent in the crime bill. Most important, he reached out to the invisible, voiceless masses—the poor, the dispossessed, the jobless, and the babies—all of whom he intended to bring under the sheltering umbrella of the NAACP he envisioned.

Chavis's calls for unity were disturbing to NAACP directors, who appeared unwilling to have the national organization identified with the urban poor, particularly those who were activists with or worked on behalf of gang members. The association was clear that it did not and could not be in "association" with those who were on the oppressed side of the economic ledger.

In his historic effort to rescue the NAACP from the brink of irrelevance, Chavis found himself challenged by the group's self-appointed bureaucracy. In addition, nervous contributors, concerned about the prospect of "diversity"—a coded reference to black-on-black classism, one of the most serious threats to civil rights for all African-Americans—were withholding their money, eroding the organization's financial base.

Anxious to reclaim its safe middle-of-the-road position and to divert attention from their own limited views, the directors latched onto the fact that Chavis had used $332,000 in organizational funds, without their knowledge, to settle a personal sexual harassment suit lodged against him. This misappropriation of funds, from an organization running a deficit exceeding three million dollars, was a fatal mistake for Chavis to make, even though his vision for our country stood in the finest tradition of Martin Luther King, Jr., and the original NAACP.

I still believe that Chavis is a valuable leader and mentor in our fight. His vision, courage, and experience, combined with the creativity and passion of the new leaders, can surely overcome the apathy that threatens us all. Meanwhile, his example should serve as a constant reminder to us of the difficulties we face as we promote a new paradigm.

Chavis has not been idle since his ouster from the NAACP. The National African-American Leadership Summit (NAALS) convened for the fifth time thirty days after the Million Man March. The summit, an umbrella organization chaired by Chavis, includes as its members the NAACP, the National Urban League, the National Medical Association, the National Bar Association, the National Society of Black Engineers, the National Association of Black Journalists, and the Nation of Islam.

For this particular gathering, Chavis's intent was to keep the spirit of the march alive, provide positive follow-up, and find ways for the African-American community "to join together to respect one another, invest in and build our community." Delegates, observers, and other summit participants gathered to draft and implement together a "National Strategic Action Agenda for Black Empowerment." By all reports, this fifth NAALS was a resounding success. It holds within it the seeds of new ideas, a new paradigm, and new leadership. We are desperately in need of all three.

Another familiar leader on the African-American scene today is Minister Louis Farrakhan. Farrakhan's uncompromising standards make him almost universally unpopular in the white community, and even some blacks are uncomfortable with his fervor. But a broad cross-section of blacks, of every faith and no faith, admire Farrakhan because he so strongly and unequivocally supports the very underclass that desperately needs recognition and validation.

The Nation of Islam continues to have a powerful and positive impact upon the poor, particularly those in the clutches of the penal system. No other religious figure or entity in America can make such a claim. Under the guidance and direction of Elijah Muhammad and now Farrakhan, the Nation of Islam has irrefutably been the only bright spot in the otherwise dark tunnel of prison recidivism.

The young African-American males that you used to see on the street corner, selling crack and heroin and worse, are still out there. But now, under the leadership of Farrakhan, they are well-mannered, dressed immaculately in suits and bow ties, and selling fruits, bean pies, or the *Final Call* newspaper. These men were transformed while they were inside maximum-security prisons, not by government, not by affirmative action, not by handouts, not even, I'm sad to say, by Christianity (which incidentally has a very mild presence in a penitentiary setting). No, they were transformed by a religious organization whose leader many black Christian ministers excoriate passionately. These prisoners were invited into a community that supported, nurtured, and challenged them to salvage their spirits from the corruption and immorality that had them in its grip. They are now employed and paying taxes, and they are positive role models for, and contributors to, the overall American community.

Minister Farrakhan's leadership keeps lapsing into the very style he criticizes. The groundswell of atonement and reconciliation fostered among those who attended the Million Man March has received no encouragement from Farrakhan. Rather, he has squandered that respect by sitting down with the leaders of repressive regimes in Nigeria, the Sudan, and Libya during his recent twenty-three-nation tour of Africa. Whether or not the State Department was at odds with the Minister or what the Israeli Knesset thought of him is not the point. Here at home, countless people await principled leadership. Urban America once again must ask, "What about us?" And Farrakhan does not seem to have the answer.

Moreover, we cannot afford race-baiting. Hate serves no one. Rather, it polarizes all those who have the nation's poor at heart. In our economic system the poor have enough natural enemies; it is a disservice to foster conditions that create new ones.

Literally millions of men and women dedicated to improving conditions within their reach have made as much of an impact on a local scale as Chavis and Farrakhan have made on the national scale. The Million Man March, held October 16, 1995, was intended to provide individual and collective validation to such black men all across the country. The March's slogan—"Million Men, Mighty Men, Wise Men . . . Our Future Is In Your Hands"—was a public declaration of empowerment and the first step in liberating them from the crippling stereotypes to which they have been shackled for centuries.

There is no denying that black men have been emasculated by society, or that the march helped to begin the healing of that wound. But to discount black women by totally excluding them is inexcusable, to say nothing of short-sighted. To state openly that the interests and welfare of black women cannot, *should* not, be addressed until that of black men has been seen to is to alienate half the race. It defies logic to exclude black women, black mothers who want to see their children live long enough to grow up, from the struggle. These women are every bit as ready, as able, and as committed as the men to apply their considerable talents and energies to the elimination of poverty.

Jesse Jackson, Benjamin Chavis, and Louis Farrakhan are the most visible African-American leaders today, but a new face is also emerging. With the NAACP's election, late in 1995, of Kweisi Mfume as its president and CEO, the association seems to be serious about finding its way back from the brink of extinction. Mfume's appointment holds out tremendous possibilities and restores hope to all those who were prepared to leave the NAACP, despondent over its internal chaos.

Mfume, former U.S. congressman from Maryland, came from poverty in a single-parent household. He was a school dropout and was used to the street life. He comes to the NAACP with a broad experience that I hope will inspire him to be mindful of the unrepresented voices in the African-American community. In his position as head of the Congressional Black Caucus, Mfume gained a reputation for a realistic and comprehensive understanding of the issues confronting African-Americans today. He was not afraid to take bold and courageous stands when the interests of African-Americans were being jeopardized.

His presence at the NAACP produces hope for a vital, inclusive future for the association. In the words of retired federal judge Leon Higginbotham, as reported in *The New York Times*, "In our new president, we have the brilliance of Du Bois, the eloquence of Martin Luther King, Jr., the toughness of Thurgood Marshall, the caring of Ms. Bethune and Harriett Tubman and Sojourner Truth." If this is indeed true, the NAACP will gain a new credibility in the country's hurting communities.

A radical shift is necessary to restore confidence in African-American leadership. If we are ready to transcend the mental condition that continues to enslave us—and I believe that many of us are—we can do so only by aligning ourselves with leaders who understand the process of niggerization and are working to escape its clutches.

These new leaders—ethical, bright young black men and women from Chicago, South Central, Roxbury, Harlem, Newark, Minneapolis–St. Paul, and Watts—are already out there inspiring visions of hope. They are former gang leaders determined to address the urban crisis and committed to the peace initiative that came out of the national gang summit. They participated in the African-American Leadership Conference in Baltimore and in similar gatherings across the country.

They attended the Million Man March in Washington, seeking atonement for past moral violations and demanding justice for the hurting communities of this nation. All across this country there are pockets of integrity occupied by uncompromising young politicians, ministers, and entrepreneurs. They toil in anonymity but are ready for their chance to lead us in a moral direction.

Finding such leaders requires careful scrutiny on our parts, combined with a steadfast refusal to vote for any candidate just because he or she fits the young-black-religious-urban-Democrat description. It is, in fact, much more likely that the leaders of the future will find us, especially as we begin to ask, louder and louder, "What about us?" Pockets of committed blacks, determined to redefine themselves, will shine like beacons. An absolute refusal to settle for second best—to be socially, educationally, or economically ignored; to live like animals; to watch our children die; to shoot each other in the streets; to kill for Starter jackets; to abstain from parental responsibility—cannot fail to be noticed. If we can be strong magnets, the emerging leaders will be attracted to us as their natural constituency. The voices of those willing to shout "What about us?" and demanding answers will overcome our history of self-destruction and make niggerization obsolete.

We have an active role to play. Every facet of our daily lives must meet the standards of respect for ourselves and responsibility for our lives. These standards should apply to the most basic and the most complicated of situations, to our families, our schools, our neighborhoods, and our own bodies. They should apply to our cities, our states, and our nation. And most especially, they should apply to our leaders.

Being black is a genetic inheritance. Being a nigger is a state of mind. It exists independently of geography, economic status, or education. Its effects are insidious, eroding our spirits, our pride, and our very sense of who we are. Deniggerization is by definition a self-administered cure. It's not something done either *to* you or *for* you. Each of us must accomplish it for ourselves. Once we respect ourselves, we will be empowered to take responsibility for our lives. From there, it's but a short step to helping each other, taking collective responsibility for our race.

———

We live behind physical, mental, and emotional barricades, literally and figuratively staring down the barrels of each other's guns, fully prepared to shoot our friends in the name of eliminating our enemies. Why is this so? The reason is, I think, that we have abdicated responsibility for our own lives, lost our sense of history, lost faith in too many of our black leaders, and lost faith in the church that shepherded us through our darkest days.

I remember the black churches in my South Philly neighborhood. On Sunday mornings my mother would send me out the door, insisting that I attend nearby St. Peter Clavers Catholic Church. She always handed me a quarter as I left the house. Even though I never understood her insistence about the quarter or what connection it had to the church, I would go to church all by myself. I kept the quarter to buy something to eat.

When I was seven or eight, I discovered another church in the neighborhood, a Baptist church. Being there felt good to me. Every Sunday I knew I would attend that church, staying there from eleven A.M. to four P.M. The other children there were clean and wore good clothes. The little girls wore black patent leather shoes and white dresses, and their hair was always perfectly fixed. I found myself wanting to be cleaner, so although I knew nothing of grooming, I scrubbed my face and my hair before I went. I loved going to that church. The people there made me feel welcome. The ladies of the congregation always cooked a big meal that would be served after the service. They insisted that I eat, and when the cold weather set in, they allowed me to take two of the coats that had been donated, because they knew I did not have even one.

The church buildings in my neighborhood were big, though not necessarily in good repair. The ministers used to come out in the streets and invite us kids inside. Every time I went, I was struck by how different it felt to be in a church. The violence and gangs, the garbage in the streets, the drugs, even my family—all were left outside. Inside felt safe. I looked up to those ministers, but I never connected their world with my own, never understood the historical legacy they and their churches represented. Ultimately, my street world proved a stronger influence than anything they could offer me.

The black church is not easily defined. The collective black church today is a body of institutions that have provided care, nurtured spiritual and religious commitment, instilled community values, and periodically demonstrated a strong sense of moral leadership in an effort to rectify social injustices.

Southern black churches were born out of slavery. From the beginning they represented sanctuary and wisdom. Their history is inextricably connected to that of our African ancestors, men and women who were forcibly brought to America as many as four hundred years ago. Viciously uprooted from viable communities, those who survived the harrowing voyage to America were immediately sold as property and subsequently treated as animals. They were forbidden to speak their own African languages, to practice their African religions, to marry whom they chose, or to keep their families together. They were prohibited by law from learning to read or write, or from intermingling with whites. Most white people thought of them not as human but as objects whose only purpose was to help develop the southern economy.

Across the South, the African oral tradition—stories of ancestors, tales of bravery and courage, silly anecdotes, and reminiscences of better times—kept the spark of humanity alive inside those slaves, the spark of hope. Those stories saved us as a people and kept our history alive. The best storytellers, the ones who could keep their audience spellbound with their oratory, were the most respected members of the community. These "spellbinders" came to be known as preachers and were considered to be divinely gifted.

Almost all of our African-American culture, right up to today, sprang from the black churches north and south. In the antebellum years the black church was our mother, the essence of our life. We relied on it to survive, investing it with our skills, our stories, and our music—every aspect of the humanity that White America denied that we possessed. We invested it with all that was our spirit, all that we shared, all that we loved, and all that we aspired to be. Only there could we exercise any self-determination. The churches became the repository of our African culture and the womb of our moral, social, and political development. And the best church leaders produced black civil rights leaders, then went on to represent their voiceless, anonymous black flocks with intellect, vision, and courage.

Too few churches today are providing that kind of leadership, and too few communities are willing to accept their nurturing. In the last fifteen years, I've traveled all over the country, visited in countless black churches, and talked with ministers and congregations of all faiths. Most appear to have no recollection of their churches ever having been mother figures in the nurturing sense I've described. Over and over, churches get mired in budgets and member counts and feuds with one another. Sheer survival too often becomes their only goal, leaving them neither the time nor the energy nor the resources to continue their historical mission. At the same time, the communities served by the churches are concerned with their own sheer survival and have neither the time nor the energy to reach out to the churches, asking for the nurturing they so desperately need.

We are at an impasse that could well have tragic consequences if it cannot be resolved. The strength of the historic bond that ties African-Americans to the black church *and to each other* must be put to better use. Resurrecting our racial unity, particularly as it is expressed in a religious context, has nothing to do with being racist. Rather, it is an acknowledgment of our unique history. Our black churches gave us respect when no one else would. They valued us when no one else did. As a result, we felt more powerful there than anywhere else.

That power is still there, waiting for us to claim it. All we have to do, clergy and congregations, is reach for each other.

Niggerized thinking would have us believe that the most we can hope for in this life is to be better niggers. Niggerized thinking says we don't deserve anything more and will never get anything more, and that we had better not teach our children to expect anything more.

Well, we *do* deserve more—for ourselves and, especially, for all our children. Empowerment. Leadership. We must claim them, then use them to correct the injustices and inadequacies that plague us.

It's time we took off our shackles.

I was a nigger in the womb. Not just black, not just male—a *nigger*. Centuries of contempt for my race were laid on my infant shoulders the instant I was born. But God's grace was there too, at the center of my soul. No matter how hard I tried to kill it, my humanness, my innate need to *connect* never disappeared. And when I finally went looking for it, starting in my cell at Western, it was there waiting.

Every single one of us must stop participating in our own oppression. No matter what our life circumstances are, we must assume the responsibility to improve them. We must stop living passive lives, content to be herded around like cattle. Deniggerization is meaningless unless we acknowledge our role in perpetuating niggerization. It's long past time for us to declare that the racial damage that we have inherited through generations of cultural assault will stop with us.

Where we begin does not necessarily represent where we will end. Indeed, many of us are born into circumstances that do not lend themselves to an easy, comfortable journey. Some have a political ideology that promotes the rather simplistic and racist notion that some intrinsic quality accounts for our negative behavior. These folks accuse us of deserving our plight at every level. Others essentially disagree with that theory but still demean us by asserting that we need special help to overcome our unfortunate circumstances. Both approaches conspire to maintain a status quo that perpetuates the misery we endure.

This book is meant for all those who are living as I once lived. If you get nothing else from it, get this: I would not be where I am today, who I am today, had I waited for "society" to rescue me. The history you have read here marks me as a blessed man. Blessed to have survived. Blessed to have realized that I held the keys to my own future. Blessed that the right people crossed my path at the right time, when I was ready to hear what they had to say and act on it.

South Philly used to be the center of my world. It seemed to have an inescapable gravitational pull, like a cosmic black hole into which I would eventually have disappeared. Some special people helped me realize that I could escape that deadly gravity and pushed me to work hard enough to break free. If I could do it, so can countless other "lost" youths. But somebody has to tell them that. Somebody has to lift their eyes to a wider horizon. Somebody has to inspire hope within them.

I finally understood that, in the end, I may not be responsible for what I was, but I am responsible for what I am, what I hope to become, and what I hope my children will become. I'm the role model now. I cannot possibly demand moral behavior from others, demand integrity and forthrightness, if my own life does not exemplify it.

Amazing Grace, how sweet the sound
That saved a wretch like me.
I once was lost, but now am found,
Was blind but now I see.

ACKNOWLEDGMENTS

Any project of this magnitude could not have been produced without the support and assistance of others. In the process of writing this book, there have been countless individuals along the way who have generously shared their gifts and talents—from reading the rough drafts, to challenging my ideas, to sharing genuine encouragement and faith.

While I take full responsibility for any limitations or weaknesses inherent in the ideas, presentation, or style of the text, I must share credit for the strength, depth, and heart of this book with the following people: C. Eric Lincoln, Jack Kirby, Robert Hinton, Stephen Butler, Jim Hornfisher, Setrina Hunter, Gary Walters, Eloise DeZwarte, Dana Herreman, Laura Bruce, Kate Kenah, Jeff Mills, Jim McCord, Grace Dils, Sally MacPhail, Jana Lowe, Anne Helmke, Zaphira Muhammad, Omar Ali-Bey, Sherry Paprocki, and the Denison University Library staff. I would also like to thank the many students and dedicated young athletes who have helped me to grow, and have inspired me to continue my struggle, particularly: Gwynn Evans, Laura Hinebaugh, Katie

Heisey, Nate Dennison, Heath Mullenix, Mark Edwards, and Shane Carmichael. Finally, a special thanks must go to Sandy Ellinger, who is primarily responsible for bringing this book to fruition. Her tireless dedication, persistence, patience, hard work, and editing skills made this project possible.

ABOUT THE AUTHOR

CARL UPCHURCH is the founder and executive director of the Council for Urban Peace and Justice in Pittsburgh, PA. He lectures widely on the state of urban affairs and has addressed major universities and conferences as well as the United Nations. In 1993 he was awarded the National Humanitarian Award by Jesse Jackson's Rainbow Coalition. He previously won the Southern Christian Leadership Conference's National Peace Award and the Fellowship of Reconciliation's Martin Luther King Jr. Award. He writes for *Columbus Alive* and attends Trinity Lutheran Seminary. He lives in Columbus, Ohio, with his wife and daughter.